Thank You

Your Opinion Means

Nothing to Me

Thank You
You

Your Opinion Means

Nothing to Me

Nancy Blair

 element

Element
An Imprint of HarperCollins*Publishers*
77–85 Fulham Palace Road,
Hammersmith, London W6 8JB

The website address is: www.thorsonselement.com

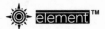

and *Element* are trademarks of
HarperCollins*Publishers Ltd*

First published by Element 2004

1 3 5 7 9 10 8 6 4 2

A catalogue record of this book
is available from the British Library

ISBN 0 00 716050 X

Printed and bound in Great Britain by
Creative Print and Design (Wales), Ebbw Vale

For Mom and Mo

Life is simple. Sex, birth, death and weather.
Toss lightly with a dash of chance, a heaping scoop of choice and season to taste.
Cook it all up and watch it change overnight.

The Menopause Queen

You don't have to be good. You do not have to walk on your knees for a
hundred miles through the desert, repenting. You only have to let the
soft animal of your body love what it loves.

Mary Oliver

Acknowledgements

I am deeply grateful to the following people, who helped bring this book to light: My beautiful mother, Frances Blair, whose unconditional, loving support throughout my life continues to give me the courage to be myself and speak my truth. I love you so very much, Mom. To Leo Morrissey, for seeing me through the many chapters of my life with patience, love and understanding. My brothers Leo, Paul, and John for being supportive of my writing, no matter what. My publisher, Greg Brandenburgh, for his keen insight, wonderful wit, undying enthusiasm, and most of all for believing in this book from the get-go. To *all* the people at HarperCollins*Publishers* (Thorsons/Element), especially Steve Fischer, Chris Aherne, Kathy Dyke and Lara Burgess, and Michele Wetherbee for her creative vision and totally hot and wonderful book cover design, who have worked arduously to put my book in the world. My editor extraordinaire, Caroline Pincus, whose brilliant guidance and joyful encouragement made all the difference. The rest is up to us. My women friends who continue to laugh, sigh, dance, cry, and howl with me through the tidal loops, fiery hoops, and hilarious uprisings of this wildly metamorphic maze called menopause, I love you all so very much. I couldn't do this trip without you. In alphabetical order, Patti Coleman, Barbara Davison, Ellen Fernandez, Joan Fericy, Pearl Gray, Patty Green, Cathy Hayes, Sandy Lehman, Jane Muller, Nancy Peters, Gale Sasson, Pamela Wyn Shannon, Jane Wilson, the WOW POWER™ group, and many more too numerous to mention who so willingly shared their stories with me. My acupuncture physician and wise woman friend, Leslie Stone, whose healing touch and presence in my life are pure joy. My Clarity Works™ life strategy coach, Kathleen Rich-New, whose gentle, kind reminders helped me learn how to breathe all over again. My cousin, Pike Powers, who so generously helped me find my way to the creative cauldron of molten glass when I needed it most. Thanks be to the trees that are the pages of this book. And last but not least, to the spirit of my ancestors, which continues to guide my creative vision. I thank you a thousand times over, every day. I am your daughter, forever.

Menopause Happens

(a kind of preface)

How in the world did I arrive at menopause and not know what to expect? At first I thought I was dying of some insidious and catastrophic disease, of course only to realize much later on that dying—becoming aware of my own mortality—is precisely what my bodymind and spirit, my mid-life board of directors, was calling me to the table for. Not that I was dying of anything specific. I remember finally going to my doctor and plunking my perturbed and cranky butt on the crinkly translucent tissue paper covering the exam table, observing keenly that my increasingly dry skin could eventually and surely be sold for this very purpose, and exclaiming to my doctor with all the knowledge I had gained up to that point, "I'm either pregnant (my period was eight hours late) or I have a very bad sinus infection."

You see, the big thing with menopause is that it doesn't have an exact and definite beginning like its kid sister, menarche, or its fertile middle ground, motherhood. There are no big and hearty exclamations with the Change of Life. No wondrous weeping moments of joy and exhilaration accompanied by proud nods and big hugs to family, friends, and anyone else who cares to listen; basically outright strangers and passersby. No. No cutesy, cryptic emails to classmates you haven't seen or heard from in years. No spontaneous leaping up onto your cubicle desk chair triumphantly exclaiming to your work mates, "Hey everyone, I have good news. I'm sweating like a horse. I'm now in menopause."

Nope. Not a chance. At least not in my country we don't.

Menopause is a slow, sliding, inevitable kind of blood mystery that saddles up alongside you and hangs out for a long time, whispering thin warnings and snarky hot currents of caution, often inciting an uncontrollable urge to chew the face off the stranger sitting in the car next to you, before you, and the Crone you are becoming, actually reach a definite destination together: no more eggs, and the cessation of monthly periods.

Well, sounds simple enough. No more bleeding. No more supersized tampons, heavy-days pads, rinsing out the crotch of your underwear in the sink during your lunch break. No more ragging on yourself for sobbing into your palms suddenly when the theme song from your junior prom plays on the oldies' station. Did I say no more PMS? No, I didn't. Because there's one thing I learned about The Change. PMS does not go away. PMS is here to stay. It's the one small barking dog that doesn't seem to want to budge when everything else feels like a solo raft ride on a class five river run. But I've come to discover there's a reason for PMS; more about that later.

As menopause approached I was certain I had a bad twin in the saddle next to me, jabbing me with her bony elbow, telling *her* truth, demanding to get *her* needs met, asking for what *she* wanted, poking me at the most inappropriate times howling, "Wake up. Pay attention." The good twin, the one who likes to please, doesn't want to upset the way things are (even if the way they are really stinks), and is willing to put up with a whole lot of bumps along the way to avoid a scene in which she may be called names, especially that B word. You know, Bitch. Meanwhile, the feisty, fuming one seems hell-bent on embarrassing the good twin to no end, barking at every turn in the road, telling it like it is, refusing to back down on unresolved stress, making it quite impossible for the good twin to stick to her N & S (nod and smile) approach to life, in spite of the fact that her ass is aching and her head is throbbing. Does it seem like my thoughts are meandering all over the page here? Well, in fact, it's hormones pushing my mind around in ever-widening spirals, pulling me off the "age of reason and rational thinking" and bringing me into the intuitive side of story-telling, which is precisely the metamorphosis of the menopausal mind. The mid-life brain actually gets rewired for a stronger interior world of dreams, hunches, and psychic "knowing", bringing keen insights and a new and different way of telling stories, our own stories, from the heart and not from the compliant places conditioned by culture. (All of which leads me to think that James Joyce was a menopausal woman.)

During the menopausal years our fluctuating hormones are really our deepest wisdom, calling us to get honest, get with what's real, and address those areas in our life that need to change for our own well-being, which is the true reason PMS happens in the first place. It's our watchdog within, telling it like it is. The more we ignore her, the louder she barks, until at menopause you can't turn her off.

It's not called The Change for nothing!

Where was I? Oh. At the gynecologist's office. Anyway, it was the first time that my doctor, bless her busy little heart, actually heard me. I was forty-ish at the time and bleeding so heavily, or as my perimenopausal sisters called it "flooding," and passing blood clots so painfully large that at one point I called my husband, L, into the bathroom screaming, "I just lost my liver. Look at it. It's floating in the toilet." To which he leaned over, peered in, and shrugged saying, "Hmm. Looks serious. Better talk to someone about that."

I also happened to mention to my doctor somewhat tentatively that I was thinking of having a baby, pouring out my soul about an upwelling of desire. Not for sex, mind you, because the urge to actually engage anything sexual from the waist down was strangely disappearing into the dusk. But the strong and seemingly last-ditch effort to create a child from my very own body, blood, and bones was getting stronger. A perimenopausal paradox in action: Want to *have* a baby, but don't want to *make* a baby. So here I am, pouring out my thoughts, stringing words and feelings and indecision all together in one of those stream-of-consciousness confessionals that surprises even me because I hadn't really talked much about having a baby, not even with the man who would have a major part in making it happen, that is, if I'd actually let him go *there* with his baby-making apparatus. I was, it occurred to me later on and simply put, perimenopausal, my brain on fire, trying to run away from the conditioned idea that I was *supposed* to want a baby: yammering at my doctor, incoherently touching on various internal discomforts ranging from suddenly watching my libido hit the skids to wanting to turn the house upside-down and dump everything out on the sidewalk and let the garbage crew take it all away. Then start filling every closet and corner back up again with, well, something different.

I knew that having a baby wasn't what I really wanted or could ever conceivably imagine taking care of in my already very selfish and erratic life. I could barely take care of my own screaming needy child, the one living in my psyche who is still mad and pouting about not getting what she needed when she was too young to actually verbalize it.

At this time, all, and I mean *all* my forty-ish girlfriends were nursing their newborns, having postponed their pregnancies in favor of a career. Given the choice between career or baby, I was leaning toward baby because I'd had a bit of success with getting pregnant in the past, but no success with getting and keeping a job. The life I'd chosen for myself, to be an artist (as if anyone actually *chooses* art) was long, hard work with very little monetary reward. Early on I realized that I was a bona fide card-carrying member of the Maynard G. Krebs school of life: "Work? Work?" No way was I going to trade my creative dreams in for someone else's bottom line. Thing is, I forgot to marry a rich man and instead fell deeply in love with, you guessed it, another artist.

I'd put myself through college, returning to school in my late twenties, an "older student," the first in my family. I waitressed my way through grad school only to find that making a living as an artist was basically, well, nearly impossible. Fresh out of grad school I applied for twenty-one teaching jobs, which was really what I wanted to do; make art and teach, and got twenty-two rejections. Go figure.

Having a baby was, it seemed at the time, the thing I ought to be doing, even though I was terrified at the prospect, every part of my being shrieking from within my womb, "You better think twice about this." Thinking back on it now with menopausal hindsight (which comes in quite handy to justify the past), what I really wanted were my girlfriends back in my life and on the phone and having a good old girlfriend time. I figured out early on that I'm homo-emotional and although I wanted a man to pleasure my juicy fruit, no man had satisfied the camaraderie of a laugh-filled lunch with my female confidantes that almost always included secret fantasies, wacky dreams and nightmares, with heart-to-heart, concerned conversations about the world of art and politics, newly unattractive sex positions like being on top because all that loose skin is just so unappealing from the bottom looking up. And, of course, summing it all up with, "Oh no, I think I'm becoming my mother."

Alas, my girlfriends had grown-up to be mothers, and were now and forever bonded in baby talk, wincing proudly about cracked, tender nipples and divining the color of poop. I tried my best to keep up, but to be perfectly honest, I was happy to see them come, bringing with them their perfect bundles of pink or blue joy, and happy to see them go, hoisting their baby backpacks on their weary shoulders, along with enough baby gear to require a burro.

What I really wanted was to grow up, make art, and be able to feed myself.

So all the time I'm talking to my doctor I'm thinking that I must sound like a lunatic, which is just another code word for perimenopause. But I couldn't stop my lips from flapping about babies; my voice coming from way far away like an accumulated echo of all the women who ever sat in the very chair I was sitting in which, by the way, was not very comfort-able. Meanwhile my palms are getting clammy and my blouse is sticking to my already damp and chilly armpits and I'm getting myself all balled up in baby talk, shifting and strumming, and then suddenly staring curiously at a cross-section of a pink plastic uterus with hot-dog-colored fallopian tubes and hard knobby ovaries with fringy white fingers reaching (desperately?) outward, which starts to look like a space-age techno fetish, or one of those transformer toys that goes from galactic princess to alien praying mantis in a few quick fallopian flips. Everything in my doctor's office seemed to stare back at me in a peculiarly cold and utterly disconnected way.

Then my meandering mind skips to the night-cleaning crew, wondering if the man who mops the floors and dusts the desks actually picks up the uterus and rolls it around in his hands, trying to twist and turn the various parts. Or, does he just dunk it in the bucket of industrial disinfectant, shake it dry, and put it back where he got it? All at once I get an electrifying blood rush emanating from somewhere around my belly button, heat gathering speed like a Colorado brush fire, my panties sucking tightly against my suddenly damp skin. This minor distraction sets me off in another, equally meandering, direction in which I start telling my doctor everything I know about the anatomy of a hot flash, which I'm sure I'm not having because I'm too young. But just in case she's interested, I've discovered there are four chihuahuas camped out in my stomach who seem to get really pissed off at very unpredictable times, day and night, and running madly around the periphery of my interior, they work up a barking force so heated that it feels like a small bonfire has spontaneously erupted in the middle of my body. The little bug-eyed beasts then get really nervous and one of them, I call her Over Reacts, pulls out a fire hose and I end up soaking wet. My doctor then lifts her head in my direction for only a second, a look of curious concern crawling across her face.

Skittering along in a mindless blab, my arms gesticulating a chihuahua trot around my belly, I'm hoping my ob-gyn will at some point look up at me and make eye contact, just to let me know she's still with me, or lift an eyebrow to signal an empathic emotion, or hold out her hand like a crossing guard to signal me to please, stop. But all the while I'm out on a shuttle mission to intergalactic gynecology, she keeps herself busy thumbing through my chart and scribbling viciously as I speak. I'm starting to think she possibly forgot I'm in the room, when suddenly she looks up at me between the canyon of bulging manila folders stacked five-deep on her desk, and in a matter-of-fact kind of voice says, "Don't worry, it will pass."

Now I'm really confused. What will pass? I wonder. Maybe I had unknowingly moved into the subject of my recurring indigestion and flagging bowels. I ask rather hesitantly, "Excuse me?" She stops writing, lifts her head, and puts her pen down to explain, folding her fingers together like she's about to start praying, but instead leans on her arms and with an air of impatience says, "Wanting to have a baby," annoyance now creeping into her voice. Then unfolding her hands, she gets back to her paperwork and finishes up in a professorial, encouraging tone, "The feeling will pass."

She then stands up abruptly, causing me to jump to my feet like a kid in the principal's office. She grabs my folder, and ushering me out the door with a pat on my back, pushes a white piece of paper into my palm saying, "This will ease your symptoms," and then rushes on to her next patient in one of the many rooms filled with women just like me, I'm sure.

Bewildered, I look into my hand. I am holding a prescription for birth control pills. She never once mentioned the word perimenopause. Not to mention my sinuses.

Being the alternative baby boomer that I am (in 1976, at the age of twenty-four, after hitch-hiking home from a wild, eye-opening sexy summer in Berkeley, CA, flashbacks and details I'll get to later on, I opened a health-food café and called it Nature's Place Restaurant, making all the pottery and living on granola and hippie-eyed dreams), I toss the script for bc pills into the garbage and begin a long and holy search on the alternative trail to find not only a health-care practitioner who has ears but one who can act as a mid-life midwife, an auntie, granny, wise woman, and Mother of all Mothers to guide me through the womanly mysteries of menopause. Naturally.

After all, my grandmother, who lived to be 90 years old, didn't take hormone replacement (as if pregnant mare's urine can actually replace my complex endocrinology). OK, so she grew shorter as she grew older, and looked a lot like those Edward Curtis photos of Navajo women, with deep leathery crevices from ear to ear. But Grammy Smith's hard-earned wrinkles never obscured her endearing beauty or her hearty laughter, which is what I'd always cherished, and was hoping I'd inherit.

And then there's my mother, who when asked to share her menopausal experience, says nonchalantly, as if I'm making a big deal out of something she can't even recall, "Oh, *that*," she says without taking a two-second break from one of her many cleaning activities (as I sit in a stupor wondering where in this, our genetically linked world, did she get the energy to fold the laundry and do the dishes in the same day), "Menopause?" She lifts her head gazing into a science-fiction dream, "I seem to remember having a hot flash or two, but nothing really." Of course she later confesses that nothing going on *inside* her body could have demanded more attention than what was going on *outside* her body: life with my handsome, creatively brilliant, and barely there alcoholic father. And then she adds with a not-too-encouraging wince, "There are no two ways around it, hon. You'll get through just fine."

Even my mother's sister, Aunt Betty, who I loved so dearly, replied with a ho-hum shrug when, during my fact-finding family mission, I inquired if she had had a difficult time with The Change of Life.

She simply replied, "No. Nothing. Really."

So I figured I'd end up with a dry river of wrinkles, like the women who came before me, along with a couple of hot flashes. Wrinkles, shminkles. After all, we are part Native American and I remember thinking when I discovered this secret family heritage: How awesome! And then in a parenthetical prayer to the sacred spirits of my ancestors I begged, *"Please, go easy on my face."*

Then on second thought (which I have *so* many of lately that I actually lose track of my first one), What's the big deal about a few lines and folds on my face? Wrinkles=experience=wisdom. But somehow the voice of one of my first, much-older-than-I-was-boyfriends still lingered in my mind, "Men get better. Women get wrinkles," he said with a self-satisfied snort. "When you turn forty I'm trading you in for two twenties." Followed by bigger, more confident, sounds emanating from his big mouth, this time adding a few knee slaps.

Yes. I know. It's really nuts of me to still have a stupid, sexist guy voice in my head, not only because I think of myself as a careful and conscious "womanist", who writes spiritual books guiding women to their own empowered goddess selves but because I've gotten this far and nobody else has figured out just how split in half cuckoo I really am. And how this old crap keeps surfacing when I least expect it, and why can't I get away from the past and its tight, spooky grip on my thinking? So I have to come right out and admit it to myself right here, right now, because a big part of my menopausal promise to the voices of my ancestors and the pile of sacred white bones staring back at me when I close my eyes at night, is that I will tell my truth, *my truth*, no matter what it looks like or sounds like. And as much as it hurts to actually share it with the world (when Mother Night knows I've tried hard to hide it), this is my truth: I'm one of those sad and scared raccoons who can't feed herself from what is wild and wholesome and real because someone took her in as a little pup and fed her canned dog food.

So, determined early on to have an easy menopause, like the women in my family before me, I imagined I would just slide right through my forties *au naturel*, with a wink and a smile and an inward goddess glow of womanly knowing, and fearlessly face fifty with a keen zest for the rest of my golden years, willing a wondrous way of life for myself. PMZ here I come. Post Menopausal Zest smiling back from the not-too-distant shores of my own lifeway.

Now let me just digress a little. First of all, I have to admit that I have never simply "slid" right through anything. I have been spontaneously erratic my whole life. When I read that menopause often mimics a woman's teenage years, I grimaced. At age thirteen I used to come home from school, drop my books on the floor, open all the windows of the tobacco-soaked "double-wide" that I grew up in (both parents smoked, heavily) and lay on the couch listening to Simon and Garfunkel's "Bridge Over Troubled Water" thinking deep thoughts about being chubby and how come I was so smart, but none of the boys that I liked, liked me back, and why in the world did my mother insist on cutting my hair in that damned "pixie" cut that made me look like a basketball with a bad wig?

I couldn't wait to get my license, which seemed like eons away, and all I wanted was a bag of potato chips and a root beer float to nurse me through the thick sludge that hung over my folded-inward shoulders. When I did get my license I headed straight for Friendly's Ice Cream to dine on French fries and hot fudge sundaes.

It's amazing how fast my hair, my breasts, and my curiosity grew from age thirteen to sixteen, startling even me. I was voted president of my junior class, and became co-captain of the cheerleading team overnight. A budding young woman, I started to "act up," and you know exactly what that means: boy crazy. In 1969 (think Woodstock and landing on the Moon), one week after I turned seventeen I married a guy I'd met at the beach the summer before. He was five years older than I was. C, an only child, drove a fancy little sports car, smoked weed, chewed mushrooms, and dropped mescaline. But he came from a good family. He grew up in a house. And I was a teenager in love, spelled H-O-R-M-O-N-E-S.

Looking back on it, I think by marrying me, a kid from a trailer park, C was enjoying his own version of upper-middle-class offspring revenge. My parents, on the other hand, although none too happy about the long-haired bearded guy who was taking their little girl away, sprung (with my brothers' help) for a big Catholic Church wedding (which was for my parents' sake because I'd stopped going to church on my own free will. Too creepy with all that stigmata blood, and thorny crowns poking holes in Jesus' head.) My bride's maids each dressed in a different pastel color of the rainbow, the girls ranging in age from fifteen to sixteen. My horny new husband and I honeymooned in the Bahamas and by the time I was approaching the mature age of twenty, I wanted out. My world as a young wife had grown way too small. The world out there was too big, and in our conjugal crisis I lay in bed hearing the sweet breath of Night calling my name.

There's one good thing that came of this marriage: I learned how to have an orgasm. I stayed home from school one day until, working fever-ishly alone, until IT happened (better late than never, I suppose). The ecstatic clitoral event took place just two months before we got divorced; the same year I graduated with honors (a French and German major), from a two-year college. In my last semester in college I took an Art Appreciation class with a wildly enthusiastic teacher and couldn't imagine doing anything but making art for the rest of my life. My father's genetic influence was making its way to the surface. I stopped shaving my legs, threw away my bra, and hooked up with a photographer and hitchhiked out to California. Berkeley, California. I was free-floating, sorting out the mysteries of life, and moving in whatever direction the wind blew. I used to tell my friends: "Yeah, I grew up in New England. But I woke up in Berkeley."

So, after all my experiences in the world at large I've come to the simple fact that the Change of Life is a built-in biological release program that begins at perimenopause. Peri meaning "around," as in around about 40 or so (give or take a few years); the cute, little raccoon realizes she isn't cute or young any more. She is growing long, sharp claws and teeth to match. She is fed up on a domesticated diet of soft fluff meant for a different kind of animal. The cage that once fit isn't the princess palace any more. She sits huddled in the corner and can't sleep at night; burping, belching, and staring into the distant places in her soul. She weeps silently, hotly, screeching and scratching around for her real voice; her authentic woman self. No more twirling in someone else's circle and putting on displays for onlookers who toss her peanuts and marvel at how amazing it is that she uses her little paws just like real humans do.

No more tricks.

No more dying to please.

Then one night when the Moon is full and the last sleepy human has gone to bed and the stars shine so brightly she sees her own masked image reflected back to her in the glint of her tipped-over water bowl, and with the power of her own deep breath she reaches through the cage door and lifts the latch, releasing herself into what is real and true, and deliciously wild.

She slips into the vaguely familiar darkness, her nose lifted to the wind, remembering the strong bounce of Earth under her feet, catches the shine of silver light dancing on round, smooth stones, sniffs the soft warmth of dewy, midnight breezes. She draws in another, deeper breath, taking in all she can get. She stops at the edge of the woods, standing tall on her own two feet. Stretching and pressing herself upward. My how she's grown!

She drops back down and pads her way into the green forest. Going first this way then that, meandering, weaving, stopping, listening.

She has changed. She knows this for sure. She is changing.

And nothing will ever be the same again.

By the way, did I mention that in my forties I also had a dream; one of those bolt-me-upright-in-bed kind of dreams that emphatically insisted I move to a barrier island off the "Space Coast" of Florida? Well, I did. And we moved. L, my husband and I were looking to get out of the frazzle of the city and a dream seemed just as likely a place to get inspiration as any other. Remember, we're artists. We trust the invisible world. I now know it was Change, acting up.

Once happily settled in a beautiful little house by the sea, things started to change. Really change.

Menopause and my elderly mother arrived about the same time.

How my mother came to live with us is no mystery to me. When I was two hours old I remember someone thrusting a miniature pen in my infant-sized fingers and helping me sign a contract that said something about a big family secret in which my mother had given up her first child, a daughter, to adoption and that I, her youngest child after three sons, would be the daughter who would forever love and adore her, never quite leaving her side. So the deal is, at a very tender and impressionable moment, I promised to take care of her into old age and beyond. The "beyond" part of the contract gets a little fuzzy.

In addition to starting her own painting career and making us into one small, happy family of three, my mother helped out tremendously doing our laundry, grocery shopping, cooking, running errands, and basically keeping herself busy around the house, cheerfully and wonderfully happy. We loved the domestic attention and kissed the ground she walked on with heartfelt gratitude. L and I spent every hour of every day pursuing our respective art careers, part-time teaching jobs, running a small business and whatever else it takes to fill in the financial gaps of life as the self-employed artist. Then one day, my mother says to me rather shyly, "I met a man and he wants me to marry him." I, of course, am thrilled that after being a widow for twenty-three years my seventy-nine year old mother has found love, in the nick of time. "But," she says with a worried look on her face, "I don't want to live with him." A tiny problem, indeed, but not insurmountable. We decide that my mother, and the new love of her life, Walter, a quiet, shy, Midwesterner, can live with us until we move into a bigger house with one of those attached "in-law" suites, of which there are many here in Florida.

Well, that never happened. The "in-law" suite that is.

But isn't that just like life? Interrupted plans and everything always changing, especially when you least expect it?

Oh. Before I forget. At forty-five I ended up having a hysterectomy. I certainly didn't plan on that either. But it saved my life.

So buckle up and hold on to your hats. The Menopause Queen is about to set the ride called mid-life in motion with a true story, my story (I've changed names, dates, and places so no one can be identified) about love, healing the past, forgiveness, changes, Big Changes, and waking up to what is real and true and wonderful: one breath at a time. And wisecracks galore.

Initiation

OK, so it feels like all hell is breaking loose.

Hel is breaking loose. She's waking up your spirit cycle.

Is that anything like the rinse cycle?

It's more like a long and wobbly spin cycle.

I don't think I'm going to like it. I don't like it already. I can't sleep, can't eat, can't think straight. Everything that goes into my stomach brings on the bloat and a bout of belching and heartburn. I'm not tired when I go to bed and I wake up exhausted. I'm nervous, anxious, and scared most of the time. I'm hypersensitive and inappropriately emotional. The other day I drove by a vacant lot being cleared for a new home and I started to cry when I saw them cut down a big oak; a beautiful tree probably forty or fifty years old. I loved that tree.

That tree was about your age?

Yeah. Well, seeing that tree massacred, hacked, and chopped down so senselessly launched me into a mournful depression for the rest of the day. I swear I heard that tree screaming. I couldn't even watch. I had to turn up the radio so I didn't hear the buzzing of the saws and that awful machine that shreds everything into tiny little lawn chips. They could have saved that tree. They could have built their stupid big house around it. That tree didn't do anything to anyone. Now she's gone forever. I feel like a child out of control.

I don't consider your feelings inappropriate, idiotic, or childlike. You're waking up to the invisible realm of spirit that exists in all things. You're connecting in wholeness to all that is. That's Hel, She who sits at the crossroads of Change and guides your inner fire—helping you do what you're supposed to be doing at this time in your life—your mid-life.

Waking up? Waking up to dying is more like it. I'm suddenly terrified of any and every disease. I have overwhelming thoughts about breast cancer, heart attacks, and losing my bone mass. All this leaky emotional energy keeps me from enjoying what little energy I do have. I wake up in the middle of a nightmare where I've suddenly collapsed in a pile of wet, rubbery skin resembling a bloodhound without blood or bones. I'm obsessing way too much about my body, turning every tiny ache and pain into some horrid terminal disease. One entire shelf of the refrigerator door is filled with small brown bottles of homeopathic elixirs. L, my husband, calls them "herbal bourbon." He says the door's going to fall off if I add another bottle to the collection.

Seeking alternative health-care solutions is not a bad thing.

No, that's not the worst thing; it's the idea of being totally out of control in my own body that's making me nuts. I feel like I've been invaded and invalidated; the incredible shrinking woman, tossed aside like outdated meat. My shelf life is running out and there's nothing I can do about it. And that bad twin, you know, the old Wise Ass sitting in the saddle next to me? I'm starting to look like her!

Well, you can think of it as an invasion or something that's being done to you, if you like. But that's not really going to help you. What you're going through is a spiritual transformation and metamorphosis, a sacred calling from the depths of your soul, from the heart of Hel's kitchen. You're on the road to becoming the woman you are meant to be, tuned in and turned on to your soul's yearning. The gifts of menopause are many.

Who is this Hel you keep talking about? Doesn't sound like a popular name.

She's the Menopause Queen: courageous inner guide who nourishes and heals. She lives in every cell in your body. Think of her as an ancestral memory, the accumulated wisdom of all the women in your genetic field. Your Wise Ass within, if you will.

Does she cook?

Does she ever.

Because that's really what I need, somebody to prepare a decent, healthy home-cooked meal just once a day. Like a grandmother. I never had that, a grandmother who cooked. Now that would soothe my nerves. A grandmother's tender touch and a delicious bowl of soup. I used to cook, you know? I used to be a good cook. But that hormone is gone, too. How did you say this Hel is going to help me?

Listen closely. You'll see.

JANUARY

January 1
8:43 am

Tuesday

° Turn fifty this year. How did that happen? What? Just the other day I was twenty-three (or was it thirty-two?)
° Feeling Bloated. Must be fluid retention in advance of Full Moon on the 30th. Remember: Fat is how "they" make you feel. Have to love myself no matter what size my panties are. I feel good. I feel good. (Are the size 9 thong underwear more expensive?)
° Order more Menopausal Tonic from women who live in the woods.
° Remember, it's not a hot flash, it's a power surge (yeah, right.)
° Would have started my period this week, I think.
° So proud of myself. No New Year's resolutions. Avoiding self-flagellation in Feb.
° Fifty? Five times ten. Ten times five. Half a century. Five-Oh!

January 3 (I think)
1:17 am

Thursday

Shit. The chihuahuas are howling tonight. A hot flash nearly blew me out of bed. I'm wide awake after only two hours of sleep and another dream about that Menopause Queen. I woke up drenched; now I'm cold. I'm actually shivering a little. Maybe I'm catching something. I feel damp and undercooked, like a premature bagel, floating face up and pale. I was hoping it was closer to 5am. That would have given me almost six hours in a row. That would have been unusual. That would have been sheer luck. Now I'll be up for at least an hour; possibly two. That means I'll be a zombie all day.

Last night I made it until 3:13, but spent another hour tossing and turning, shifting and sighing before finally getting up. E, my acupuncturist straight from heaven, told me to take advantage of the free time. That's what she calls it, Free Time. That's not what I call it. I tell her she's an optimist. She says to start writing. She told me to buy a special, no-lines, blank journal and start making some notes on whatever pops up: recurring thoughts, daydreams, and especially what I'm thinking about when I can't sleep; and exactly what it is that's waking me up (as if I can actually name it!). She says there are messages in my dreams and I need to get them all down in detail, if I can remember them. I wish I could forget them. I have this recurring dream where I'm looking at my chin in the mirror, a very close-up mirror, and there's a bristly black hair protruding and it turns out to be an enlarged and hairy leg of a fly embedded so deep only surgery can remove it. And no doctor will take me. Like Sisyphus I'm doomed to drag my hairy chin uphill into eternity.

E told me to get a red candle. She said the flame would help me relax. I told her I don't do candles. Especially after I read that lonely women and candles are replacing women and cats as the new sad trend. E said not to believe everything I read. She says I am now entering the "fire of my life" and keeping a journal is going to be my escape route. She repeats with a big smile, "Pay attention to memories. They carry healing energy." And she reminds me to breathe.

Thank goodness I decided to take this year off. Not that my measly, part-time teaching pittance made much of a difference. But in my mind I need time more than anything else right now. Time for *me*. I'll miss my students, all wide-eyed and happy to get their hands in clay and express their twenty-something selves. They don't know it, but they're the best teachers I've ever had. I get to experience "beginner mind" every time they light up with creative joy. I guess I'll be depending on my own mind to light me up now. Yikes!

January 4
3:13 am

Friday

It's weird how my eyes just open and there are the green, glowing numbers on the alarm clock waiting for me, staring at me. Sometimes I play a little guessing game before I open my eyes. Is it 2:43 or 4:23? Is it 3:51 or 1:35? Funny how I'm a good guesser when it comes to time. I know when 20 minutes is up and almost to the minute what time it is when asked. I would have been a winner on "Beat The Clock." Without a good night's sleep I'm not feeling I can beat eggs.

How in the hell my husband can snore all night long and not have a clue that I'm rabidly awake rattles my nerves to no end. I'm envious of his deep sleep. I want it. I want to reach over and poke him and wake him up so I can steal his deep sleep away from him (a demitasse of testosterone wouldn't be bad either). I wouldn't mind some of his dreams, too. Actually, he doesn't really remember his dreams and that too would be a relief. I haven't told him I'm having this much trouble sleeping. I don't want him to think something is wrong with me, like I'm defective now that I've reached my very late forties.

S says she hasn't told her husband she's in menopause. Doesn't ever talk about it at home. She doesn't want him to know she's, well—getting older. I wonder does she think he's blind, too?

January 6
3:43 am

Sunday

The truth is I have a secret second life. It begins sometime after midnight and can last all the way to 4:30 am, sometimes even 5 am. More often than not it begins around 3 am. Maybe 2:47, to be precise. My secret second life isn't sordid or ugly or glamorous. It isn't expensive. It doesn't involve the Internet, thank goodness. And it doesn't require new clothes. Usually I'm naked. But that's only because my secret life begins with a fiery sweat causing me to tear off my clothes like I used to when a different kind of wild and wicked urge kept me naked, thrashing, breathing heavy and wet all over until the wee hours of the morning. My secret life these days is usually sexless, solitary, and very very quiet. But that doesn't mean I'm not thinking about sex. I am, in some ways, that is. So here I am, sitting upright in bed, naked, my hair limp and damp from another hot flash from hell and tired of twiddling my thumbs and waiting for sleep, sweet sleep, to return to my side of the bed, when out of nowhere I get this rascally urge to dip my finger into my yoni. With a quirky smile on my face I run my pointer finger up my silky slit like swiping a carrot stick through an eggless fish dip. Next, and I don't know where these interior instructions come from, because it sure feels like someone else has a hold of my mind, I unflinchingly hold my glistening finger right under my husband's handsome nose. He's sound asleep and I just want to see if he'll twitch and quiver like a dog having a dream about raw meat. I'm curious. That's all. I don't really want to wake him up because then he may expect me to actually do something sexy. That, I'm not interested in right now. I'm very busy doing olfactory research.

I push my finger a little closer, waving it back and forth in short, waggling sweeps, like waving a miniature flag, careful not to make contact. I love L's nose. It is so perfectly aquiline and direct and—well, penile in a very primal and gorgeous way. If I were into worshipping anything, which I'm not, except for the raw wildness of Nature, I'd be prone to pray to L's nose the way devout Hindus drag those hypnotically perfect lingam stones rubbed smooth by the Ganges river and prop them up in their homes as the divine penis of the God Shiva. And then rest them ever so subtly in a yoni stone shaped like a cereal bowl to symbolize the original creative spark of Shakti, animating soul of the Universe, without which no god, no life at all, could exist. Their sexual union, a communion of souls. I remember masturbating once with one of those lingam stones when L was out of town. I'd given him the lingam as a birthday gift oh so long ago. After I was done pleasuring myself, I washed it all off nice and clean and then put it back on the nightstand and never told L about it. I thought of his nose the whole time, and Shiva and Shakti squealing in love's rapture, dancing around the bed.

These little secrets keep popping up in my head. I don't know what to do with them—except write them down and get them out of my head.

It's said that many miracles take place in the presence of the yoni-lingam.

I keep praying.

Just the other day I read that the penis first came onto the scene during the Reptilian age some umpteen thousand years ago. The image tickles me to no end: Tyrannosaurus Rex dragging his big, bad rippling schlong around trying not to trip over himself or knock himself out when it stiffens and bongs him between the eyes when he catches sight of his mate of the day wiggling her wrinkly rump around the mountains. This article, which I thought was quite brilliant, also said that long before the penis appeared, all life on Earth swam in an oceanic tidal flux; one vast sea of lunar female fluids. So somewhere in our ancient memory there's a primal dream of floating loosely and languidly on the waves of a big blue womb; a huge scaly penis with beady eyes looming on the shores ahead.

Yep. I'm becoming very familiar with my primal dreams within, that silly organ called my Menopausal Mind, the ticking of the clock, and my fleeting pheromones that are at this very moment backing out of my body, tiptoeing down the hall and running out the front door shrieking wildly.

L doesn't move. Doesn't flinch. I pull my finger away and take a sniff. Hmm. I love the smell that is the juicy inside of me—or as juicy as it gets these days. How my huz can sleep through my secret life is beyond me. Especially when I'm burning up inside, the little volcano that could.

January 8
7:52 am
                                    Tuesday

I endeavor to do more yoga, not less. More meditation, not less. More magic, not less. And much less *thinking*. What the hell does endeavor mean, anyway?

What I'd really like to do is grow up, especially since I'll be half a century old this year. Have a nice little job that I love and get paid for (correction: get well-paid for; I need to be very wish-specific here) with a check that comes in like clockwork every week or two; a regenerative kind of sustainable future creating things I love and sharing it with people who like the things I make. My mother says that when her friends at the Senior Center ask her what I do for a living, she doesn't know what to say. "Tell them I'm an animal trainer." She laughs an uncomfortable giggle, "Oh, Nancy." She waves and flops her hand at me, "Go on."

"Tell them the truth," I finally confess. "That your daughter is an artist."

Yeah. It makes no sense to me either when I actually say it out loud that at this big old age, I'm still playing with clay, making totally fun and functional pots on a spinning wheel; playing in a metal sand box and ladling molten glass from a roaring furnace into the negative impressions made in the sand, then standing around in mind-boggling awe waiting for the color of the glass to go from orange hot to clear ice and then in a flash rush the stiffened glass to an oven and let it cool for days. And then when I'm not doing any of those things, I gather stuff that I find on the beach and make what the voices in my heart tell me to make—mostly spirit figures who have something to teach me when they're all done and staring back at me and feeling really happy that I followed their instructions and just let it all happen.

I'm hoping that some day it will make sense to me that I stuck with this unpredictable, totally insecure, passion that keeps an important interior part of me propped up and happily tuned in to intense moments of pure bliss, but all the exterior parts of my life falling into quivering little piles of unpaid bills and never knowing what's next. Art-making is the only place where I can lose myself and feel found at the same time.

Blissful moments are their own reward.

It also occurs to me that I probably can't keep a job. I'm too sensitive to people's feelings; too wrapped up in my own way of doing things, and I have a neurotic fear of perfume. There isn't a place for this kind of thing on a job application and I don't think I'd want to bring it up in a job interview situation. *It says here, Ms. Blair, that you have a fear of perfume. Can you explain further, please?* And I can't. Well, I can, but who wants to hear that in order for me to work in their office building? I'd have to make up little signs and post them everywhere: "For your scent-sitive new co-worker, please refrain from using any scented body products. That means hairspray, too. And by the way, this is a reminder to the night crew: no toxic cleaning products. Use only the Earthfriendly kind, please." *Hmm. Am I reading this right, Ms. Blair, it also says here that you need at least a three-month vacation every other month?* "Well, that's just to be on the safe side." *And that you'd prefer working about two hours a day so you can have enough time to do what you really want to do?* Well, yes. If I don't make art I'll get very suicidal and then, well, Mr Human Resources man, then I won't be able to work at all, will I?

Thank you Ms. Blair, he says as he lifts himself up like a rocket launching in slow motion and escorts me to the door, discreetly dropping my application in the garbage. *We'll call you when something opens up*. Like a hole in the wall he will. This scene runs through my head whenever I think I'm a big girl and can go out in the world and earn my own living (although these days maybe a job at 7–11 is all I can handle). So to console myself I get busy making more stuff in my studio because my hands are like breasts and they want to nurse the world.

My friends, who have real paying jobs, think I have a very cool and easy life. I haven't told them that it heats up around the time the car payment, the health insurance premium, the mortgage, and the credit card bills are due. And as much as I think of myself as an independent woman, I'm almost entirely dependent on my husband, and my parents, to support me. And I'm going on fifty years old already!

So what do you think this living-a-little-feminist-lie does for my self-esteem?

Nada. Zippo. Zilch.

I'm an independent thinker with a noose around me purse.

J says if I just keep doing what I love and affirming that money is my friend, it will all work out. So I say these little prayers every morning and write notes to Money's Mama and ask if money can come out and play with me and if money is just energy (Energy with a capital E!), and if it's infinite and there's so much of it to go around can somebody please just wink a little pile in my direction once in a while? I'd be really grateful and I promise I'll be a very happy artist friend. And I put these notes, like big begging hints, on the altar above my computer desk because I'm worried that Money's Mama is too busy taking care of Martha Stewart, whose prayers are written on fancy note cards, all color-coordinated and gold embossed with a fancy S, and my trailer-park hen scratch is on a neon-orange post-it pad.

I've just about driven myself into a hunger frenzy...again. If there's one thing that's gotten more out of control than my imagination these days, it's my appetite.

High Protein Grown-Up Breakfast
When You Want More Than Flakes

Slice of your favorite high-fiber bread (at least 4 g per serving)
1 serving slice "firm" tofu
3–4 fresh basil leaves
Thick slice ripe red tomato (I choose organic)
1 tsp olive oil (I love the full-flavor virgin variety)
Thick slice red onion (give up the big deal about onion breath; consider it a charm to ward off invaders of quiet space, and enjoy one of Nature's gifts of good health; cooking without onions is like dancing in the closet!)
1 or 2 slices of veggie/soy cheddar cheese

Broil tofu just enough to heat up. Toast bread lightly. Use a timer if you're like me and can't seem to do much to bread these days but blacken it. Build your breakfast, one delicious slice at a time, beginning with tofu. Layer next four ingredients, drizzling oil over tomato. Return Grown-Up Breakfast to toaster oven for a minute on low bake just to warm up the tomatoes and onions. Do not cook or broil. Again, use a timer if you have to. Top your hearty, healthy, and delicious new breakfast food with a slice of cheddar.

Do not stand up while eating. Digestive juices flow better when you eat sitting down. Chew slowly. While eating, do not do anything else but eat. Keep your mind on your food, and all the cells in your body getting really jazzed about eating good foods that are good for your menopausal mindbody.

Self-care is the number-one priority of menopause, and it can't be crowded out or moved down on the priority list, no matter what is going on around you (or in you), in the kitchen, in the neighborhood, in the world.

Self-care is not negotiable.

Breathing In. Breathing Out.

Take time to smell the olive oil. The olive tree and its fruity food have a long and delicious history throughout the ancient world. The olive tree was sacred to Athena, Goddess of Wisdom, and honored as the Holy Virgin (the word virgin originally meant "a woman who knows how to take care of herself" and only later became associated with chastity). Athena's more menopausal aspect is that of the Holy Crone, Medusa, who was able to turn men who dared defile her to stone.

Extra virgin olive oil is definitely a wise choice when using vegetable oils. It's recommended most by nutritionists as an excellent source of healthy, highly digestible good-heart fat. Good fat is also a very important nutrient for building healthy cells and hormones. Avoid all hydrogenated and partially hydrogenated oil products. Our bodies can't digest them and we don't know where they end up in our organs; most likely predisposing us to diseases and early aging. Read labels carefully.

Note: To the love goddess within: Olive oil makes an excellent, all-natural vaginal lubricant! Keep a small (refillable) container near your bed, within reach, and use liberally. And I do mean liberally. It's a great massage oil to get the love juices flowing. Either alone or with a special, loving friend.

January 9
4:14 am

Wednesday

It's not fair that I'm menopausal; my stepfather is battling cancer, my mother is losing her mind and memory all at the same time and my marriage is wandering in the Gulag looking for a thin slice of warm fun (L says life is often cruel, but never fair.) A says I should be grateful that I don't have a teenager to boot. When I think of it all wrapped up in a mid-life package I start to wondering if evolution had such a well-thought-out plan for us. L and I talked about marriage counseling, after days of dreadful silence. I'm scared as all get out that he'll wake up and realize that the past nineteen years were all a big mistake, and end up with some sexy blonde strapped in faux Manolo fuck-me-here-and-now heels and leather thong underwear who giggles and laughs at all his jokes and pushes her breasts into his face without first having to pick them up off her belly button. In my pathetic fantasy I'm standing in the kitchen wearing my way-too-fuchsia, 100 percent cotton mu mu with larger-than-life hibiscus flowers plastered all over it and hanging off me like a tangled parachute; a glass of green barley drink in one hand and a jar of herbal libido boosters in the other. "But honey," I call out desperately, "I promise this new supplement is going to do the trick this time. Honest. Look. I feel sexy already." With that I bend down and lift the hem of my dress with my teeth, waving at my crotch in an increasingly hopeless and desultory way. My huz and his new thirty-something giggle and wiggle their way out the door and never once look back.

When I look down the turnpike of our marriage I want so much to see us happy and grab-assin' and leaping like rutting gazelles in spring. But all I see is two people pulled over by the side of the road, wandering that grassy swale just off the shoulder where drunks stand with their backs to the oncoming traffic with their hands in their crotch (do they think we're stupid?), and mothers bend over small squatting children, telling them to "Hurry up. We don't have all day." In this spot, called Pull Over Now, L and I are wrapped in loose gauze from head to toe, the walking wounded, arms outstretched stumbling and bumping into trees, saying very politely whichever way we turn, "Excuse me. So sorry. Have a nice day. Ta ta."

And all I want to do is play and have fun and laugh and live like there's no tomorrow. I want to feel alive again like I did when I was hitchhiking across country and didn't own a thing. Hell, I didn't even have any keys, then. Was it so long ago?

When F called yesterday to do our weekly "Women Making Magic" session I told her how my guts were all freaked out and wrenching about where my overactive TV imagination was taking our marriage. "Wonderful," she shrieked, which really pissed me off. I hate when she reminds me that every moment is perfect the way it is. And then she continues as if she's channeling a spirit guide from the Psychic Network, "Now is the time to adjust your deepest intentions and lean all your hopes and desires on love and joy." I hear myself start to respond with a "Yeah but…" (I've been yeah-butting myself all over the map these days and F is tired of hearing it.) This time I catch myself in mid-"but" before my "but" has a chance to trap me.

"*All* your hopes and desires," F says, as if reading my thoughts. "Your whole being." She pauses and then continues with the voice of Sister Mary Margaret from my Saturday catechism class, "Nancy," she says slowly, "Now is the perfect time to get honest with yourself, and with L. Let's face it. You don't know what the future is going to look like. Your only responsibility is to speak your truth." She reminds me to make every thought a spell. Every act a ritual. She says I can't allow any other possibility to enter my mind but joy and love. "Because," she says. "The beauty and wonder of love is that it's self-grown."

I guess that means I have to stop adding up our assets, subtracting our liabilities and dividing by two just to see if I'll end up a bag lady pushing my mother down the street flopped in a shopping cart, her legs spread-eagled and dangling over the sides, the two of us howling like banshees in between a litany of curse words aimed at the sidewalk.

"Think simple, fearless math," F says. "Love plus joy."

Just when I decided not to think.

I think I need to do a love spell. I'm obsessing wildly about losing my husband. Or maybe I'm paranoid and projecting. P says she's had a bit of menopause paranoia herself. Seems it just comes over her and then vanishes like a thin fog in the sun. I read in one of those relationship repair manuals that we tend to blame the other person in our lives for issues we ourselves don't want to deal with. This means that I'm planning to leave L for a blonde? Can't be. Read three horoscopes from women's magazines while standing in the check-out counter at the supermarket; each one more ridiculously off the mark than the last, with ever-too-predictable predictions of that "special tall, dark, handsome someone on the rise." L is short and bald. On the way home I got to wondering if I ought to take any magazine seriously that uses a twelve-year-old model on the cover, gussies her up to look like a teenager and then runs a by-line that says, "Shake those flabby thighs thin in thirty days or less."

On the way home caught myself channeling a song from years ago, *Keep your heart open cause love will find a way.*

I want inner peace so bad it's making me nuts.

January 10
11:35 am   Thursday

I sit and write with pen in hand, my fingers stiff from gripping too tight, and I am overwhelmed with silence. The electricity went off suddenly this morning. Usually this happens during a storm and I have fair warning to shut down my computer and find some other activity to move to. But today the shut-down came without the usual warning. No flash of lightning or rumble of thunder. At first I'm pissed. Damn brewing storms. Damn power company. Damn remote island.

Always something unexpected intruding on my plans. Yet this abrupt intrusion leaves me jarred by the natural silence that suddenly fills in the spaces that happen without electricity. No humming of the clocks, sudden clanking on of the refrigerator motor, rattling of the dehumidifier, clicking rush of the air conditioner.

Suddenly I'm thrown into the natural world around me. Rather, it's the natural world that now can penetrate the noisy barrier that buzzes between me and life, itself. I can hear the stiff, whizzing song of tree frogs coming from the lot across the street, the cardinal pair in the hibiscus bush just outside my window bleep, bleep, bleeping, and an occasional slow, passing car. Water is dripping somewhere in the house. My nervous system feels suddenly calm, the way my body sighs in relief after an intrusive loud-radio-thumping coming from the car sitting next to me at a stop light leaves me in the settling dust of my own thoughts after pulling away.

Yes, I must admit it; I prefer this natural silence to the electromagnetic strain that clatters all around me.

In the solid, natural silence that surrounds me, a memory floats up like a bubble in a pond.

After my first marriage failed, at the tender age of twenty-one I returned home to live with my parents in the trailer I grew up in. When I was twelve they had moved out of the trailer park onto a two-acre lot on a long country road that linked two towns together. Our move put us just over the border and I had to change schools. I finished my junior year of high school before meeting C and got married a week after I turned seventeen.

My teens were tumultuous years in that trailer. I arrived home from school every afternoon to an empty house. My three brothers were signed up in various branches of the military and my mother worked second shift at the plastics factory. She had already left by the time I got home. My father would be home in two, three, four hours, depending on how many bar stops he made along the way. The bus dropped me off at the end of the short driveway and I'd open the heavy back metal door to the lingering smells of cigarette smoke, sticky wine, and total silence. I'd drop off my books on my bed, change my clothes and take up residence on the couch to listen to sad songs; stupid, sad songs that spoke directly to my heart. I'd lie there crying—sobbing for hours over swirling thoughts and heavy emotions I couldn't put into words.

In the world outside the trailer I looked good. I was an A student, president of my class, co-captain on the junior varsity cheerleading squad and dating one of the star shooters on the basketball team. On the inside I lived the life of a child of an alcoholic family. My father, a brilliant artist working as a sign painter, was a very unhappy man and when he drank, which was most of the time, he let everyone know just how unhappy he was by telling the same sad story over and over again while sitting at the kitchen table, his chin in his hand, a cigarette clutched in his fingers, a beer, or whatever he was drinking at the time, placed perfectly in reach in front of him. His story goes like this.

"Those sons-a-bitches hit our ship. Arty MacArthy, my good ole buddy died. We used to have a good time the two of us. Now what have I got. Nothing."

There were variations on the same theme of my father's few years in the navy during World War II. Sometimes he'd elaborate on offshore episodes with his buddies, or how some wrong was perpetrated on him and that's how they started a fight. I heard his war stories every night of my life for as long as I lived in that trailer. I hated storytelling for years to follow. I hated when anyone started to tell a story about some miserable event in the past. I shut down, closed my ears, went into fantasyland, hoping not to have to respond.

Worst of all the stories or drunken babble that my father eventually got around to were the ones about my mother. He'd go right from the war abroad to the war at home, blaming my mother for his miserable little life. He called her every derogatory female curse in the book, and more not in the book.

"Your mother's nothing but a black bastard whore."

I didn't even know what those words meant, except it wasn't a good reflection on my mother's virtue. He accused her of having affairs with everyone she met.

"Shut up. Shut up about Mom. I hate you. Shut up." I'd scream from the couch just in the living room, coming to her defense. If I squeezed myself hard into the right side of the couch I was far enough around the corner so at least I didn't have to look at him. My father didn't hear me no matter how loud I shouted or how small the trailer grew with each passing hour. He kept rambling on and on. I could smell his sticky sweet story from one room to the next; from one lousy episode to the next. No matter where I went in the trailer, his story commanded all my attention. How lucky my mother was to be working. During the week she was spared the onslaught of accusations.

She left me with him. She left me alone to do what she couldn't.

He only hit me once. Decked me real hard after another hair-brained screaming match; me finally yelling my deepest, maddest feelings at the top of my lungs, "I wish you were dead!" which were the worst words I'd ever said to anyone. I didn't know my father was behind me, chasing me down the skinny hallway to my room, my brother right behind him. I turned quickly to slam my door and caught my father's fist on the right side of my face. I'm not sure if it was the force of the blow or my own surprise that pushed me clear into the closet, where I didn't stay for too long. My brother pounced on my father, easily knocking him down and almost smothering him. I had to pull J off with all my might for fear he was actually going to kill dad, creating right before my eyes a self-fulfilling prophecy.

Later I would take on the survival technique of living by leaving, which I figured out later on was my mother's answer to life.

The day I got my license—my ticket to ride—I left my father's story as fast as I could. But no matter how far away I got from home, his slobbering litany came with me. I packed it up in my mind, where it continued to replay for years, until the day we buried him.

I didn't hate my father all the time. And really didn't want him to die. Just sober up and be good, because when he was sober I adored him. I loved watching him paint signs, bringing words to life in bright colors. His hand always perfectly steady and every long stroke of the brush perfectly straight. How I marveled at his skill. He'd smile at me in the middle of a pause for a cigarette, putting his brush down on the torn piece of cardboard that acted as a palette. The minute his hand left the brush it was my cue to pick it up. I wrapped my little fingers around the thin wooden handle and, mimicking my father's every move, every gentle gesture, I slowly and deliberately wiped the brush back and forth in the little pool of paint he left in the middle of the palette, gathering enough in the long soft animal hairs of the brush to be able to write my name without having to go back for more paint. Sometimes he'd give me a little instruction.

Hold it lightly. Don't squeeze. Let the brush take you with it. There you go. Keep the line fluid through the a and open at the c. OK now, come back at the bottom of the y and curl it up, lifting your brush at the very end. Spacing is everything. You can't do it by the rule. You have to let your eye lead you.

I love making letters, Dad. Can I do one? I mean a real one. Not just my name. Can I make a letter on the sign? Sometimes he'd let me fill in between the outside lines of a vertical stroke or the sweeping curve on a capitol O. I could fill in the empty spaces, but he wouldn't let me start a new letter.

Don't get used to it. It's not woman's work.

As much as he loved having me next to him, my eyes lovingly riveted on the magic he managed to create on a simple square of plywood, my father did not have hopes for me in the sign business. After taking his last drag off the tiny chewed stump of a cigarette and flicking it under his foot, he'd pick up where he left off and with a few quick moves wipe out my squiggly name on the palette to begin again his serious work.

The many times I spent standing next to my father watching him paint, first as a young girl and later on in my twenties when he was sick and needed me to do more than watch, are the ones that fill my heart with love and joy to this very day, over twenty-five years after he died. I reveled in the quiet moments we stood together, caught in the creative flow and me soaking it up by proxy. He transmitted something enduring and eternal during those precious times together; his love for creating something from nothing. My father had enormous talent. Men in the sign business called him a genius, a true artist. I proudly shone in this, his positive reputation. Men in the sign business also said, Leo Blair's the best, if you can catch him when he isn't drinking.

He was the best sign painter; there was no question about it. I loved it when he worked in gold leaf. That was my favorite time to watch, when he turned dull white letters into a glimmering treasure. Working with thin sheets of gold tickled me in a nervous, sacred way. Was I feeling my father's tension? The incredible skill of getting that flimsy, uncontrollable perfect square of precious metal to stick exactly where you wanted it was pure magic.

Don't breathe until I say it's OK.

I nodded my head knowing that any sound out of my mouth, any movement, would blow the thin gold skin like a hurricane force, tearing it down the middle, rendering it useless, a waste. He used a wide, squirrel-hair brush that he fluffed against his hair to pick up enough static electricity to lift the dazzling sheet of gold from the small pink pad of paper, where each square sheet lay snug and nestled. He then carried the radiant sheet carefully and slowly to its destination. I held my breath, watching intently, as if he were rescuing a small child from a pond on the end of a rope, hoping the treasured cargo didn't slip off in the middle of the maneuver. Until each gold sheet was safely secured atop the tacky adhesive painted on each letter did I dare take another breath. My father moved swiftly and attentively, like a surgeon in the operating room, like a priest at the altar. As soon as the gold was caught and laid out flat on the surface of the sign he quickly switched tools, laying the brush down on the table next to him, without taking his eyes off the gold, and picking up the small, soft red velvet ball that looked like a piece of Christmas candy wrapped and tied with string, he patted and tamped the gold until it was firmly adhered in place. He then gave a little signal, nodding his head, and we'd exhale together, breathing freely for a few minutes until the next nod, when we inhaled together, holding our breath again in the gold leaf ritual that lasted for hours, until the sign was finished.

I still have all my father's tools. When he died my mother asked me if I wanted anything from his painting studio; The Shed, as we called it. I knew exactly what I wanted. I walked in, picked up all his brushes strewn around the room, packed them neatly and carefully in the tool-box he carried to every job and where he kept his lettering brushes, gold leaf tools, charcoal, pens, pencils, erasers, and razor blades. I looked around to make sure I hadn't missed anything. Before closing it up I spotted his leather eyeglass case with his name, Leo, embossed on it in all capital letters. I grabbed it, too, placing it squarely on top of everything else and then slowly closed the lid. I carried my father's tools out of the shed and I've had them with me ever since, packing and unpacking them with every move I've ever made.

My father died in 1976.

It would be nearly fifteen years before I opened the box.

One of the reasons my first marriage didn't work was because C wasn't an artist. I didn't know it at the time, but the man I was going to spend my life with had to know—and love—the exquisite power of the creative process and the deep soulful satisfaction being in it brought. The man I was going to spend my life with had to be an artist. In the quiet moments spent with my father as an adept of art I was setting the precedent for relationships to follow. The fact that I ended up marrying a man with the same name as my father, well, that's just another mystery worth smiling at.

Even after I got married (the first time), I kept going back home. On weekends I'd make the one-hour drive back to the trailer, taking my cat, Munchie, with me. It's not that my marriage wasn't working. I loved being married. I finished my senior year of high school, transferring to a large city school so C could finish his last year of college. In my new adult life I was introduced to the world of hip thinkers, parties, alcohol, and drugs. Many drugs. This was 1970 and Vietnam had our eyes glued to the TV. I remember watching one night as the draft lottery numbers were being posted. We shifted restlessly, knowing that any one of the young men in our living room that night might die on a decision made by some old man sitting in a stiff suit somewhere very far away. C and I breathed a sigh of relief when, by some luck of the draw, he came out on the high end.

We had an easy marriage the first year or so. C was an only child in an upper-middle-class family and money flowed freely from his doting parents. Every Friday his mother and father arrived, their arms filled with grocery bags. Not only had his mother arrived with food, she had already prepared it. I was lucky, too, then but I didn't realize it.

I kept returning to the place that caused the most pain in my life, the way a fingernail roams over skin, returning to a crusty scab to pick away again and again. My family. If I wasn't able to visit I'd call. I've been calling home every weekend my whole life. But it wasn't my father that I longed to see. In the middle of every return moment home it was my mother I thought about. Her smiling face, her open arms, her unconditional loving ways.

The one visit that stands out in my mind happened after I left home the second time. After getting a divorce I moved back in with my parents. When I arrived and let my parents know I was getting a divorce, my mother just held me. My father was mad. "Who's going to want you now?" was his only response. In my mind I finished the sentence he didn't say "...now that I'm used goods."

Oh Dad, that is so last-century thinking.

Memories, like pink lightning, appear out of the vast reaches of my mind, light me up momentarily, and are gone.

Only I can control my thoughts. I don't have to think about anything I don't want to. I can change my mind. Why not? Everything else is changing.

January 11
3:11 am

(named after the Norse Goddess, Frigg, a friggin' good sign)

Love spell: Decide to gather up all the stuff that's broken that I haven't gotten around to gluing back together yet. The house is all quiet and half-lit by a pale crescent Moon, pacing slowly like a cosmic boomerang across the sky. I didn't know why at the time, but a few weeks ago I bought this big clear glass vase that looks like a ginger jar. I like trusting my gut, even when there isn't any real logical reason for doing something. I figure artistic license.

Insanity, maybe, but it's what keeps me busy. Logic shmogic. Who needs a reason to be creative?

Today, the empty glass jar makes perfect sense. Magic sense. Decide to fill it up with whatever I find around the house, or out in the yard, or on the beach, making little prayers and positive affirmations as I place the pieces in the glass jar and arrange them really carefully. I concentrate on breathing and making sure the pieces are lodged tight against each other nice and snug, like I want to be with L. Snug as a bug. Love bugs.

First to go is a hand-blown blue cup with a few big white polka dots scattered around the edge. Turning it upside down, I arrange the largest white orb facing me. It is a good place to begin, the Moon facing outward, staring at my heart. Then there's the little clay mask that my friend B bought at a flea market because she knew I had to have it. Last week in my frantic fit of "got to get my office organized" it fell on the floor and shattered to tiny, dusty bits, except for a long thin section that included the left eye, one nostril, and the little tiny pinhole that is the mouth. I threw all the bits away and kept the shard. It seemed almost too powerful, half a face staring up at me from the floor, to throw away. I was stunned at how it cracked so perfectly to leave so much and so little at the same time. I placed it in the jar to the right of the Moon, with a long, deep breath, "May all that breaks apart come together again in love and deep trust." Then the tiny yellow onyx bear that I gave my Mom for her birthday a couple of years ago, carved by a southwest Native American artist. The front paw is broken and the ear is chipped. She dropped it dusting. I reach into the jar and lean it against the blue cup along the back-side, the background of my being. "Help me with forgiveness and patience." Then there's the dead butterfly L found at the end of the driveway last week. It's still pretty colorful. Picking it up ever so carefully it falls from my fingers and lands just under the moon shape. Perfect. I didn't even have to try.

What next?

I turn and walk around the living room breathing deeply and not "trying" to find something. I am drawn to a bowl of rocks that L and I picked up at the beach when we were in Seattle last summer. We had a great time and I want that feeling of closeness to be what stays with me always, no matter what the future looks like. I let my fingers be drawn to the one with two parallel stripes of white quartz, like rings; wedding bands. I call these striped rocks Friendship Stones, because the circle never ends. I say nothing when I place it next to the butterfly because the beautiful and complete stone says everything I cannot.

The jar needs some very big thing next. Something to sit on the overturned glass cup and direct the energy of the spell.

I know exactly what to do. My hands instinctively reach for the ceramic statue of Minerva that I bought in Turkey with L. He got really sick when we were in Ankara and had to have the bus driver stop the tour bus every fifteen minutes so he could fly out the door and barf. I got really scared that L was so sick. Finding the sculpture seemed to help me. The look on Minerva's face is solemn and strong. She's wearing a Medusa breastplate for protection, snakes wrapped around her face like rotelle noodles. It's not a great sculptural work of art. It looks like a kid did it using a chopstick to carve the details. But it seems perfect to me. Perfectly primal; like the yearning in my heart.

Yesterday while L went swimming I strolled the beach. The waves were too big for me. So I went looking for some interesting shells. The winds have been out of the east lately, driving a hard shore pound against the sand. Always a good condition for treasure-hunting. Found a twisted and gummy purple balloon with a pink ribbon still attached and two little light bulbs, the kind that go in refrigerators or fancy chandeliers. One about four feet from the other; all crusty green around the metal part that goes into the socket, tangled in seaweed, the glass part still perfectly clear. The little filament still in tact. I just love that they had taken a mysterious long journey and ended up on the same beach within feet of each other. Decided to keep them and now I know why.

I placed the pair of light bulbs close together. One face up. One face down. Kind of like a 69 oral sex position for light bulbs. I wasn't thinking that when I did it. But when I stepped back that's exactly what came to mind (what mind?). I then placed the lid on the glass jar and closed my eyes. *"Great Mother of the Yoni-verse. Help me float my way through this mid-life maze."*

January 12
1:49 am

I feel a funk coming on, in spite of it being the beginning of a weekend. Feels like a deep creep. A petit (I hope petit and not grand) case of the blahs. I felt it yesterday and tried to ignore it. I was slogging my way through yoga, not at all wanting to go from Dog Looking Down to Cobra Looking Up when a slow dull heaviness crept up on me and I couldn't lift a leg. Then it moved rapidly to my hips. Oh my aching hips. I am paying for those nights, twenty-seven (can't be!) years ago, when I hitchhiked to California and didn't get a ride through Las Cruces and had to sleep in the ditch by the side of the road, all night worrying about someone pissing on me. I'm going to give up wheat. W says it made a world of difference in her joints. Chocolate doesn't have wheat in it, so I think I'm OK there.

While in DLD pose it also occurred to me that I'm not a very good lover. I don't know where this idea came from or how it popped into my head when it did. Maybe it's because B told me that she and her new lover spend hours in bed, and they're not sleeping. Staying in bed for hours makes me anxious. And the other thing is, I can't stand to go slow when we're doing it, and I hate small talk. Let's face it, I have an agenda. I figure the shortest route between the flatlands and the mountaintop is the road for me. For some reason, this has suddenly started to depress me.

What's up with this line of questioning, doubting what I've been doing so matter-of-factly for so many years? Well, I'm thinking that maybe I'm missing out on more of the good stuff and don't even know it. B says I have to take my time. "Hel-*lo*. Whose time do you think I've been taking?" I scoff back. Now I have something else to worry about. Taking my time. Slowing down. Enjoying the moment.

January 19
(Where did last week go?)
2:35 am

Saturday

After yoga I got in my car and started crying and didn't stop sobbing until I got to the red light at the corner in front of the beach park entrance on A1A. Thank goodness for red lights. I can say that now. When I lived in New Jersey I'd be cursing at anything that stopped my fast-forward pace. Now I throw myself on the mercy of someone else's timing, grateful for a still moment to take a deep breath and sigh, or cry. Do I know exactly why I was crying? No, I don't. I try to sort out my feelings only to realize I'm trying to think my way out of an unthinkable paper bag, brown, dumb, and mushy. But some part of me wants to put a finger on the heavy emotions that wash over me unexpectedly the way brushing the edge of a glass suddenly causes a nerve-jolting crash and the milk that was once sitting so placidly containerized is now spread all over the floor in a flat white animal shape and all I can do is stare at it, blankly, hoping it doesn't come to life and bark or bite. My yoga teacher says it's not uncommon to have emotional releases after a yoga workout. The body holds emotions and loosening and stretching the body can release what may be trapped in muscle and sinew. She's so kind to mention the word muscle.

While stopped at the light I reached into the back seat to grab a tissue and caught sight of a young man on a bike, waiting to get across the street. He was maybe twenty, dressed in surfer baggies and nothing else. No shirt. No shoes. No hat. He had shaggy straw hair and was all butter-browned skin. He didn't get off the bike to cross the street. He was leaning on the big cement pole that held up the traffic light, his feet still on the pedals, pedaling backwards the way bikers do when they have to stop but want to keep the momentum going, even if it's not in the direction they're heading. This backwards motion with the pedals caught my eye. Not because I'm particularly fond of anything going backwards. I'm all for forward momentum myself. Backwards is where I grew up and it's no place I want to be right now, even though I can feel an emotional tugging in that direction, sniffling and dripping from my runny nose. In the middle of my reach backwards something completely unexpected caught my eye. The young man, full of his own future and waving at passers-by like he's running for county commissioner, except he looks like he's enjoying talking to people, spinning his wheels and looking like Adonis on high, has an artificial left leg; a shiny plastic prosthesis with what looks like a gray metal shoe horn for a foot. As if hearing my quiet gasp he glances in my direction and smiles, waiting for me to make the turn. I smile back. I let the sun shine through my teary eyes. I must have looked pretty sad because he kind of lifted his eyebrows and then unexpectedly gave me a thumb's up motion as if to say, "Don't waste another minute." I kind of waved to acknowledge his friendliness. But before I could get his attention he pushed off, hunching over the handlebars, riding off toward the sweet soft salty sea, like Lance Armstrong rolling onto the Champs Elysee. In the window behind him I see a row of tee shirts. All are printed with the same slogan: *Life is Good*.

January 20
3:30 am

Sunday

Bolted upright in bed, breathless from a vague image of me dangling on the upside of a seesaw laughing and squealing all girlie-like when suddenly and without warning the person I'm playing with, who is only vaguely familiar, jumps off and runs away, causing my side of the seesaw to hit the ground hard. I am left alone in an empty playground, my hands wrapped tightly around the dull gray metal handle, my stomach pushed into my throat, a flame of fear burning my cheeks. Every bone stinging from the sudden shock of hitting the ground, tilting backward in an acute state of lopsidedness.

B called yesterday morning. Says I need to get with a breathing coach, especially since I'm in the big M, feeling uncontrollably anxious and having nightmares. Tells me she's been doing Breathwork and it's opening up a whole bunch of stuff for her, helping release old emotions, healing the past, and making room for the joy of life. She encourages me with more glee than I can handle, "If not now, Nanc, when?" I tell her I've been breathing with the lizard that hangs out on the window ledge in the bedroom, doing those funky little lizard moves. I call them pizza-push-ups because their little bodies go up and down and this funky thing called a dulap juts out from their throats and looks like a slice of pizza. There ya go, I tell her, some people are having conversations with God, angels, aliens, and fairies; I'm talking to reptiles, which are not exactly easy to love. They're so—well, so dry. "His name is Lenny," I try to sound very convincing. "And he has a very simple take on life, a kind of one-track mind: Rest. Blink slowly. Learn to love bugs."

B loves the lizard wisdom, and still thinks I need to breathe, and let go of the accumulation of emotional gunk that gathers and hides out in the area around the heart. "Where all the old pizza gathers?" I'm trying to make light of the weight-bearing truth. She says it can't hurt to try, in any case. She makes me promise I'll check into it after I tell her I have an intense fear of finding myself living in a cardboard box under the freeway on the Beeline Express with Lenny on my shoulder whispering his very meaningful reptilian advice, the two of us nibbling on one very plain piece of cold pizza.

January 21
2:43 pm

Monday

"There is no returning without going," I hear out of the blue this afternoon after all the morning butterflies have left the flame bush and Walt has been fed and Mom is napping. I'm squatting in a half-daze next to the rosemary plant, squeezing the short pine-green needles, brushing them back and forth under my nose and minding my own obviously very shallow breathing business, hoping to get a fresher look at the day ahead of me. I spent another delirious night slogging my way from 3:05 am to 4:13 am with a dazzling array of thick worries that show up when I least expect them. All of them accompanied by the liquid night crew of Sweat and Chill. Last night I got caught in the swirling maze of "I shoulds…" and I know better than to let anything should me around like a windbag bully. But this is how it always goes: Maybe I should go back to school and get a degree in something I can actually make a living at…Maybe speech pathology or web design…I hear they pay well (gagged thinking about sitting in a classroom with twenty-somethings calling me Ma'am)…Maybe get a degree in gerontology…No lack of work here in Florida…Or, maybe I could become a mortgage broker…or a nurse…Got enough experience there. Speech pathology pays well.

Oh, stop it! Get a grip. What is, is.

Then straight out of the "Shoulda, Coulda, Woulda" triangle, I got myself all wound up in what ifs. What if I'd never moved to Florida…What if I'd taken up heavy-equipment operating, or engineering or banking…or midwifery?

Not sure if I woke up depressed, disinterested, disgusted, or downright hungry beyond belief.

While I'm sniffing in the vibrant joy of rosemary, my eyes catch hold of a giant swallowtail butterfly dipping across the stand of Spanish needles, delicately coming to a soft landing on the fennel that I planted last year. These marvelous and mesmerizing winged creatures are attracted to the lacy wisps of licorice fragrance situated along the back patio. I get real still, breathing very slowly in the presence of these magical beings. I'm hoping she'll land and make the fennel her nursery so I can watch her fat and ravenous yellow and black larvae gobble up the tasty greens growing rounder and longer by the minute. Then one day I'll come out to check on their progress and the caterpillars, as big as my thumb, will be gone. I'll wonder again how I missed this quiet phenomenon when it's right under my very nose.

Your energy just shifted, she whispered, calling me back from my butterfly meditation. *Did you notice it?*

"Yes. Most definitely. I was here. Really here."

That's your job. Watch. Pay attention. Breathe. Nature is your teacher.

"What about the past? How can I live in the present when the past haunts me like a cheap ghost?" I am talking to the plant fairies. The green divas. The Menopause Queen of my new mind.

Stop fighting what was. You can't change it. Can't rearrange it. She sounds like Phyllis Diller about to launch into her own rendition of *Down On Me* then pulls up real close and moves her lips without speaking. If there's one thing I've learned about this sometimes cranky Queen: she is downright honest. And rude. I lean closer, squinting, watching her lips and stretching my mental capacities as far as they'll go. I string together the words: *Underneath the cheap costume is a lonely ghost. Invite the ghost for tea. Write. Breathe. Dance. Listen to the yowling. The past is not your enemy.*

"The past?" I shriek. "The past sucks."

Precisely. Black holes sucking away energy and life force. That is, unless you chase it down and own up to it.

I smell a New Age crapfest coming my way. But I keep my comments to myself.

This is not New Age, she grumbles, insulted and obviously spying on my mind again. *It's healing wisdom. As old as the hills.* A quirky smile returns, wrinkling up her already wrinkled cheeks. *And that's pretty darned old in my book.*

What book? I'm hoping she doesn't get religious on me. I just can't take religious zealots, especially marauding around in my loose and liberal mind.

The Big Book of Natural Law. Where there's fear, there's big healing. It's just that simple.

How about this pain in my ass called night sweats, nightmares, and obsessive worry whirring around my anxious brain?

Avoiding your feelings is giving away your power. Better to conserve it for the rest of the road trip.

Road trip?

The trip you're on. You know, life. You're an old hippie. Don't act stupid. You know the jingle.

"That's lingo."

Whatever. You know what I mean. A few saved breaths can go a long way when you're gasping. Even the butterflies rest between flowers.

"Do I look like I'm gasping?"

You are when the ghosts come calling.

"Easy for you to say."

You need to manage your mind, she says, oh so simply.

"Oh, that silly little organ."

You'll figure it out. But for now, know this: You cannot eat a half pint of chocolate fudge cake ice cream two hours before going to bed, even if you're sitting on the beach and it tastes like you're mainlining manna and the Moon is full and you're finally taking a deep breath.

"I was treating myself." I'm defensive and pissed.

That thing you ate last night, my little lovely, was no treat. Caffeine makes your breasts ache.

"I'm weak," I'm slinking like a dog on her belly, trying to hide under the couch in a thunderstorm. "Is that what's making my breast feel like it has a toothache."

Yup. Well, you're human. But at this point, caffeine is exactly the thing you ought to be avoiding, not the fact that you have an opportunity to see Walt through to the end of his life and help your mother as she deals with her own emotions. At the same time you're going to have to learn how to be a better Mother to yourself. A handful of blueberries and a long walk are the real treats to go for. And a cup of chamomile tea works wonders at bedtime. Think about it. Nourishing treats, that is.

With that she flicks a dismissive wrist at me, utters a fond *Toodlee Do* and vanishes, disappearing into the roots of the sea grape bushes all tangled with tiny new green shoots. I pinch off a few sprigs of rosemary, shaking my head, thinking if someone had a video of me I'd look like a mad woman. Oh well. Who cares what I look like on video? I pull up a few stalks of lemongrass to brew up later for tea. Damn. That ice cream sure did taste good. But it's not worth a night of bad juju, that's for sure. Better take some time to write in my diary and see if I can't invite the ghosts to tea. Hope they like lemongrass. I remember reading in Eric Maisel's *The Van Gogh Blues, The Creative Person's Path Through Depression,* that the only homework I have to do in any one day is to honestly chew on something. Yomp. Yomp.

FEBRUARY

February 2 (Halfway to spring)
11:14 am

Saturday

° Full moon on the 27th . I love the big tides
° Walt's 80th on the 26th. What to do?
° Month of the yellow moths

February 4
2:14 am

Monday

So, I'm afraid I'm going nuts. I may be halfway there, so I'm thinking I don't have far to go. I'm all over the place, like egg whites in boiling water. My anxiety is like a bad dog that keeps chewing on the same spot in the rug, no matter how many cheese-flavored doggy bones I give her for lying quietly by the chair. Sometimes I have to take her out for a walk to wear her out so she can sleep at night.

The thing is, my dad went nuts when he was fifty-six and the closer I get to that number, the more I'm hoping it isn't contagious. I was sixteen at the time and I'll never forget the look on his face and his last words to me the day the state police came to take him away because he thought someone was going to burn down the house. I came home from school feeling my usual sullen teenage self, walking slowly down the driveway, kicking dry clumps of mud with every heavy step and trying to sort out the intriguing words to the musical, *Hair*, wondering what exactly a "mystic crystal revelation" might look like, only to look up and find my father running in and out of the trailer, piling up a shitload of junk out on the walkway. He was real quiet and looking mean, squinting narrowly through dark eyes. I knew right off the bat that something had snapped. It's not as if we lived a normal "Leave It To Beaver" household. Frankly, I didn't know anyone who did.

All my friends came from screwed-up families. It was normal in my neighborhood to have one or both parents drunk in the middle of the day, the car pulled too far up onto the lawn, the driver's side door wide open and a passed-out parent leaning over the steering wheel. "Oh," we'd say nonchalantly. "Don't pay any attention to Linda's dad. He's been working late." We all knew the code, nodded, and never talked about it. My father spent many a night in the driver's seat. He was a binge alcoholic, drying up for months at a time only to fall off the wagon at the tiniest infringement on his fragile state of sobriety or "at the drop of a hat" as my mother called it, going from a soft-spoken Dr. Jekyll to the manic-monster Mr Hyde.

I grew up hating when he was sober, even though our lives had a modicum of stability because at least when he was wildly drunk I knew what to expect: utter chaos, violent emotional outbursts, angry arguments with my mother, and most of his paycheck pissed down the drain. When he was sober I lived in a perpetual state of waiting for the left shoe to drop. He was pleasant and kind, but I didn't trust it for long because tomorrow his teeth would grow and his palms would sprout fur. That day, however, felt unlike any other. In some deep part of my being I felt my life unraveling to no end. My dad hadn't ever gone this far before. Hadn't ever stepped over the line into looking so completely filled with World War Two terror. I stopped short of the kitchen table, where a letter I'd gotten from my boyfriend the day before, waxing poetic about the "cloud-shaped" semen stains left on his sheets from my last visit, had been obviously read and ripped in half right down the middle.

I grabbed for it, my face hot and flushed. I spun around on my heels to find my father standing right behind me, staring at me, his eyes wide like onions. "That bastard," was all he said before running into the bathroom, jabbering fast and incoherently about someone, some alien invader "asshole know-it-all" about to destroy the world, as he was taking everything out from under the kitchen and bathroom sinks and cleaning out all the closets, removing bottles of detergents, spray paint, solvents, lotions, soaps, because the alien was going to use these "flammable" products to blow up the house. He walked fast to grab another armload of flammable liquids and ran out quickly, fending off his personal pool of demons in broad daylight by cleaning the house and speaking in tongues, his voice like a tape recorder on fast-forward, all the time trying to convince me that he had the inside information on the whole plot. I remember thinking in a numb stare, What's he doing home in the middle of the afternoon? He'd quit drinking again for the umpteenth time in six months and I was pretty scared just to be there alone with him. How the state police got involved I don't know. Maybe I called the operator for help and they didn't have an ambulance available. Maybe it was the alien. The details from this point on are pretty fuzzy. There's one image, though, that's very, very clear. With the officer holding his arm, my father was being escorted out the back door. Burned on my brain is the look on his face just before they tucked my father into the patrol car, bending his head down like I'd seen in so many cop shows as if the perp suddenly forgot how to get into the backseat of a car. His face looking all screwed up and just about as scared as I felt, my brilliant, bad father looked over at me, standing frozen in the doorway and said,

"Thanks, Nancy. Thanks a lot."

I can hardly bear to think of this old, cruel memory. It wasn't my fault that my father went nuts with the DTs and had to be escorted to the mental hospital in the back of a police vehicle. My adult self knows this. My father had his own built-in self-detonator in place long before I was born. But I can barely get the scene out of my mind, knowing that the one flammable liquid that my father failed to remove, the cunning demon set to ignite our family on fire again as soon as my mother signed the papers to release him from the nuthouse, was the pint of vodka hidden under the mattress.

No, my father's broken life was not my fault. I was not the parent. I was the child.

It is finally released. Take a deep breath. Bring the quiet light of this moment into your heart.

February 5
11:15 pm

Tuesday

Mom did the laundry this afternoon (or was it yesterday?). She tries so hard to get it right these days. The darks and lights and then the sheets and towels. Her clothes and mine. L's and Walt's. I don't want to take over the one job she can manage to get through with some pride still intact. Taking away her driving privileges has been so hard on her (and us). My mother, the woman who coped by getting in the car and driving her way to nirvana, doesn't have an escape route, except maybe the narrow tunnels of her own mind. This morning, half awake and stumbling to get dressed, I reached in to grab a pair of underwear and pulled out a pair of her blessed bloomers, big honking size 11s. It scared me half to death.

I'm terribly anxious.
So.
My heart is pounding.
Think of the alternative.
I have no idea what I'm doing.
Who does?
I'm sweating.
Natural air-conditioning.
I can't sit still.
Nothing is still in the Universe.
Can't think.
Thinking is overrated.
I hate that I can't control what's happening inside my body.

Now, you're on to something we can work with.

Seems I can't control anything.

You don't have to.

Yeah but, Mom is losing her memory big time, I mean to the tune of can't remember where she was for lunch and keeps asking me over and over again, "Where's Aunt Ruth?" who's been dead forever.

Everyone has her own way of coping. Her memory loss doesn't stop you from loving her with all your heart.

I feel like a chicken with my head cut off running around trying to hold it all together.

You're wasting your energy. There is no holding it all together. Time to face your fears and get on with living; the real lesson of dying. Breathe. Breathe deeply, even when it feels like there's no air. Do not play dead. Play alive. Play at living. It works all the time. Enjoy every moment.

February 6
7:11 am
(I'd be a winner if I were playing craps)

Wednesday

I'm not so sure about writing down all this stuff that keeps coming up. It's like a blowout sale at Macy's. You let the first screaming shopper in and the rest frantically force their way in behind. I'm hoping the sale on outdated secrets will end soon. Another memory shook loose yesterday while I was helping Mom strip Walt's bed, holding the pillow under my chin to slip on the fresh, clean flannel case with little pine cone designs all over it. He is cold all the time now. He likes the soft flannel against his skin. The past popped up again, surging like a dull wave through my mind, while changing the dressing around his feeding tube. I was thinking and thinking and thinking about a very bad moment triggered by, of all things, pillows. Then spent the rest of the day trying not to think about it, either my childhood memory or the gaping hole in Walt's stomach that oozes brown goo and then crusts over and cracks open. But like the white elephant in the living room this heavy old ghost just won't go away.

Do not run away. Remembering and letting go is a healing ritual. There is wisdom in a memory that wants to speak. What stays hidden haunts forever.

When I was about seven or eight my father used to play what he considered a hilarious joke on me while I was napping. I don't know how long he played this little trick or if he did it to my brothers or just to me. I never talked about it, actually. Never told anyone. And it wasn't like he said one day, OK

Nancy, I'm done with this silly, stupid game and you're free. Nope. He never said that. But suddenly the game stopped. Maybe I grew up and got stronger. Maybe I stopped taking naps. Anyway, I used to fight real hard to push him away and maybe he grew tired of fighting back. What he did was this: When it was time to wake me up he'd put a pillow over my head and hold it there until I came to and realized, of course, that I couldn't breathe. Then I'd start twisting, kicking, and flinging myself from side to side from the neck down, flailing my arms around in mid-air, screaming as loud as any kid could scream with a big, soft, suffocating pillow in her face. The pillow was only half the game. It was what my father said that drove me thrashing mad and sweaty-wet with terror. I mean the pillow trick was bad enough, all by itself. But then he added just a little something extra that really set me into panic. The whole time I'm trying to get free, get some air, and basically get away, my father is laughing a loose and drunken snarl and pushing the pillow tighter to my head, telling me over and over again the words that horrified me to no end, "Wake up, Nancy. Wake up." He'd taunt. "You're mother is leaving. She just walked out the door. She's driving away in the car. She's leaving for good. She's never coming back." Yup, my father knew exactly what it was that would torment me, the little girl who wouldn't leave her mother's side, "Mommy's shadow," he used to call me. "She's a baby. She'll never grow up," he'd tease. Yes, my father knew exactly what it took to put the finishing touches on his game called torture. He'd put his head down close to the pillow and whisper in a strong and serious voice the one sentence that if I could have summoned enough strength I would have pushed the trailer over on its side and crushed my father under it. But the strength I summoned to win the game wasn't of the physical kind. It was a slow-moving interior force that taught me a very serious, winning trick of my own. Just before my father got to the words I couldn't bear, the words that tore my heart inside out, I played my last card. After fighting as hard as I could for a short period of time and then suddenly stopping, letting my whole body go limp; if I got real still and didn't move, I mean dead still without as much as a twitch, it would be my father's turn to get real scared. While I was holding my breath and waiting, taking really tiny breaths without moving a muscle, my father would suddenly realize that the game went too far. Then in a flurry of his own fear he'd stop the teasing and taunting and suddenly lift the pillow. I'd stay frozen for as long as I could while he shook me, yelling my name in a desperate way. Then when I couldn't hold my breath any more I'd open my eyes real wide. Pop. Just open them up big and round and wide awake. He'd start laughing, nervously and relieved at the same time. Then, like a bored cat that walks away from a mouse he's had under his paw for half the day, my father would simply turn around and walk out of my room. Game's over. And that's when I'd throw the pillow at him and flip him the bird and mime Fuck You, which I'd seen a boy at school do behind our science teacher's back. Fuck you. Fuck you. Fuck you. I'd be miming for the rest of the day. Fuck you, Dad. But my father never saw me or heard me say such a bad word. The only thing he said when he left the room was, "You'll always be a mamma's girl." But I didn't care what he said. In the end I figured I'd won. I stopped the game before he got to say the one sentence that he knew I couldn't stand. Couldn't bear to hear. This time, he didn't get a chance to say the words I feared the most, "You'll never see your mother again, ever."

February 7
8:49 am

Thursday

Woke up craving eggs. Decided to invite the ghosts for breakfast. I set the table for three. Only three. I have my limits. Sitting down, I take a deep breath. Yes. Breathing is good. I close my eyes.

Breathing In. Breathing Out.

Who are you, thin, filmy spirits? Who wants to show up and talk? We need to get to know each other, whoever you are who visit me in the middle of the night in the name of Anxiety and Dread. You know who you are and it's time to talk it out. I'm ready. I'm willing. Right here in broad daylight. I'm scared, but I'm ready. I want to let go of the old crap so I can move on. I'd like to run for the hills, but don't have the energy.

Forgiveness comes when you're ready. You don't have to know how and you don't have to force it.

Dad? Is that you? Of course. Yes. I figured you'd want to come. Who else? Anyone else want to join us? Bring anyone with you? Forgiveness? You brought Forgiveness with you? Oh. I start to cry. Hope you're both hungry, I ask, brushing tears from my cheeks. I'm starving, myself. I've mixed up a big batch of scrambles with veggies. Yes. Only veggies. Healthy stuff. You want ham? Oh. Um. How about Soysage? That's cool? OK. You look good, Dad. Nice clean shirt. Trousers ironed. Sneakers? Dad, you never wore sneakers. Yes, it's true. They are more comfortable. Yes. I'd like a hug. Yes. Please hold me. Please tell something you never ever told me when you were alive. Please tell me that you love me. I need to hear it, Dad. Need to hear it from you right now before the eggs burn and really stink up the house with that awful egg-burning smell.

I love you, my darling daughter. I always will. I brought Forgiveness with me. I'm so very sorry for the pain I caused. Please forgive me. You'll release us both and make way for a greater joy in your heart. It's true what those Beatles said you know, "Love is all there is."

Dad, you hated the Beatles.

Time changes everything.

I love you Dad. I always did. But I was really angry too. I hated you a lot.

Understandable. I hated me, too. I just couldn't change. I just didn't know how. It's easier for you. You have so much help. By the way, you're going to have to someday forgive your mother, too.

One at a time, OK? I didn't scramble enough eggs this morning for all of us.

This is the perfect time for healing into love. She needs help now. I'm glad she's with Walt, but he won't be around for much longer.

I know. I feel very sad most of the time. Watching him die reminds me of you.

Dying is dying. Another transition on the cycle of life. Stay awake. You have a lot to learn here. You can stop apologizing for things that weren't your fault. It's not up to you to fix or control the outcomes. Your job is to pay attention. Listen. Remember that sweat lodge you did years ago?

How do you know about that? Oh. Never mind.

Remember when it got really really hot and you lay down on your belly and tried to secretly lift the flap and get some air?

Don't remind me. I thought I was going to die.

You were actually experiencing your birth. Remember what the old medicine woman said to you at that very moment.

Yeah. She said, "Wake Up." She actually shouted it.

Right. She also said, Don't go to sleep now.

Wow. You remember all that?

It's all accessible out here, every tiny thought, floating in space. So, just remember. Don't go to sleep now. You know what that means don't you?

Oh yeah. No chance of that. Don't get much sleep these days.

You're waking up and that's much bigger and much better than sleep-walking. Oh, before I forget. There's one more thing.

What's that?

Beware of the Drama Drain.

You mean, what exactly?

Other people's stuff. Don't get caught in their emotional spin.

Gotcha.

February 10
3:13 am

 Woke up from a strange dream about the house on Fletcher Street, where I
lived for the first five years of my life. I figure this is an invitation to healing
(remembering and letting go) so I decided to stay in bed a little longer and see
where I end up. Closing my eyes I bring to mind as much of the house as I
can remember. I am drawn to walk quickly through the living room, taking
long, wide steps. My heart is racing. Someone, something is waiting for me. I
hear a little girl crying. I come through the archway and see her standing on
the kitchen table. She is me. I am four years old, maybe five, but no older,
because right after I turned five we left the house on Fletcher Street. Packed
up everything we couldn't sell, and towing it all behind us in one of those
rinky-dink two-wheel gypsy wagons, we moved into a skinny tin trailer with a
thin sky-blue stripe wrapped all around its middle like a gift box half-finished
and set down in a trailer park on the edge of Route 6, facing a bowling alley
and a tiny little airport. There is mystery surrounding this abrupt move out of
state. The house feels uncomfortable. Turbulent energy like the static from a
radio is buzzing all around me. But I don't know what it's about.

    At four or five I am standing on a chrome-legged kitchen table with
a shiny laminate surface painted in mottled reds and grays. A floral pattern
dancing around the perimeter. When I think of it, looking at the scene from
a distance, it's a perfect opening shot for the movie of my life. A little girl
wearing mahogany-colored Buster Brown shoes, scuffed and cracked dry,
worn thin at the toes, baggy corduroy pants that at one time were almost as
brown as her shoes, but are now faded and tan at the knees, and a maroon and
green striped tee-shirt pulled a little too tight across her belly, revealing a thin
band of smooth pale skin. She doesn't know exactly how she crawled onto the
table, but she is nearly frozen on the inside at the thought of trying to get back
down. Her face is pressed up against a large window. She is screaming. What
startles me most is not the ill-fitting clothes, obvious hand-me-downs from my
older brother. No, it's not the furniture or the very plain interior, almost empty
of frivolous decorations, or the fact that she is alone and it's late in the day and
her bangs are cut too short and crooked like a zig-zag stitch. It's the screaming. The little girl that is me, is standing at the big window that overlooks the
open field between our house and our next-door neighbor's and is hollering
and shouting as loud as she can, banging madly, as madly as any five-year-old
can get, on the window frame to get my brothers' attention. Her face is red
and her eyes are puffy.

    How long have I been there? Crying out for help.

    My brothers are outside, in the field. They are laughing and shouting and playing a game of baseball, taking big, strong swings at fast pitches, throwing bats on the ground, slapping each other on the back and banging their shoes with the bat, just like the big boys do, and they are not looking in my direction at all. They can't hear me calling for them. They can't hear me yelling at the top of my lungs, "Help me. Please somebody, quick. Help me." My right hand is hot and tingly from banging hard against the white window frame, yellowing with age, paint cracked in perfect square chunks, lifting and trying hard to separate from the other pieces that surround it.

So much time and memory ready to drop, yet still stuck and hanging on by a breath. Her left hand, pudgy and open wide is leaning on the cool window pane, leaving a foggy round print mark on the glass like an ancient cave painting; a thin trace of memory come and gone long before. Suddenly she stops screaming. The little girl who looks like a little boy, who is terrified to go upstairs alone to the bathroom at the end of the long dark hallway, who has in her pocket, shoved down into the seam with loose threads and fuzzy lint, a little hunk of dried dirt that just yesterday she peeled from the chocolate-colored mud puddle half dried in the driveway, now rolled into a ball like a prayer bead for safe keeping, knows exactly what she has to do.

She hikes up her pants, falls to her knees and slowly crawls across the table, sniffling and stopping to drag her sleeve across her nose. She looks back one more time, through the window, one long look, just in case, then moves across the table. She must look like a baby, she thinks. But she's not a baby. She's a big girl. She can do it herself. She doesn't need anyone to help her. She'll show them. Anyway, they're boys. They stink.

When she gets to the edge of the table she looks down at the chair. It looks so far away. Her head feels all fuzzy and she closes her eyes to make the room stop moving in heavy waves like the scary, fun house mirrors her mother took her to at the carnival. This is not fun. With her eyes closed she makes up what she wants to see: beautiful butterflies singing and smiling, brightly colored birds that whistle happy songs, women with wings who hold out their arms to her and talk with smiles. *You can do it. You're such a brave girl. You're strong. Take your time.* She loves the places she can go inside her, the world behind her eyes. She wishes she could stay there forever, dreaming up what she wants the most, softness and wide-open spaces to run and play. Imagining, making up exactly what she wants. Opening her eyes she concentrates on every move, so she doesn't fall or slip. She stretches one foot out and then the other. She can't fall now. They'd laugh at her if she did and she hates it when her brothers laugh at her just because she's a girl. She slides off the edge of the table until the tips of her toes touch the chair, her hands still holding tightly to the table's edge. She eases herself slowly onto the chair and then hops down to the floor with both feet. She brushes her hands together and grabs hold of the chair, dragging it across the room. The shiny edge is cool and soothing to the touch, the sounds of the hollow metal legs scraping against the already scuffed, dull linoleum fill the room. I'll show them. I'm a big girl.

She pulls and tugs and doesn't stop until the chair is exactly where she needs it. Climbing again, this time up onto the chair, she pulls down her pants, hoists herself up backwards, feels the cold white porcelain against her bare legs, and pees in the kitchen sink.

When she's done she quickly pulls up her pants, jumps back down and pushing the chair back over where she found it, she crawls under the kitchen table and falls asleep.

The camera zooms out.

This is obviously the place where self-reliance and determination were born. And a piss-poor attitude about men, and spectator sports.

I open my eyes for a second and wonder, if at five years old I could crawl up on the table, drag a chair, lift and hoist and create some pretty big solutions for myself, why couldn't I turn the doorknob on the kitchen door and go outside to get someone to help me?

OK. So what if the door was locked and I was left alone and the house is growing dark and I'm scared.

It's obvious I have unfinished work here.

I close my eyes and go back into the kitchen. I'm in a Free Willy kind of mood this morning. I feel a rescue mission in the making. The little girl whose rage is fresh and real, whose needs were not met, whose resentment has boiled over and burned the pot, must be set free. Nobody was there for me then, but I can be here for me now. That's all there is to it. I close my eyes and drift backwards again, rewinding the film to that place where my girl child is waking up from an afternoon nap and the house is really quiet and she calls out for Mommy and no one calls back. Enter the adult me with an entourage of Goddess Guides to cut through the crap and get to the heart of feeling and healing. I walk into her room where her father has painted the ceiling above her bed like the night sky with white stars and yellow moons and green and pink planets swirling in a powder-blue background. I wrap my arms around her and take her to the bathroom, talking softly and smiling, brushing her damp hair back away from her forehead, kissing her cheek and making sweet-sounding noises. *You're safe now*, I whisper. She drops her head on my shoulder and I rub her back. *You are innocent. I love you, my dear sweet child. I love you so much and I will never ever leave you. I am here for you and I will always be here for you when you wake up in the dark and call out my name and need a hug and smile and a loving song to sing. You are with me always and I am taking care of you now.*

I hold the sleepy five-year-old next to me, close to my heart, rocking and singing a soft lullaby until her arms relax around my neck. She is five going on fifty. She is tired of pretending and wants relief.

We breathe fully and freely. We are finally together.

I open my eyes, the morning light streaming in through the blinds. Tears are running down my cheeks. The zebra butterflies are flitting around the peach-colored hibiscus. A young green lizard slides up a thin, brown, knobby branch, rubbing her head like she's got something stuck behind her ears. She is molting. Thin, translucent skin is peeling off over her nose and eyes. She is turning almost on her back now, wiggling to get out of her old skin. It looks like a dance to me, a writhing sensual lizard strip tease. The new skin has already grown under the old one, already in place before the old one started to crack away. Somehow this makes me feel better. She doesn't have to go around with her heart and bones all hanging out, waiting for a new skin to grow. Everything is already in place before she lets go of the old.

10:28 am

E just called. I tell her about Fletcher Street. She says to go out into the back-yard, in my menopausal garden, when the Moon is full, and do some shadow boxing; real wild and loose like, howling my pain out loud. Says it's better to box with the shadow than let the shadow box you in. "Time to get real trans-parent," she coaches in a sing-songy voice. "Then the shadows disappear."

Yes. I am learning how to cry out loud for help, opening doors instead of banging on walls. I know how to offer up my yearning to those who can help me. When it's clear that those I'm looking to for help can't provide it, for whatever reason, I move on, knocking on doors until they open up wide, so I can go out and play.

I remember reading somewhere that you can't find a solution to a problem at the level it was created. I think Einstein said it. In my very unsci-entific mind I figure you have to make yourself real big and go at the deepest shadowy parts with all the courage you can carry, ferociously roaring with Mother Love.

I'm also really glad I didn't invent a profound theory about energy, time and distance that got all twisted up in the hands of idiots and ended up turning into a couple of big bombs that killed a few million people, especially when that theory was conjured up by a pacifist. Talk about the irony of life.

February 11
11:36 am

Monday

Today feels like a mess already and it's not even noon. I feel so fucking angry, so anxious, so nowhere and everywhere at the same time, like a storm is brewing and I can't see the clouds, but I can hear the thunder in the distance. I am a raging capped volcano. I'm starting to feel like that bumper sticker I read the other day: *I do what my Rice Krispies tell me to do. Snap. Crackle. Pop.* Mosquito Control called. They're spraying the area tonight. "Again?" I screamed. "You just sprayed two days ago." I then asked them to register a complaint in my name. Too much poison. Too much spraying. The mosquitoes are not going away. It's obvious they're mutating, growing stronger, and multiplying by the gazillions. Don't they know what's happening? Research has proven the more you try to annihilate a species the faster they reproduce. And by the way, isn't anyone else concerned about this poisonous assault on humans? I slam the phone down.

Heart palpitations. Big sweat. Pacing. Rocking back and forth.

I can't stand being in my skin and want desperately to run, hide, cover up, and pray hard so that the sound of my own begging drowns out the sound of my anger throwing my bones against brittle hopes. It is useless. I can't win this battle with the Florida authorities on mosquitoes.

Slow down. Time out for a quiet few breaths.

L took Mom to the Senior Center this morning and I cried when they left. I'm alone with Walt. He is breathing raspy hard sounds. I don't know what to do with myself. I pick up Anne Morrow Lindbergh's *Gifts of the Sea*, hoping some key words will jump out to help me, distract me, lift me off the planet, or at least out of my thin and shivering skin. I quickly flip open a page, any page, my eyes falling on a short few words that snap me to attention: "In fact, the problem is how to feed the soul."

Soul, where are you? Are you in there still? Can you be still while everything is whirring mindlessly around me? Can you hear me through the whining and yammering and free-floating anxiety that pulls me in a long, thin, wispy thread and then turns on itself, winding and wrapping me tight and tired? What fed my soul yesterday, the day before, this morning doesn't work any more. Everything, every day is changing. And that's what I really have to get used to. But first I have to find a solid thing, an immovable pearl of beauty or, skipping beauty (too much cultural baggage), I want to find a little piece of myself I can trust and love and keep safe. Where are you, little safe soul of mine? Are you hiding and scared, just like me? To this soulful sadness there are no immediate solutions. *No amount of grasping is going to give me peace of mind.* Nothing "out there" can sustain the "in here" that sits shivering like a cold and hungry dog. Come here, little mutt. I love you no matter what you look like. I'm scared too. Let's listen to some really nice music and have a cup of tea. A nice little doggy treat will do. No, we're not feeding our emotions. Not this time.

I sit and wrap my arms around my knees.

Breathing In. Breathing Out.

A consistency of calmness would be a gift of cosmic proportions.

February 13
3:25 am

Wednesday

I'm taking inventory of my menopausal friends and feel like a shit for comparing myself to everyone else. It is such a waste of energy but I do it anyway: D is living on Valium; M is doing another new antidepressant coupled up with a new anti-anxiety med (she calls them her pharmaceutical familiars, Auntie D and Auntie A); B has a new lover with a big penis (I tell my mother this one day just for fun and she replies without skipping a beat, "Yeah but does he have a big bank account?"); F is eating herself into a coma; X is exercising every other minute; C is on Jesus and Xanax; Z is working herself into mindlessness with two jobs she despises equally; K is on happy hour; O is on HRT; R is smoking pot; Q quit smoking but says she is still "burning up" inside.

I'm living on lemon balm, black cohosh, motherwort, and chocolate chips. And I'm thinking I may have to get on antidepressants, but feel like a failure when I can't do this trip myself.

There is no right way. Only choices. You have nothing to prove to anyone.

I looked through an old journal because I know I've been here or somewhere close to the edge before. Maybe not that long ago, either. I remember writing a kind of healing recipe for the "Bad Days." I find my notes after spending hours looking…looking for myself. This is what I wrote over a year ago:

Dear Nancy,

Here are three simple and easy Healing Reminders for the Deep Creep when feeling suddenly surrounded by rapidly changing and uncontrollable events, creating a very real need for a heavy anchor or light, diaphanous wings. You decide. This recipe for healing works especially well when you find yourself lying on the couch with a bag of frozen peas and carrots on your hot head and asking yourself, "Where's the book on the One-Minute Menopause."

Remember. You can take care of yourself.

° Stew a pot of lemon balm tea. It works best for jittery nerves, jumpy stomach, and insomnia. Lemon balm is a nourishing green diva plant. She is called Melissa, the Greek word for bee. Avicenna, the 11th-century Arab physician said, "it causeth the mind and heart to become merry." Obviously an Elizabethan translation here. But get this: ancient beekeepers used to rub the fresh leaves on hives to encourage the bees to return to the hives, bringing more bee buddies with them. I love the idea of "encouraging" bees. A sweet little reminder in case they get lost. A kind of Coming Home ritual for the flower dancers.

° Take a spiral walk. You can keep the frozen peas and carrots on your head if you want. It will definitely slow your walk and keep you cool at the same time. You have a labyrinth in your own home. You don't have to travel to the exotic cathedrals to get there. Besides here is where there is. Imagine walking the great spiral of your own life exactly where you're standing. Start in the center. This is where you are in this very moment. Take short, slow steps moving around the center place, making tight little circles at first. Think of it as unwinding tension or unraveling the knots. Breathe slowly, deeply. Start humming. You're a bee, a sweet and wondrous fuzzy buzzing bee on her wise, wide walk reaching ever-outward and inward at the same time. Find a rhythm that brings your steps in harmony with your breath. Slow your mustang down. And stop listening to that melancholy music from the past when you're feeling a slump coming on. Go ahead. Think about death if you want to. It's certainly part of the living picture. It isn't going to go away just because you're scared. But with every other step, think about taking one more living breath. Just for now. So what! You feel "out of control." It's OK to feel like everything is going to hell. Actually it is, in some ways. Hel is the Old Woman at the crossroads. She sits at the center of the fire in the deep, dark roots of the underground guarding the gates of Big Changes. Trust the journey. She's the wild one and don't think you can avoid her. You can't. She's everywhere. You're learning how to hold on and let go. All at the same time. Think about this. To your ancestors, hell was the nourishing warm goodness of the Great Mother Earth.

And if I have to I'll get a prescription for antidepressants or anything else my Wise Ass within tells me to do.

Time is the Big Snitch. Eventually she tells all.

11:01 pm

All I want to eat today is cheese and bread, bread and butter, cheese and pasta, ice cream—all those luscious, high-fat, mucous-making foods. My head is pounding with humidity. The top of my head is ready to blow off and my face close behind it. My sinus cavities feel stuffed with wet cotton and slime-green mold. I am a raging, snake-hissing Gorgon. In the back of my mildew-ridden mind I realize, of course, that I cannot control the weather. Damn. Two more days until we leave for NYC and winter, which is just what I was running from eight years ago when we moved here to the Sunshine State.

Thank goodness P will watch Mom and Walt while we're away. What would I do without my girlfriends? Feels so hard to leave my parents alone. But I can't give up *everything*. I feel suspended on a rubbery tightrope bouncing between two fires burning in my direction.

Better get used to the bounce and the hot breezes. And asking for help.

February 17
3:21 am

Sunday

L and I walked in the snow today up Broadway. The city quiet in a soft furry white blanket. Young women laughing made me laugh without knowing why. Those who dared the confusion came out in small bands, giddy with the light fluff piled head-high. All of us walking in single file to cross the street through the narrow channels carved in snow banks. Yesterday we went to the Picasso–Matisse show and afterwards dinner with G and S. Haven't seen them in over five years. Does anyone ever change? Really change? Of course we have slowed down. Our conversation is less animated. Without speaking about it, I think we are all tired, weary with the news of impending war. A heavy memory crouches on the street corners here, in spite of the levity of the weather softening hard city sounds.

February 19
8:34 am
Tuesday

Sitting in the hotel room alone. L has gone to his conference. The bathroom fan sounds like a tortured cat squirking for life. A clomping horse (yes, horse!) slogs along slushy streets, pulling my attention from the bathroom fan to the world outside the window. Garbage truck. Bang. Bang. Bang. Horn honking. Cars slipping and sliding in the mushy snow. Winter brings a kind of soft muffle to the street. Sidewalks disappear. The drought, they say, is over here. Spring will come and no one will remember the snow.

I feel comforted by the wet, heavy snow in a strange, otherworldly way.

February 21
11:42 pm

Morning with G in Chelsea going to art galleries. Most of what's in the galleries is completely uninteresting to me. Booooooorrrrrrrrinnnnng. The exhibit at the Asia Society of Montien Boonma's work, however, was astoundingly rich and sensitive. Awesome, really. One installation of hundreds of bowls stacked up in an arc facing a corner of the room, where a gold lotus blossom dangled from the wall, intensely captured my spirit. Simple. Serene. Eternal. I couldn't pull my eyes off the glittering gold leaves that sparkled and whispered a soft word, Peace. The bowls were all black and stacked lip-to-lip and rim-to-rim, a prominent shape outlined in the negative space between the bowls. Defining what is there by what isn't there. I love, too, that he uses (used; he is dead, died of lung cancer after his wife died of breast cancer) plant essences and aromas to stir all the senses. These natural fragrances do not irritate, but rather soothe. Near the entrance to the main gallery several big Buddha heads are mounted on stilts, inviting the viewer to stand beneath them to *be* and *breathe*. The interiors painted all bright red, the stuff of life. I am stirred by this spiritual artmaking, creativity as a reverent response to the passions and passing of life, transforming pain into poetry and prayer.

I cannot talk about what touches me most. I feel autistic in my own thin skin. Words fall like envelopes ripped open and turned inside out. I return to the first installation and walk slowly through the exhibit a second time. When I catch up with L later on I can't even remember what I saw. Like a story so profound that once said it is immediately forgotten, I'm left alone with the sound of my breath and the thin edge of a golden lotus floating in my mind. I tell him he has to see the show. But he doesn't. He is too busy meeting new people. Networking.

Along 23rd Street G and I stop at thrift stores. We walk arm in arm. I love G so much. We have been friends for over twenty years. She can make me laugh when I need it most. We are two squirrels in New York, jabbering and playing catch-up in the cold wind, wrapping around our smiles.

Decide to buy another pair of black jeans. These are stretchy and give where I don't, or rather where I'm giving a little too much. My waist and thighs are stretching on without me. This new pair is already soft and worn in and comfy. While in the dressing room I hear the woman in the stall next to me giggling in a sexy voice. I noticed her while on the floor, shopping with a cell phone tucked between her chin and her shoulder, pushing hangers one by one and pulling out gauzy blouses, satiny pants, and slinky, low-neckline sweaters only half-heartedly paying attention to what she was doing. All the while talking and laughing and being in two (three? four?) places at the same time. In the dressing room she is whispering, "Let me tell you what happened yesterday." Big pause. "I have to be quiet." Her voice growing smaller. "I'm so embarrassed," she says laughing with a snort. I can imagine her friend on the other end, "What? What? Tell me."

"Well," she says, pausing a little excitedly. At this point I've already tried on my jeans and slowly, very slowly, gotten dressed again and, with one shoe on, I'm almost ready to exit. Instead, and I don't know why except that a force bigger than me, call it the big V (Voyeurism) sucks me into someone else's seemingly exciting life: that of a tall, thin, thirty-something New Yorker. Here, I lean closer to the mirror (big mistake—I catch sight of long dark hair growing sideways off my cheek. How could L let me go out without mentioning it?), pressing my ear into the gap along the back wall, already starting to sweat from either a hot flash or an anticipatory moment of mystery. Up periscope. At this point I can nearly reach around through the space that separates us and touch her. I think about it only for a sadistic second, imagining just how high she'd jump. I hear her confess with a hint of excitement, "I accidentally kissed a woman on the lips." Maybe I'll try the black jeans on a second time. I'm really hopeless as shit. I don't even read stuff like this. I hate soap operas. And still my ears are lifted and clinging.

"Yes, believe it," she squeals. "It was sooooooooo strange. My friend Thomas at work was introducing me, yeah, the Romanian man who works in the cubicle next to me. Yeah, that's him. Well, I met him and his girlfriend at the doorway on my way into the building..."

Suddenly a loud knock lands on the dressing room door. I turn around so fast I nearly trip over my untied shoe.

"You all done in there?" Obviously the voice of an irritated and curious attendant. She must have bent over and seen my feet standing in one place for too long to be actively trying on anything new. Probably figured I was picking my face.

"Yup. Be out in a minute." I was hoping I hadn't missed the juicy parts.

"So like I was saying," she continued obviously distracted with the investigation. "You know how Europeans kiss each other on the cheek. Yeah. Well, when he introduced us, we leaned into each other and as I was going for her right cheek she went for my left and we smacked lips in the middle. I mean smacked. We were both kind of weirded out." Suddenly she got real quiet and began again louder than she'd been talking before, almost angry. "No. Of course not. No way," she nearly shouts back. "I am not turning lesbo. What's wrong with you anyway? It was only a kiss." To which her voice grew quiet again. "Actually it wasn't all that bad. It was kind of soft and unexpected and caught me funny like. I can't explain it now. It wasn't terrible. Well, it was an accident. But it wasn't that weird. Yeah, I did. I did kind of like it." Silence. "I gotta go now. Talk later."

Met L for dinner. Ate at a Thai restaurant. Got back to the hotel late, walking up 55th Street in the sleet, stinging cold against my cheeks, holding hands with my husband, an urban soul, who is happiest when in the big city. I am so tired and yearn for sleep. Sweet, sweet sleep. Resting between one have to and another, I finish the drawing started in the morning; my daily meditations on paper. They calm, center, and focus my mind, like throwing pots on the wheel. I think about the Buddha heads, the black bowls, and dust balls in the corner of a secret, thrift store whisper.

I have never kissed a woman on the lips.

February 26
11:14 pm

Walt's birthday today. He stayed in bed all morning and hobbled around all afternoon. Took him in the car to the park so he could watch the sunset. He is growing so small. His hands are still so large. Skin shrinks faster than bones.

March 1
3.17 am

° Give more stuff away. Do not keep anything that doesn't fit.
° Say what I mean. Mean what I say.
(So what if I change my mind a hundred times a day?)
° Say *I love you* to Walt and Mom every day.
(L, too, even if I don't feel like it.)

Feeling totally meno-postal. Managed very easily to waste one entire day acting all pissy and shifty and being mad at L because D found a video of her husband having sex with their tennis instructor. In their new bed! And he taped it no less! She also found a bunch of porn mags in the trunk of the car, hidden under the mat where the jack is kept. What she was looking for I don't know. She didn't say. I'm starting to think that all those planets coming together, rattling old patterns for "exalted consciousness" might be pushing a little too hard against our fragile human emotions. I fumed about it like it happened to me. I couldn't even tell L why I was so crazed. He figured I was mad at him for leaving his socks in the living room again. D is out of her mind, raging. Says she's going to take a chainsaw to the bed. (That's not exactly the first direction I'd head with the chainsaw, but I don't tell her that.) Says she can't possibly sleep in it again and gives it a wide berth every time she passes it on her way by. Then she spits on it. Nothing I could say consoled her. I just listened, wishing I could be there to hold her in my arms and cry with her and let her know how much I love her and that everything would be OK, even if it feels like raw shit at this very moment, a gift would eventually come from the hurt…and that I'd make the first cut on the headboard if she couldn't. What is up with the porn shit anyway? Nothing exalted there. It's times like these when I want to send all men back to Mars launched off the end of a burning tire jack. And now that the Red Planet is moving closer to Earth, maybe we can get a reduced rate on airfares. I told my mother about it just to vent and she said, "Men. They never stop hunting." She may be losing her memory, but her delivery is impeccable.

8:48 am
Woke up exhausted. My eyes crusty and sealed with dried tears. My first thought: If I've grown old and blind overnight, Great Mother, please let me at

least be able to taste. Then I remembered the dream that woke me up. I am sitting on a park bench waiting for a bus. I am seated between two very large people, who I keep thinking must be Republicans because they are looking straight ahead and acting very self-righteous and ignoring me because I'm wearing my work shirt all covered in clay and a button that says BHL (Bleeding Heart Liberal). The sky is really wide-open blue and I'm in one of those "I am the world" kind of moods. All of a sudden I start crying; sobbing deeply and trying to explain to the Republicans next to me that we are All One, that we are all related and isn't it magnificent and awesome and can't they just feel the glow between us? They are not listening, but continue to stare straight ahead. At this point I see our auras merging and at first I get scared thinking I'll become one of them, but I'm so "in the zone" that it doesn't even matter. The Republicans are getting really scared and slowly inch away from me clutching their grocery bags. I think, Oh, of course, they don't get it because they voted for George Bush and that means they're splotted; whatever that means the dream didn't indicate. Just splotted was all I remember. I continue talking to myself and anyone else who passes by, yelling out loudly, "What is essential to the heart is invisible to the eye." I wake up thinking I have to re-read, *Le Petit Prince*. Again.

10:56 pm

OK. So, I'm menopausal and it feels like I'm pregnant. I've had a very bad case of heartburn for weeks and suddenly I've forgotten how to breathe. This morning, after my acupuncture treatment, I realize that in fact I am "pregnant." I'm giving birth to myself in a new way. First thing, I begged E to put the needle in the top of my head; that makes me feel exceptionally high and happy. She smiled and then after inspecting my tongue and taking my many pulses, opts instead to needle into one of my liver meridians. E says the liver is the "governor" of life, giving me the elbow she winks and adds, lifting her eyebrows, "Liver, as in living."

She uses the word "governor" a lot when referring to my internal organs and their corresponding energy meridians and all I can think of is Governor Jeb Bush and how living in Florida is an everyday embarrassing production in the Theater of the Political Absurd. So when she begins talking about these governors and their role in my body I wince. While my liver meridian is opening and flushing and pulsing long silvery needles running up and down my legs, I keep having this vision running over and over again through my mind where I look down between my legs and see a little pink (I know, pink, where's that at?) infant attached to me by a throbbing red root, all pulsing with blue veins, and this little girl baby that is covered in cheesy clots is mouthing something very important, but I can't hear her because I'm too busy screaming in utter terror. It occurs to me that in spite of the simple fact that I don't have a period any more, I'm having a baby. When I mention this vision to E she says in a matter-of-fact way, "Oh that makes perfect sense." She then immediately leaves the room without further explanation, whistling a happy tune that sounds like, "Oh when the saints come marching in." At this point I'm starting to sweat, profusely. It's obvious that my liver meridian and Governor Jeb Bush are having an all-out face-to-face aura cleansing and all I can think about is the desperate look on the baby's face hanging upside down between my thighs, now holding out her arms like she wants me to pick her up. When E comes back into the room, which seems like a week later, she says, "Looks like you'll have to get really quiet so you can hear what that baby has to say." And all I can think about is I'm at that point in the birth process where women in labor start swearing at their husbands and screaming, "Just get this thing out of me."

March 4
4:14 am

Monday

I think an alien entity has taken over my being. I'm sure of it. I keep dreaming about a Queen who wants my total attention. She's competing with indigestion. Everything I put in my mouth turns to a mad dog in my gut. (At first I wrote *mother* and crossed it out. *Everything I put in my mother turns to a mad dog in my gut!* What's up with that slip?!) I want nothing but chocolate. P said she considers chocolate one of the main food groups. I have to agree. Though when I eat my favorite truffles (expensive, too) my breasts ache like an abscessed tooth. I'm suffering from CRS (Can't Remember Shit). From one room to another I lose my thoughts and have to retrace my steps back into the hallway to see if I can find them. I'm not interested in my husband's sexual advances. Hell, I'm not interested in anyone else's either, except in my dreams, where they're wildly orgasmic; men and women romping in white marble temples and singing bird songs.

     Sometimes you just have to go out of your everyday mind, the little pea brain steamed and sautéed by everyone else's tastes and desires, and find your own way; the true core and delight of your woman being. It simply takes what it takes.

10:12 am
The Sky So Blue I Can Taste It, except that I feel so freakin' fat I can't breathe. I am shrinking and expanding all at the same time. That's all I have today.

March 6
12:16 pm

Wednesday

Had lunch with J on our way back from a drive through the Redwinds Wildlife Refuge. I had called her in a tizzy, feeling overwhelmed with Walt. I'm just too sensitive to deal with the medical merry-go-round of phone calls, appointments, prescriptions, insurance papers, and second opinions again today. The week just wore me out with daily trips to the hospital and repairing my mother's emotional mess as well. My mother is resting comfortably, so I thought I'd give my dearest friend a call. J is a few years younger than I am. She's always so upbeat. I tell her it's because she hasn't stepped onto the menopause launch pad yet. She usually just laughs. She says I can be the pathfinder and then help her through the gate.

J and I have known each other since we were teenagers. We met in Florida after she ran away from what she calls a "perfectly go-nowhere middle class family" from the New York City suburbs. She's creative and happy and loves my mother, which is so important in a friend these days. An impulsive idea, I asked J to take a bird-watching break and check to see what migratory birds have arrived south. She said yes. Said she too needed to commune with our winged friends. I picked her up and drove the nearly twenty miles to the right-hand turn off Route 1 to the quiet, bleached-out white sand road that bumps and winds around a broad, flat expanse of Florida salt marsh looking like a photo from the turn of the century. Dotted with an occasional hammock of skinny palms, wispy boughs of slash pines and a mangrove-lined pond, it's the Florida I love, the Florida that existed long before the developers got their greedy hands on this pristine land and raked it clear to build cookie-cutter subdivisions that continue to spring up overnight, squeezed between the beach and Interstate 95; the long road that brings "northerners" to this peninsula called paradise. Once here, the out-of-towners begin immediately to scrape away the existing native plants and wildlife habitats only to replace them with water-guzzling green rug lawns (just like the one we have "up north"). Then come the tons of pesticides, herbicides, fungicides, and chemical fertilizers required to keep them so unnaturally green 365 days a year in a kind of forced feeding that denies the natural cycles and seasons of change.

As we turn off the racing buzz of traffic on Route 1 I immediately feel my energy slip from tense and tired into the tranquil beauty and serenity of this magnificent marsh with its relaxed, meandering streams and graceful grasses leaning westward against the thin whisper of an ocean breeze. The Spanish moss catches my attention instantly. It hangs from the oaks like wiry gray hair, moving loose and free in the wind. Tall and skinny palms bending in every direction like birthday candles drooping in the sun form a jagged silhouette against the clear blue sky. Streaks of lilac-colored clouds with shiny pink patches pull my breath deep into my belly. I sigh a lot when I'm in nature. "Hey," J pointed out with a giggle. "I think that cloud formation looks like a big mauve vagina, smiling."

"Yeah. Don't you just love the color mauve?"

Just the other day I was reading about the scientist who developed the color mauve, or rather the scientist who spent his life replicating the natural color he called "mauve". I don't know what came over me, but at one point I looked up at my husband and asked, "Do you think he was inspired by the color of his wife's labia?" L laughed, adding that he could understand it. He's been greatly inspired by his wife's lips in just about all his work. L is an artist and I love him for his gentle sensitivity. We are truly joined at the soul in that way.

It's not easy to drive and bird-watch at the same time. But as we turned the sharp corner that takes visitors past the first quarter-mile marker post I spotted what looked to be a close-knit family of wood storks roosting in the shiny green branches of a mangrove bush, all hunched-over like white-haired seniors asleep on a park bench, all facing the same direction; their long, dark-gray bills tucked tightly into their chests. Another deep sigh. J and I were both silent for a long time. J and I are friends for a number of reasons, but also because she understands at times like these that it's not necessary to fill up every moment with chatter, commentary, and noise. We are comfortable with quiet. We decided to get out of the car and I grabbed the traveling binoculars that I keep stashed in the glove compartment.

Looking closer I noticed that the wood storks had a guest, a single roseate spoonbill looking a bit out of place with her pretty, pink feathers. I wondered if she was there first or was gliding by and decided to drop in on her distant cousins. These spoonbills make me laugh. They look prehistoric and just a little too exotic for Florida. I mean: pink feathers! It just tickles me well to no end.

J then pointed out a large flotilla of ducks, American coots to be exact, gliding around in the pond just in front of the wood storks. With their short, white beaks contrasting against their shiny tuxedo black bodies, I wondered: Where did the term "old coot" come from? I vowed to look it up when I got home in my favorite resource guides, Barbara Walker's, *Woman's Encyclopedia of Myths and Secrets*. I'd met Barbara years ago when I lived in New Jersey; a brilliant scholar and wise woman. I'd heard that she too had moved to Florida. All of us crones moving south for the winter, I laughed. Just like so many coots.

As we watched the ducks dip and dive and tip their tails straight up into the air, their heads submerged in the dark water in search of food, I became aware of a complete and total silence weighing lightly all around us; a sweet and soothing breath against my neck. I noticed, too, no anxious somersaults in my stomach. No tightness in my shoulders, chest, or fingertips. In the middle of enjoying my awareness of what it's like to feel relaxed, if only for a few moments, I heard a foosh, foosh, fooshing and quickly looked up, spinning around to find the source of the almost eerie sound. I almost fell backward as I lifted my head to catch sight of a magnificent bald eagle swooping just above us. She was so close it felt like I could jump up and lightly press my fingers against her ebony underbelly. I was certain we made eye contact and for a moment I knew I wasn't breathing. The sky was breathing for me. I was totally out of time for that single moment, feeling like I too was flying with my wings spread wide and my head held high and strong against the wind. I could feel the rush of air against my neck, my feathers rustling and free. I don't know how long I stood there totally transfixed by the empty space that for a few seconds held the weightless form and spirit of an eagle. I don't know how long I had been crying when J walked over to me and gently tucked a tissue in my hand, waking me from my trance.

"Everything is going to be all right," she whispered, draping her arm around my shoulder. "You'll get through. You'll be soaring like an eagle in no time."

Later, at the take-out Chinese restaurant where we had lunch J asked me if I thought a sacred ritual was in order to honor my transition into menopause. I told her I thought it was about time. I fiddled with the cellophane wrapping on my fortune cookie before cracking it open. It was empty. No fortune inside. I was going to let it go, figuring the eagle was fortune enough for one day. But I decided to assert myself. Even though I'm endeavoring not to live in the future, I deserved a fortune I told myself. The young Asian woman smiled and apologized, bringing me another cookie with a fortune tucked inside.

You have at your command the wisdom of the ages.

We had a good laugh, too, at the little smiley face that followed.

March 7
4:01 am

More Fatty Food Fantasies: My mother's macaroni and cheese, piping hot and crusty on top.

° A thick slab of cold butter on the end slice of a French baguette.
° A pint of Ben & Jerry's *Karamel Sutra*™ all for myself.
° Garlic-roasted smashed potatoes with shredded parmesan.

° A flaky chocolate croissant and a cup of frothy rich hot chocolate from that place in Paris next to the Louvre.

° A slice of New York-style chocolate chip cheesecake from the Lower East Side.

° Gorgonzola cheese on a slice of ripe red Bartlett pear.

March 8
5:06 am

Have to do something with my hair. It has a mind (and body) of its own. I really don't like going to hair salons. First of all, I can't stand the smell. The price of hair these days tends to leave a bad taste in my mouth, too. Besides, L has managed to trim the ends in the back and I tend the bangs. This hair partnership has worked for years. At least no one has taken me aside to warn me otherwise. My sister-in-law says you can tell what a menopausal woman's high school graduation picture looks like because it's the hairstyle she returns to (she may as well have said "grasps at") when she reaches mid-life. In high school I had a chin-length "page-boy," no bangs, parted in the middle. That was, of course, only after years of that awful pixie. Ugh. I hated how my mother cut my hair. Whenever we look at those photos of me with jagged bangs and a billboard-wide forehead sticking out, I'd ask jokingly, "Mom, didn't you like me?"

"Mousy." That's what the young woman, the "shampoo attendant" called my natural hair color. "Kind of mid-life mousy," she said unapologetically. "It happens to everyone."

I wondered how she knew about *everyone*. Then I wondered how in hell I ever let my bad twin within talk me into going to a hair salon. Ugh. I felt trapped.

Then something weird happened. I heard myself say: *Thank you, your opinion means nothing to me.* I can't believe I actually said it because it was exactly what I was thinking. I immediately felt bad, but said nothing to follow up. The woman glared at me and spun around on her heels, leaving me alone to face myself in the mirror.

The voice seemed to come from somewhere below my belly button.

I didn't get a haircut. I grabbed my bag and paid for my shampoo, telling the receptionist I wasn't feeling good. Heat was washing over me and my upper lip was covered with tiny beads of perspiration. I felt dizzy.

I drove home a little shaky and took a long nap, dreaming of mice.

March 9
3:13 am

Saturday

If I have to give up chocolate I don't know what I'll do.

4:03 am
My New Mantra: I do what the hair on my head tells me to do.

March 10
11:45 pm

Sunday

Z called this morning. He said that if I look at life as a burning candle, and dying as the process of letting the flame burn out it doesn't seem so bad. I didn't say: That is so trite. But I wanted to with all my might. I'm not sure Z really hears me anyway. Z is a former co-worker and part-time teacher. He said he wanted to talk to me about something important at work. I said I'd call him back when I had more time. Besides, I reminded him that I have taken the year off and am minding my own business, away from office politics. Z likes to gossip and I'm just so not there. I want to get back to my new sculpture waiting for me in the studio. This something "important" makes my stomach twitch. I find myself avoiding Z lately. I end up going down the drama drain with him at least once a week. I either need to talk to him about it or be willing to give up the friendship.

> *You'll know when you know. Trust your gut. Your life is all about you.*

March 11
10:36 am

Monday

Going out for lunch, alone, at Thai Thai (or as my mother calls it, Thigh Thigh. She can't seem to get the correct pronunciation of these "foreign" words, in spite of my numerous corrections). I really should get my ass into the studio to finish up the Ancestral series, but I need a break, need to not talk about nursing home options for Walt while trying to eat. I've arranged for him to get a hospital bed at home so he doesn't disturb Mom in bed at night. He tosses and turns and coughs and spits up most of the night; Death knocking on the window.

> Why do the people who greet you at the restaurant door say, "Just *one*, (big emphasis on the ONE) today?" Is it such a freak show to eat alone?
>
> Yes. Just one, you twit.

4:18 pm

E's right. You never know how anything is going to turn out. I was standing in the kitchen this morning leaning against the sink, peeling the skin off seven soaked almonds (one for each chakra?), thinking about nothing at all and feeling relieved. Of course until I catch myself thinking of nothing and then my secretary within reaches through the door and hands me a list of messages that I missed while my mind was out to lunch. But it's quiet now and that feels good, too. E, my wise woman acupuncturist, says I need protein and sprouted almonds are "pure potential power" and a good source of calcium. I think all I really need is a tranquilizer. V seems so happy now that she's on prescription medication for anxiety. She says it takes the sharp edges off, especially in the morning when she first wakes up and feels like she's caught in a bear trap. And here I am peeling almonds with my thumbnail.

Walt is asleep. His breathing is slow and liquid-like. Mom is having lunch at the Senior Center. I'm starting to relax a little. I don't know about the protein power, but the act of peeling such a tiny little nut is deeply rewarding. All seven are finally peeled and sitting on the edge of my mother's one and only piece of cobalt blue and white Staffordshire dessert plate. She found it at a thrift store and didn't know what it was, but liked the stamp on the bottom. It said, "Commemorative Plate for the 350th Anniversary of the Founding of the Nation 1607–1957." The almonds looked lonely and naked resting next to the sketched–in "Old Church Tower" of Jamestown, Virginia. In 1957 I was five years old. That was the year we moved from Fletcher Street across the tiny state of Rhode Island and into the southeastern corner of Connecticut, where we found ourselves living in a trailer park of other lost and fumbling blue-collar families with too many kids, wandering dogs and cats, and rampant alcoholism in one or both parents. I always felt lucky that only one parent was drunk. My mother never drank and for this I am ever grateful. About that move I don't remember much. When I was in my early twenties I saw a psychic named Mitzy and she asked me what happened when I was five years old (uh oh, here comes a hot flash).

Breathe. Breathe. Breathe. Don't run away from this dance of fire. Bring your awareness into your belly. Gently bring the heat down through your belly into the soles of your feet. Let the licking flames of fire travel down your body into the green fresh Earth; the core of creativity; the grotto of the Great Mother. See how she stretches up her cool and soothing hands, reaching from the quiet ground at your feet. Let her hold onto the back of your ankles, squeezing gently, releasing any pressure you may be holding. Let her gentle, soft touch relax your belly, throat, and hands. You are safe.

"Why did you move from Rhode Island?" The bleach-blonde Mitzy asked curiously.

"I don't really know," I said flatly. "I think it was because my father got a job in Hartford."

"That's not the real reason," she mumbled as she peered tighter into my handprint. She was a palm reader. She had smeared cheap red lipstick onto my right palm and pressed my hand hard, a little too hard I thought, onto a piece of what looked like grade-school math paper. I remember how bad red lipstick goo smelled, like a vinyl shower curtain dipped in dime-store perfume. She then stared at the cryptic language of my palm print, and after a heavy and anxious few sighs and a loud and startling cough (Mitzy was obviously a heavy smoker and hadn't read the writing on the Surgeon General's wall), she began rather furiously circling little open spaces, hash marks, and lines on my red hand print. As she did she called out words, towns, people's names and other disconnected events, asking immediately afterwards very open-ended and what I thought to be suspiciously generic questions:

"Have you ever been to Chicago?"

"No."

"Well, you're going."

"Do you know a Tom, Ernie, or Jay?"

"No."

"You will. They're all assholes."

(I was forewarned about her use of various critical assessments of men.) I was growing bored after what seemed like an eternity of guessing-game mumbo jumbo. I was already paying more attention to the way one single clump of hair fell out of the basket of blonde curls neatly piled on top of her head. I was starting to count the various shades of gold, platinum, and straw contained in that one curl, at the same time reciting to myself: "There was a little girl who had a little curl right in the middle of her forehead. And when she was good she was very, very good and when she was bad she was horrid." Later on, many years later, I would come to realize that Mitzy was very, very good. But I had no idea what she was talking about then. I stopped my blonde count at 12, when she suddenly looked up and said quite curiously and with more than just a little concern,

"There's something sexual spinning around that move your family made."

"Really?" I quickly pulled my attention away from her forehead and riveted a blank stare instead on the tiny red lipstick smear she just circled with blue ink on my palm print. I remember I didn't like her pen much either. I'm a pen junkie. Always have been. I think it might have something to do with the fact that my mother brought home pens as little treasures when she worked cleaning the junior high school across from our Fletcher Street house. She'd climb the front stairs, still wearing her full apron with the little dance of pink and turquoise coffee cups, white vapor wisps floating above each cup like a thin aromatic ghost, and hold out a pen with a big smile on her face: "Here baby, look what I found. Just for you." I'd nearly leap off the top steps, grabbing the pen on my way into her arms. She'd wrap me in her smell all like pine and floor wax and sweet kisses. "How's my little Bunny?" she'd say tenderly, whisking me up the stairs and into the house. I'd bury my face in her neck. "When I found this pen, I knew it was meant for you," she'd whisper in my ear.

I was distrustful of Mitzy right away when she used, instead of a sleek black and silver number befitting of a palm reader, a pink and white plastic click top with the name of a local dry cleaner company half worn off on the barrel. Mitzy's hands were now off and running, rapidly racing across my map of destiny. She'd hit pay dirt. My belly seized up and my heart crawled into my throat. If I had been in menopause at the time I would have been soaking wet clear through to my underwear.

Instead I jabbed my right finger into my cheek, pressing the inside fleshy skin right into the sharp edge of my back teeth, tearing off a little bloody chunk and nibbling on it with my mouth puckered up and crooked. I remember one time dating a man a few years my junior. (He was still at the top end of his teens, but in my early twenties I didn't even notice.) He used to yell at me saying, "One day you're going to bite a new mouth in the side of your cheek." It's a bad habit I've almost given up. But satisfying in some atavistic, cannibalistic way.

"What do you mean 'something sexual' ?" I snorted.

"I don't know…exactly."

"You're a psychic." Now I was certain that everything she said after this was made up.

"Your father, and your mother, too, both know," she said never lifting her head to look at me, "but they're not going to tell you. There's a big gray cloud, a family secret, hanging over them like a wet tent. You'll find out much later on. So try to forget about it. OK?"

I grabbed my purse, pulled out my own royal blue Paper Mate pen to write out a check, the total of which I can't remember. It seemed like too much, or not enough. Holding up my pen like a torch I said, "This is a real pen. This is a pen that will tell the truth. This is a pen that knows."

I didn't realize until later that night that I had left the palm print and jumble of notes sitting stubbornly silent on Mitzy's desk, never to be seen again.

March 14
2:12 am

I was stopped at a red light this afternoon, staring into space, a dull, tight stupor freezing my attention. I was tired and jumpy. I wrestled the morning away with three calls to Walt's oncologist, two to the radiologist, and one to his primary care doctor, waiting for return phone calls in between, which didn't come. Each receptionist I spoke with suggested I call one of Walt's other doctors. I didn't think it was such a big deal to get a prescription for antidepressants for an eighty-year-old man with a terminal disease. Walt wasn't smiling and didn't want to eat. He didn't even want to watch TV. His emotional disposition was wearing on my mother. I thought about what the nurse at the hospital had said, that in her opinion, anyone given a diagnosis of cancer should at the same time get a prescription for antidepressants. Half my friends are on pharmaceuticals just for recreational purposes, and here Walt has cancer and I'm getting the run-around. I was steaming at the end of four phone calls, no return calls, and still no results. I decided to hop in the car and drive over to the doctor's office myself, bringing a copy of the Power of Attorney paperwork for their files. At the stoplight I took the opportunity to zone out (not that I have any control over it these days) when I was suddenly startled into raw-assed terror with a loud rap on my car window.

My heart picked up ten speeds, pounding madly against my chest, adrenaline preparing me to jettison through the roof. Out of the corner of my eye I caught sight of a man bent down and peering in at me. For a moment I thought he was holding a gun. It turned out to be a cell phone. I think I even gasped with a little shriek. His cell phone went dead and he wanted to know if I had one he could borrow. His car had stalled and he needed a tow. I never opened the door or rolled down the window. I shook my head without even looking at him. I stared straight ahead, my eyes glued to the red light, desperately prayed for release. My face was scratchy and hot, my hands shaky. As soon as the light turned I raced away. It took about three miles for my heart rate to return to normal, or at least a pace that allowed me to take a deep breath. All afternoon I couldn't shake the thin gray film of fear that clung to my skin like a sticky, wet shower curtain on the way out of the tub. His silent, shadowy outline was burnt into the backs of my eyes. What exactly am I running away from?

March 15
9:36 am

Walt is watching the food channel — that is, when he's not reading his Weight Watcher's cookbook. Seems so weird. He can't eat any more, since the feeding tube went in, at least not through his mouth, and he's losing weight by the minute. After feeding him (which has taken us all a bit to get used to; pouring liquid nutrition directly into his stomach) my mother says she figures she'll wind up on Emeril's show some day. Not as a guest, but as a tender, sweet-baked bluefish, "The essence of Frances," she laughs.

"How so, Mom?"

"Well," she says, drawing out the e like an old storyteller. "When I die I want to be cremated. Right?"

I hate when she brings this up. "Do we have to talk about this now?" I tilt my head in Walt's direction, hoping she'll have some feelings for Walt. My mother isn't paying any attention to me.

"And my ashes thrown in the ocean. Right?"

"You hate the ocean," I remind her.

"Then I'll get eaten by some guppies. Right?"

"Ouch." Now I'm in the swing of it and play along.

"Then those guppies will get eaten by some mullet and those mullet will get eaten by some bluefish, who will get caught by a fishing boat. Right?"

"I hear a bluefish bite is pretty nasty." Walt nods, approvingly.

"So, some of those fish will end up in a fish market in New York, right?" She lifts her arm making a swish in the direction she thinks is New York.

"That's Miami, Mom."

"Well, when I'm a bluefish I'm going to call out for Emeril and he's gonna hear his name coming out of that shiny fresh fish and that bluefish who ate the essence of me. We're both gonna up on live TV," she says with a grin erupting from ear to ear. "Right?" She is so proud of herself.

"Don't touch that dial, Mom."

Walt closes his eyes, a slow smile spreading across his face. "That's my bride," he says, before shifting into a muffled snore.

March 17
8:58 am

Sunday

Cloudy, hot, humid. Chance of rain. Ugh. Muggy again. Will I ever get used to the heat here? On days like this I feel like a prisoner in paradise. Low tide at 3 pm. Don't care if it is raining, I'm walking on the beach. The wind will bring in some interesting debris. Found a football-shaped, Russian-made light bulb last week. Will see if I can use it in my new sculpture!

March 19
11:59 pm

Tuesday

I'm enjoying my new Chi Kung class. The instructor is a Vietnam Vet, former Special Forces paratrooper, martial arts instructor for federal agents, Christian minister, psycho-neuroimmunologist, former military surgeon's assistant! I never thought my healing guidance would come in this form. Oh well. He's close to sixty and is one of those guys who has worn his hair the same way since he was twelve. Military style. Short, with a 1950s dry sweep upward that looks like an upside-down paint brush. Like one of those baritones on Lawrence Welk. He's deep into Chinese healing modalities (learned while in China and Asia), subtle energy healing and making sure we root ourselves into the Earth with every breath we take. Sounds suspiciously like a pagan to me. But we never discuss our personal paths and he's said "God" only once and that was in the first sentence of the first day, which I immediately dismissed. I think he uses the Christian thing to smell good to the southern Bible belt mind. A kind of Christian camouflage. Seems too eclectic to be of the fundamental species. Anyway, there is no proselytizing and he is a good teacher. His medical background, unfortunately geared toward male physiology, is very informative. It's not the Wise Woman tradition by any means, but it's a solid learning experience. And I hope I never stop learning my whole life. At eighty I'll be doing some Then Age quasi-medical exercise for my soul!

T is the only other student and it's been an incredible experience getting to know him. T, with his healing story and all: simply decided while in hospice care that it wasn't time to die. Too much to do. Immediately afterward a blood vessel ruptured in his throat where the cancer is located and he started coughing up blood. He said the healing began at that moment. Eventually released from hospice (an almost unheard of reversal) he's feeling better every day. When he arrived at Chi Kung two months ago, he could barely stand up. Now he does 20-minute standing poses without much effort at all. It's really an intense kind of thing that goes on in that short, but difficult time while in posture. The postures are simple and still. Always breathing long, slow breaths from that place two inches below the belly button (the womb zone!). There are a few "warm up" movements similar to T'ai Chi before we start. Then the standing still begins. It is strong and subtle medicine. While T and I are in posture, P stands behind us doing some healing energy directed at us one at a time. It's very intense. I feel totally energized when the class is over.

So I go three times a week and look forward to it. That's different. We do it at Long Street Park, so we are outside on the river. It's a natural thing, with the birds chirping and the squirrels running around us. We are practicing Jam Jong Chi Kung, which translates to "Stand Like A Tree." It's one of many branches of the tradition, which is the root of all other martial arts. But Chi Kung is not a martial art. I asked P if Chi Kung was a male tradition. And he adamantly shook his head. I think he knows something he is not admitting. I have this intuitive feeling that it, like yoga, was developed by women for all the changes women go through with the blood cycles. The martial arts were a take-off of Chi Kung, developed by men for fighting and defending. Of course. Where else to go with all that testosterone?

March 20 – Spring
3:49 am

Wednesday

Dream. I'm holding a little monkey close to my breast; one of those little ones used in experiments with the big black eyes and fur the color of cappuccino. For some reason my brother handed her to me because he said she was lost. We were on our way to the airport and he found her by the side of the road, separated from her mother, so he decided to bring her with us. I'm now concerned that I'm not going to be allowed on the airplane with the monkey. There's no paperwork and I can't even begin to explain the situation. I start crying, not for me, but for this scared and lonely monkey, who I have now begun calling Mono. I look into her sweet and pleading eyes and she too is crying. We begin communicating silently with our stares. She tells me she wants to return to her troop; her group in the wilderness. She's really lost and doesn't want to get on an airplane with strangers. She wants to be with her own kind. She wants to be with her mother. I'm sobbing and rubbing her back and holding her close to me. Her feet are wrapped around my waist; her long and trembling arms around my neck. I wake up crying.

I looked up Mono. It's Spanish for monkey. Mono, one. All one.

March 22
10:56 pm

Friday

Yoga was hell this morning. I couldn't concentrate on one single complete breath. My mind starts to chew on its own paw when left unattended too long; sucking, licking, and gnawing away at itself. I don't stop until I taste blood. And then it's already too late. I'm wounded and limping; the salty, metallic taste welded to my tongue. The sun salutation takes on a different meaning when I'm raw and ragged from my own brand of mental terrorism; my mind on random scan. Reaching up I think surely L is leaving me for a younger woman. Bending forward…all that loose flab on my thighs. I am part-animal, an abandoned Shar-pei dog with too much skin and sad eyes all junked up with brown goo. Why wouldn't he? Right foot back…I better get used to the hours at 7–11 because that's where I'll end up working…Plank Pose sucks…I feel like I can barely keep myself afloat…Life as an artist…Argh…Cobra Pose…I'll bet L's snaking money aside for a hasty departure…Left foot forward…There goes that paranoia again…I can be so quick with suspicions…Downward Looking Dog…Again?…Oh, my… Those thighs haven't improved much since I last saw them…Right foot forward…I really do miss my sex drive…Downward Looking Dog…Enough already with the Downward Looking Dog Pose…I don't want to end up homeless…I'm sweating…Knees to mat…Rest…At last…Lick, lick, gnaw…Child Pose…I'm freaking about money again.

I finish yoga; ending with one quiet minute. Well, maybe it was only a quiet moment. Breathing In. Breathing Out.

It's called meditation practice for a reason. Practice being kind to yourself. Kindness has a long shelf life.

March 25
(What did I do this weekend anyway?)
7:58 am

Monday

Mom is rustling in the kitchen, clanging her spoon against the cereal bowl. This is her non-verbal signal, like a toddler demanding attention: I'm here. I'm alone. I'm done eating. Take care of me. She is making sure we are awake so she can get a ride to the Senior Center. It's L's turn today. He's been in his studio for over an hour. We are like burned-out parents getting up early and staying up late to snatch a few sacred silent moments to ourselves, and when we finally do we sit and stare into the empty spaces that float around us and try to remember who we really are.

Mom is dressed early. "Well, we have to leave in 20 minutes. Got to be there by nine." I remind her that Bingo starts at 10; that it's almost an hour before they have to go. She wants to wait in the car and I talk her out of it.

"I'll get arrested, Mom. It's too hot for any living thing to sit in the car for an hour." I convince her to check her email.

This is my morning plan: Yoga, then make my favorite morning miso soup. Then enjoy a few hours alone. C, at the University of Miami, emailed, inviting me to give a glass workshop for fall this year and next spring. I want to go over the proposal just to clarify the details. Just last week I called L from the cell phone absolutely ecstatic that finally I had come to an important decision leading to happiness: "I'm giving up art." I was almost hysterical with the discovery that I didn't have to do anything I didn't want to do. He was happy that I offered him my part of the studio. Of course, I'd reneged by dinner, but in that perfect moment I was flying high and feeling generous. Seems whenever I make these kinds of declarations I am always tested by some wisdom larger than my mini-mind. The email from C arrived in perfect, divine time. Of course I'll teach the workshop. Pouring hot glass out of a raging white-hot furnace puts me in touch with something wild and wholly primal dwelling in that happy space behind my belly button.

"Nobody ever writes to me. I guess they're all too busy." My mother is sulking, because in her world if the recipient of an email does not respond within 20 minutes, she feels abandoned, unloved, forgotten.

"You have to write to be written to." I sound like a broken, boring mother.

March 27
9:35 am
Wednesday

After a disastrous yoga session, I am glad to have water to stir and gaze into; my focus blurred and whirring. It helps loosen what is far too tame, and grounds what energy has gone astray.

> **Quiet and Patient Miso Soup**
> *1. Bring to boil a cup of water.*
> *2. Add chopped scallions, Add crumbled seaweed (kombu is my favorite), grated carrot,and spinach. If I have leftover kale, collards or broccoli I drop that in, too. Greens are good for the heart.*
> *3. Add chopped tofu. Sometimes I'll substitute a scrambled egg.*
> *4. Remove from heat and think about what is good and true.*
> *5. Stir in a heaping teaspoon of miso and count blessings. I am lucky that I don't have high blood pressure. I like the taste of salt.*

J called. Low tide is at 9:52. We meet at the beach, but I decide not to take a walk. Already it is way too hot, or as I heard one southerner put it, "It's hotter than the hinges of hell." I wasn't sure how one would come to know that except by experience, but I never brought it up. We find some shade and watch a huge flock of dark, sleek-bodied birds swirl in slow-motion tornado formation out over the ocean, occasionally dropping and diving like dead weights into the liquid steel-green surface of the sea. My jaw is finally relaxed. "I think there's something big out there, J, underneath the surface."

"Birds are the indicator species. They know and tell." She has a memory like a trap. Well, she's young still, and remembers everything I need to know.

"What do you think they're telling us?" I ask out loud, talking to myself without expecting an answer. I become immediately aware of tension draining from my body. My shoulders soften and fall away from my ears. The rustle of the new growth of shiny rust-red sea grape leaves takes on a quiet melody, whispering between the louder lyrics bouncing off the waves hitting sand. I think about the Australian Aboriginal tradition where each child inherits a stretch of the Dreamtime by way of an ancestral song that marks that place on earth where a mother first feels the quickening in her womb of her child-to-be; an indication that the ancestors have impregnated the spirit of the child from that Earth place in the Dreamtime. The child's "deepest self" is rooted in that Earth place, and becomes intricately woven within it, contracted by the ancestors to be its offspring and protector. A child's soul is so connected to that place and the song associated with the place, that upon looking at a tree growing there, she says, "That tree is me." According to tradition, each person returns to his or her Earth place to die, as a way of re-vitalizing the dreaming Earth in a continuous cycle of song. I know for certain I am water-woman born by the sea. I am most at home in the wild places where the Moon moves the water.

"Go with the flow." J says, as if talking to herself, too, and reminding me at the same time of the song in my soul, waiting ever so patiently somewhere beneath the stinking hard balls of blue cheese left over in my mental baggage.

March 28
3:39 am

I better figure out who I am now that I'm not cute or young any more. Otherwise I am going to be a very depressed and bitter woman. And there's nothing uglier than a bitter old woman. Some days I think I have a grip, but then I just slip into a very small snake hole and get sucked down screaming, "Give me a freakin' break once in a while will ya, huh, Big Mama?" Then I see my mother leaning over the edge holding up a life-sized mirror to me all day long singing, "Have you looked at yourself lately?" She's a cross between Napoleon, Felix Unger, and Bea Arthur on LSD. And I love her so much I ache when I kiss her goodnight and she says, "You're my little girl."

3:38 pm

Every tiny seed and root that entered our yard is now full grown, blossoming, and screaming, "You can't control me. Nah Nah Nah Nah Nah!" Holy Shit. I love it, really. Or at least I'm surrendering to it. I especially love the backyard. It's the closest thing I've seen to a flowering meadow down here in the land of scrub oaks and chinch bugs. It looks like a huge field of wild flowers from one of those picture books. Only it's my unshaven backyard. The growing mass of green is swallowing up my sculpture, my chairs, flowerpots, and anything I left outside for the taking. In some way it's nice to see only wild flowers from my kitchen window and not a mess of stuff. Stuff. I can't seem to buy into the waste of gas, time, energy to mow the ground to make it look good for my neighbors. At least not today.

So, after trimming up the hedges with the big clippers, I came in and trimmed my bangs. It's my version of, Change the Things You Can. I got a little carried away. I look like Mamie Eisenhower, and I don't relate well to Republicans.

APRIL

April 1
(My father used to put peanut butter on
my nose while I was sleeping. April Fool!)
3:47 am

Monday

I'm starting to see myself someplace else in the summer, when it's so hot here that I can't even breathe. Little images of me pop up when I least expect it. In my future vision I'm sitting at a wonderful little café in a university town that has like-minded eco-spiritual types, artists, green thinkers, strong men and women, my Earth tribe thinkers, a great little alternative theater, a great place to take yoga, Chi Kung, tai chi. A swimming pool where I can do my silly laps. In my summer town there are great little restaurants. It's brisk and cool and refreshing outside. I have a garden in my back yard. I'm taking good/excellent care of myself. I see me sipping something really delicious and loving it. I'm happy. Even if it's only in my mind; it's a place to be.

I have to get back to the present. Breathe in the moment. I cannot live in the future. It will drag me out of the gift of breathing fully and freely, even though it doesn't feel so full.

April 2
11:11 am

Tuesday

Woke up in one of those New Age moods. One of those made-for-women's TV, "Life is Wonderful", kind of movies. This kind of thinking scares me first thing in the morning. It feels like a manic attack and I'm a little concerned that I won't have anywhere to go with it by lunch. After thinking about it, I'm actually getting pissed about my good mood because now I'm going to spend the rest of the day looking over my shoulder, waiting for the shoe to fall.

No. I'm not going to waste my time waiting. I'm going to focus on the now moment and if the shoe falls, I don't give one flying foot about it. I've worked hard to think positively. Goddess knows I've taken all the workshops to prove it. I was beginning to think I was addicted to self-improvement. Then woke up one day channeling my first macho hero, Popeye, and knew I'd made a turn-around with, "I ain't scared of nuttin." Then started eating raw spinach.

I'm careful not to hyper-transcend into a whirling dervish with these ephemeral, happy moments, though. My mother used to tell me: "Start out laughing. You'll end up crying." Now why would any mother say that to a happy child? I remember seeing this bumper sticker on my way to the post office the other day: Zero To Bitch In 3 Seconds. I laughed in sisterhood with the unknown driver, careful not to nudge her fender while pulling close to her back end to read it.

April 4
3:33 am (Numbers are so weird.
So nothing and everything, depending
on how you look at them.)

L and I were up until midnight pawing over the paperwork for our income tax return. We finally, or nearly, finished the taxes if there is such a state of being. The piles of paperwork, receipts, scratch pads, and copies of previous tax returns have covered the kitchen table for two days. Meals have been buffet style from the kitchen counter top, sometimes eaten standing up. With a bite of leftover tortellini in my mouth I'm having to defend a receipt for $33.99 marked with my handwriting for "updated shoes."

"How is this a write-off?" L asks. He's the fastidious one, the artist-cum- accountant. He's the detail man of my dis-organization; the ocean to my lava flow. It's obvious I'm the Idea Woman, as I search languidly for the creative response.

"Updated shoes?" I reply dreamily. "Post it under R & D."

"Research and development?" he queries, with a wrinkled brow right out of a Dickens novel.

"Whatever." I reply, tossing my fork into the wind. "It's meaningless in the big picture."

"The IRS *is* the big picture." My husband reminds me. His smile came and went.

I have a dentist appointment and I'm out the door. Anything is better than taxes. Before actually getting in the car, though, I tried on no less than three outfits. The first was a black pair of stretch pants with a black tee and with the wind and all I topped it with a pink, floral French terry cardigan. I slipped into my black, stacked heel mules. I looked like the Easter bunny dressed for a funeral in NYC. This will never do. Off with the fluffy cardigan and on with the purple batiked, Balinese over-jacket. Better. However, in spite of the fact that I've washed the jacket a dozen times to soften the 100 percent cotton stiffness common with wax batik prints, it just doesn't hang right. Actually it doesn't move. It's stiff and sticks to my butt when I walk and the front feels like a piece of plywood. Besides, it's long sleeve and it's almost 80 degrees already. I'm definitely not going out with that on. Not even to the dentist.

My third try put me in the same basic black foundation and a beige, linen slash rayon blouse; loose and comfy. I brought it back from one of those outlet shops in Secaucus, NJ. It may be a little too loose as the split seams open a little too wide and the front droops down so much that I keep having to adjust the shoulders by pulling them up; shortening the front and letting the back slip down where it belongs, covering up my butt. Now I'm running late and once again I've played beat the clock without a prize.

Unlike 90 percent of the population, I like going to the dentist. I look forward to a few moments in an easy chair, where I can open my mouth and not have to say anything; not be pressed to comment, converse, or construct an excuse for having nothing to say.

As I pull into the parking lot that faces the park, I notice for the first time that someone has carved dolphin heads in the remaining branches of what was once a large tree, now leveled to stand about six feet high. Four dolphin heads protruding off four separate branches from a tall stump of what looks like a dead live oak or a gumbo limbo. Fascinating. How did I ever miss that? I then noticed that the tree wasn't dead at all. Several green shoots where pushing through the stump. New branches were forming. I got a rush out of the dolphins jumping out of a new-sprouting tree. I just sat in my car, staring at those wooden dolphin heads, seeing them for the first time.

I walked into the dentist's office and remember in a flash as I glanced over at the magazine pile why I don't like this particular office. Their magazine selection is too conservative, too not me: *Fortune*, *Golf Digest*, *Southern Living*, and *Working Mothers*. What did I expect, "Ms." or "Bitch?" I probably won't have to wait long, but my menopausal medusa within tells me "I better *not* have to wait long." I find a *Smithsonian* magazine and settle in, putting my glasses on begrudgingly after I've read several paragraphs, realizing that I was squinting and the magazine was at arm's length in front of me.

A sweet voice calls my name and for a fraction of a second I freeze, not knowing whether to take the magazine with me or not. Decisions. Decisions. I hadn't been in the waiting room long enough to get into any article in depth. An article on gigantic squid, netted and stretched out to full length to be studied by scholarly scientists in white lab coats. On the facing page there was an artistic rendition of a Greek myth in which a gigantic sea squid is about to eat up a boat and its crew in the raging waters of the Mediterranean. I felt sad looking at the photo of that poor squid, who once roamed the sea in freedom. I didn't get into wondering if it had a family and would her squid babies cry when she didn't come home after hunting for food all day. "Don't go there." I hear the voice of my emotional editor warning. Please, somebody, protect me from myself.

On other equally heroic pages there were photos of proud university men holding dart guns on expedition in Africa to study gorillas and elephants. Why can't they leave them alone, I snark, turning the page with an agitated crackle? Let the wilderness remain wild. Mostly I browsed the black and white display ads in the back, mildly interested in an eco-archeological expedition to Patagonia.

"Hi, Nancy," the woman in green scrubs welcomes me very cheerily. "I'm new here. My name is Betsy. I'll be right with you. I just have to wash up and get my gloves on before we begin. Make yourself comfy and I'll be right back." Uh oh. I'm in trouble. She likes to talk. What's worse is she sounds like a teenager. As she begins cleaning my teeth I realize she's probably forty-something. What would it be like to have a job where you think you have to talk in a little girl's voice to get a pay check, I wonder, staring into the crinkled green splash mask and protective goggles she wears across her face. In the dentist chair, blood equals death. I wish I had my camera. What a close-up shot this would make.

I try to fold my hands in prayer posture, closing my eyes to give the signal that I'm not interested in participating in conversation. Out of luck here. It doesn't matter whether I'm awake and shining or stretched out like a dead squid, she's going to talk. Doesn't matter if I'm awake or asleep, or even interested. She begins by telling me that her sister will have to wait a few days for her purse. With tax time she can't get near the post office. Her sister left her purse on the seat of her car when they got back from church. There wasn't anything in it—just a lipstick and tissue. She didn't really need it. The dental hygienist couldn't believe it took her sister two days to realize she'd left it in the car. Not only does she chatter on incessantly but she has the irritating habit of stopping work on my teeth to tell the uninteresting details of her story, demanding that I watch her magnified eyes and tiny, latex-covered hands as she gestures the story in a dramatic way.

Each time she stops working on my teeth I look up to see if something is wrong. Looking for reassurance in the only part of her face I can see. As our eyes meet, she takes the opportunity of my forced attention to go on about her sister's purse, her kids, the new bathroom tile in her home, and her husband's contracting job. In that fragment of a second when our eyes meet, I feel that supernal experience of melding deep in my gut that reminds me that this stranger, this chatty woman with an undeveloped voice, who may have missed her theatrical debut, this forty-something woman and I are linked in some ancient mystery dance when blood was sacred and teeth were painfully ground to the gums by chewing dirt caught in roots and weeds. As I'm feeling the pulse of some cosmic connection with my dental hygienist, I get the goose bump experience momentarily and sigh deeply, waiting for her to rinse the gritty cleaning powder out of my mouth with a hose that makes sucking sounds.

"Does your husband do remodeling?" I ask when she unclips the pink bib from around my neck. I'm already thinking about the studio L and I have talked about adding to our house. It's a pipe dream, I know. But I'm practicing positive thinking. Having a contractor whose wife cleans my teeth can't hurt either.

"Sure does." She replies in a cheery squeak. "Want his card?"

"Sure. I want to build a bigger studio."

"Are you an artist?" She nearly whispers, almost reverently, raising her eyebrows. This is the first question she's asked that I'm able to answer now that her hands aren't in my mouth.

"Yeah."

"Really?" She raises her voice, acting far more enthusiastic about it than I am. "I always wanted to be an artist." Unexpectedly she throws her arms out wide and steps forward to give me a hug. I surprise myself, deeply absorbing this stranger's sudden affection.

I make a dash to my car in the thin, drizzling rain. The dolphin heads are now glistening gray and dripping wet, jutting from the tree as if struggling to get back into the ocean.

Maybe it's the mercury in my fillings that's making me so moody. I'm too young to feel this worn out. Really, now.

April 5
8:22 am

Walt was up all night, shuffling. I don't have the motivation, or my usual drive to get up and go into the studio, at all. Want to call someone; anyone. Want to do the laundry. Want to sit on the couch and stare into space. Want to do anything but be a middle-aged artist and create one more thingy that will sit in the garage and stare at me, reminding me that making art and actually selling it are two entirely different endeavors. And I know nothing about the latter.

It's OK not to work. It's OK to simply be. I can do whatever I want to do. Maybe, I'll do absolutely nothing. Maybe just sit and watch the Earth turn and see what I can learn.

A cloud races in front of the morning sun and sucks the light out of the room, throwing a gray blanket in its place. That's how my heart feels today; heavy and hiding under a small quilt of growing grief.

April 6
4:14 pm

Saturday

Mom is parked in her seat at the kitchen table facing the street. She's French-styling the string beans I bought at the health-food store yesterday. It is 91 unseasonably hot and humid degrees out there in the fungal jungle and we are both happy to be inside where the temperature is comfortably cool. Mom is wearing her new reddish-orange blouse. She looks good in red. I don't. After cutting each bean intently first down the middle lengthwise, fileting each bean like a veteran fishing woman, she then cuts them in half the short way. "That's how I like to do it," she says. She is answering defensively a question I haven't asked. I sit watching her in remote silence. I am simply watching her hands move; her eyes focus and concentrate. Her hair is a bit fuzzy around the temples today. Actually it's a cross between fuzzy and wiry all at once. She is so beautiful in all her Is-ness.

"Did you roll your hair after you washed it?" I ask.

"Nah," she half replies. "I just stepped out of the shower and shook my head like a wet dog." That's all she said about that.

Now as I watch her splitting beans, keeping a large stash of whole ones clutched in her left hand while her right maneuvers the knife ever so deftly I shake my head like a dog too. Holy Crow. Whatever comes into her mind just slips right out her mouth. And I love her for it after all. I think it better to acknowledge the instant thoughts so they don't have a chance to ruminate, ferment, and stagnate somewhere in the middle of muscle tissue or delicate cell walls turning into a cramped dis-ease later on. Better to say it when it pops up. So this is my new mantra: I practice saying what immediately comes into me, speaking it easily and comfortably, without attachments. I am not a hateful person so I can trust that my inner tongue, my Franny channel, will not lash out to sardonically trash someone. That's not what Franny does. Like a kid she just tells it like she sees it, whether I want to hear it or not.

Franny is my new guru: Ma Zen. And she's so accessible, too. Somedays too accessible. I don't have to go anywhere or read any books or take any courses. Everything I need to know I learn from my mother. I'm sure the first religion was Mother-Daughterism.

Actually I think this thing about saying what bothers me instantly is really a very healing thing. Why hold on to any discomfort whatsoever? To make others feel comfortable I make myself dis-eased? Where's that at anyway? So now when someone says something that doesn't settle right, I immediately address it, not reacting or processing, just saying it. I will do what my insides tell me to do. I don't hold back to make others comfortable. I make my insides comfortable. This is intuitive, touchdown practice. No more carrying discomfort around in my precious body temple. When someone makes a cutting comment about my new mu mu. Smack. I give 'em a Franny-ism, "Yeah, right. Whatever." Or, "Ouch, that put-down just hurt." No more holding onto stuff...other people's stuff. It's a new lesson in how to avoid the knot-in-the-belly syndrome that lingers long after the hurtful conversation is over. As with everything else, I'm sure to be given many chances to use my new way of being.

April 12
3:55 am   **Friday**

I just read what I wrote last. Holy Cow. A whole week has passed and I've been around the world inside my head and house and heart, and Mom and I had a little fight in between. I just want to let her be herself without the pressing need to sermonize or make her change into the perfect Mother Goddess I want her to be. I'm tired of trying to convince her do things "my way." So I decided to try something new. I just let go. I just drop the subject, shift gears, change my direction. I don't even have to say anything. Basically I give up trying to prove that I know what's best for her. It occurred to me that I don't have a clue what's best for anyone. I can barely sort that out for myself. So I've noticed this thing that happens the minute I let go of the power struggle with her. In some mother/daughter psychic, unconscious way she feels it. And then: this is the interesting part, she then comes my way, walking slowly, almost tottering, with her arms open wide and wanting a hug, which melts my resistance inside and out.

I need her as much as she needs me.

I think about Bell's theorem and how two particles got split up; one sent into space and one kept in the lab, and how whatever was done to the one particle in the lab, the particle in space, which was being monitored by very sophisticated scientific equipment, responded in the same way the particle in the lab did. Even though they were separated by thousands of miles, the two particles were still acting as one, in this non-local continuity kind of thing. So, in my mind (which is always meandering in space) I wonder if the DNA that binds mothers to children isn't a lot like those two particles. No matter how far away they are they have the same response to outside stimulus. A kind of cellular inseparability.

And maybe I knew all along in my child psyche that my mother gave her first daughter up for adoption and it really messed her up and when I was born we clung to each other like scared mice, knowing that it could easily happen again; the two of us traumatized by leftover feelings and small particles that get prodded loose in the middle of the night.

Maybe, just maybe, it's one fear I don't have to carry around any more because it doesn't belong to me.

April 15
11:32 pm
Monday

I walked up to the door of the health-food store this morning and read a small, nondescript sign posted on the door just slightly above my head: "The store will be closed on Tuesday to honor T." My friend from Chi Kung class. I immediately knew he had died. After shopping I asked the young woman at the counter if there was going to be a memorial service. I knew I had to go. "Yes," she said. "Tonight at the beach, where First Avenue meets the sand. Wear bright-colored clothes," she called back to me as I headed out the door. "That's what T wants." She then corrected herself. "I mean wanted."

When L and I arrived at the beach there wasn't a parking spot left in the lot. We circled several times, ending up in front of the little mom-and-pop drug store in that strip mall with the new karate dojo and the new fresh produce shop. We walked toward the dock that descended onto the beach. My heart fluttering, my nerves electrified by the sight. There were well over 100 people there. My eyes watered not from the wind off the ocean, cool and strong that night, but from the sadness in my heart and the gratitude for my own gift of life.

Everyone was gathered in a semi-circle facing the ocean, an altar in the middle. There was T's Buddha statue and candles in hurricane lanterns so they didn't get blown out. Flowers and other small altar objects were placed all around the Buddha. A microphone system was set up and a man began talking about what T wanted. "Tonight A (T's wife), is going to speak, then her daughter will read one of T's poems, then we'd like to ask anyone who wants to share anything about T to please come up to the microphone." A rose from the inside-front layer of the circle. She was clustered with her and T's three children: two daughters who I've all met at the store and a son who I've heard about, but never seen before. She walked briskly, against the ocean wind, to take the mike and face us. Her long mahogany-brown hair blowing all around in front of her, nearly covering her face as she spoke, her long dress and flowing brown shawl were also blowing straight away from her, looking like a strange image from a movie set like there was a big fan behind her giving a dramatic effect to the scene. But no technical machinery was needed to give this scene drama.

A spoke slowly at first, with a tight wince on her lips. "I just want to say thank you. Thank you each and every one of you for your support over these past three years." Her voice picked up speed and intensity. There was no sadness. "This is the hardest thing I've ever done in my life." Her hair kept whipping up and as she talked she moved from side to side, her whole body abbreviating each word with a sharp staccato movement; all the time her hair flying straight out in front of her.

"She looks like a witch," I whispered to L. "A powerful, shape-shifter moving the wind." I was caught in her movement and emotion. I choked back tears, but wondered why in the hell am I trying to hide my grief. So I let myself sob, lightly at first. I was afraid that if I let go, I mean, really let go to this deep mourning I would wail and scream. I was surprised that when I did let go I did not come undone. And I felt relieved to affirm my body's need to cry and release my sorrow.

When A sat back down her youngest daughter got up to read one of her father's poems. She began quickly and seemed to rush through it; maybe she too was afraid of letting go, sinking into the sorrow. I wanted her to slow down with the words. But she was scared and nervous. And then she was done.

I knew I had to talk about T. But I was scared, too. All those strangers. But without much hesitation I found myself walking right to the front of the crowd. I wasn't even thinking about it, just moving...or something moving me. The man with the gray ponytail handed me the mike. I wanted to go slow, real slow. It's the one thing I remembered from all those courses I took in public speaking. Go slow. My voice was really cracking, but I took a deep breath and let myself open up wide. I said I didn't know T for very long. Only knew him in his dying. But in his dying he taught me about living.

Those months in Chi Kung with T were very inspiring. I talked about how I would come to class with my little moaning and whining about my sinuses, the weather, my cramps and there was T fighting for his life and standing in meditation pose with dignity and courage, not ever complaining about his personal pain. I learned to keep quiet in that class with T. I learned to breathe and sink my roots deep into the ground and let go of my mind chatter and live in the perfect peaceful moment of my loving heartbeat. I learned to watch T closely to see how he managed to stay in the difficult poses without a peep. "If T can do it, so can I." That's how T helped me. T touched me deeply, in my breathing and my heartbeat. And I gave the microphone back to the man with the gray ponytail and walked back to L's side. I was a little shaky, but glad I did it. Glad I talked about T;

remembered him to others.

Mourn means "to remember."

Later on that week I talked with a woman who was with T when he died. She said it was like somebody turned the volume down on his breathing and he just slipped away. He decided to stop eating or drinking only two days before dying. No medicine, no nothing. He was at home with hospice care; the family all around him. He had made arrangements with A that after he died he would stay in the house two days before calling the coroner. T had wanted to stay three days, according to the Tibetan Book of the Dead. They believe it takes three days for the soul to leave the body. A told T he'd start to stink after three days and they finally agreed on two. Don't forget it's illegal to have a dead body in your house. Another one of those rites/rights the medical authorities have taken away from us: to have an at-home funeral.

O, the woman telling me about T's last days, said that when he died they anointed his body with oils, A, the children, and O. They left him in the bed and A slept with him (his body) for two nights. A told O that she had placed a heart-shaped stone above the bed, just below the Buddha sculpture that T loved so much. When A woke up the first morning after T died she said there was a stream of morning light coming in through the window that illuminated the heart and then went right down on T's face; the ray of light ending at his heart. A was so excited that she ran and got her camera and took a picture of T illuminated. The Tibetan Buddhists believe the soul leaves the body from the heart up through the head. A was awed and shaken by the image.

When the time came for T to go to the crematorium the kids didn't want A to be around when they put T's body in the bag. A decided to climb up on the roof and watched from her bird's-eye view as the black van drove away. A was waving with a hawk feather that T had found and given to her. When the state worker needed the "wife" to sign the legal documents the kids said, "Oh, she's up on the roof. Do you want us to call her down?" The state worker said, No, she'd climb up and talk with her. So she did. O said the whole scene was quite amazing; the state worker standing on a ladder talking to A, sitting on the roof with the hawk feather between her teeth while she signed the official state documents. When the state worker climbed back down she shook her head and said, "Well, I've never done that before." Good, I thought, as O was telling the story.

Death teaches everyone something new.

April 24
7:55 am

Wednesday

Thank goodness the Earth turns, bringing another day, another opportunity to marvel at the awe and mystery of life. Another day to take a deep breath, get my roots in the ground and start all over again. Breathe in. Breathing out.

There's this one saying that I learned from my Buddhist friend and I used it all this week when I found myself standing in the hallway and not knowing what direction to turn: *When you don't know what to do, do nothing.* I stood in the hallway for almost twenty minutes. Not knowing anything at all. It felt really good.

10:31 pm

L's plane has touched down in Germany by now. He's on his way to an art conference. I found a little heart drawing in the shower this morning. By now he has surely found the little note I tucked into his wallet. These little memos are important to me.

This morning I was dreaming something clear and strong about leaving the lid off a can of bright red paint. Now I can't recall the details. A kind of jumpy tummy feeling lingers.

Showered. Ate. Took a walk around the loop. First to the ocean to check on the waves, then heading north around the perimeter of the 'hood. The winds are out of the southeast and the ocean is swollen and floppy. The lips of the waves are wide and white, foamy and fuming. I like this blue-green ocean. So turbulent and timid at the same time. The winds foretell of warm weather in the brew and the chance of showers. The oak trees are also pollinating and the yellow dusty film is gathering on the cars. Another sinus season on the way.

Today I want to remember to go at an easy pace; a slow rhythm. No more Giddy-up Girl. I can't take the rushing around any more. I suddenly remember that a voice in my dream said that I was "misguided about valuing myself."

I'll have cereal and toast for dinner.

April 25
8:12 am

Thursday

I miss L. Usually this lasts a couple days, then I grow comfortable without him, then resent him coming back into *my* space, then love him up all over again (blah, blah, blah: it's always the same emotional cycle). Anyway, I read this article about the ability of the heart to "remember." How the heart is the controlling organ in the body, not the brain. Studies show that in order to influence the outcome of a particular event you are more likely to have a positive effect by "being" in the outcome, having fun, and being relaxed. Thinking hard, working at it, and trying too hard has less effect on the overall outcome than simply "being." Hello heart. Are you listening to me now? Do you know how much I want to be in the moment and enjoying life? Help me begin, OK? Keep me out of the future where my overactive imagination, which just so happened to grow up on John Wayne and Doris Day, can't make up its mind. And, please, don't let me watch the news before going to bed. It's all about our prez pretending he's John Wayne. Not that I'm voting for Doris Day, but her ammunition is less lethal.

Dear heart, let me find a nice, soft pillow of inner peace. I promise I'll share it.

I worked in the garden in the dark last night. Seemed so natural. Besides, the plants were calling. I called out to my mother, who was leaning on the washing machine contemplating the rinse cycle, "Come on Ma. Grab a flashlight. It's gonna rain tonight and we better get those berry plants in."

"Good idea," my mother muttered, following me out of the garage, shuffling over to the cupboard where the flashlight is stashed. "You've got two flashlights and only one has batteries," my mother said in a disapproving way.

"Well, guess you better bring the one with batteries," I laugh.

Night gardening. It has a romantic ring to it. Or pure lunacy. My mother doesn't think anything peculiar about it at first and totters alongside me as we find our way to the west side of the house. That's the shady side and I'm certain a better place for berries, where they won't burn in the blasting sun.

She's got the flashlight and is more fixated on looking for mosquitoes than she is interested in holding the light for me.

"Mom. I'm digging over here." I call out, just to get her attention.

"I'm looking for mosquitoes. They're after me because I'm standing still." My mother is bug-phobic. She is concerned now that she has gotten herself into something she didn't anticipate.

I quickly dig three holes. One each for the blueberry plant, a muscadine grape, and a blackberry plant. I want to plant the grape near the passion vine trellis so that I can train the grape to share the trellis with the rampant passion vine. I'm not really sure about the sharing bit, although passion and grapes do seem to have some affinity.

While digging I'm concerned that my mother, who is not 100 percent stable on her feet, will topple over while flailing at a mosquito with the flashlight. After each hole I hand her the shovel so she can lean on it. Then I backfill each plant with the compost from last year's pile.

I'm just finishing up the last plant in the last hole when I hand the identification label to my mother and ask her to read it to me. "That's the grape, right?" I ask with only a hint of agitated doubt in my voice. "Says blackberry." My mother returns with a short voice: "This one says blackberry."

"Well where's the damned grape plant?" Now I'm knowing in my heart that this was really dumb because if I've just planted the blackberry in the grape hole, every time I come around the corner where the trellis is I'll be scratched by unexpected blackberry thorns. The other part of me is also sure that the neighbors are gathered at their window wondering what in the world we're burying in the dark.

"I don't know. Must be the one next to the blueberry. Oh well." My mother giggles with an unexpected and nonchalant humor that I am certain is a sign of impending senility.

I laugh too and grab my mother under the elbow, guiding her back to the patio. She then parks herself under the patio light, holding the flashlight at my feet where I've just poured seaweed concentrate all over my toes. "What's that stuff? It stinks like dead fish." My mother whines like a child.

"Seaweed juice," I explain slowly. "It helps take the shock out of transplanting and nourishes the tiny green shoots." I'm feeling like a displaced teacher has crawled inside my voice box and I'm compelled to explain everything like a lesson plan in that sing-songy voice that I loathe so much when it comes from someone else. I hope I'm not sounding too patronizing (or would it be matronizing) in my mother's mind because she gets really put off when I start sounding like I'm the mother and she's the child. When that happens she just walks away in the middle of one of my sentences, throwing one hand in the air and telling me as she's walking away, "Gotta check the laundry."

April 26
2:56 am   Friday

Last night I made a list of things to do without the TV. Tonight I'll be with my friends in the park for another candlelight vigil; a peaceful protest, singing softly as we walk over the bridge: "All we are saying, is give peace a chance."

°Turn off your TV. Better yet, take it for a walk to the end of your
 driveway for garbage pick-up.
°Make love.
°Breathe.
°Read your lover's lips.
°Hold your own hand.
°Plant seeds.
°Touch yourself all over.
°Dig a small hole in the backyard and fill with wishes.
°Cup your hands over your ears and listen curiously to your own
 breathing.
°Stretch your arms wide and hug everyone you can imagine.
°Stand still.
°Celebrate spring.
°Remember the sound of your mother's laughter. Repeat.
°Scratch yourself where it itches. Repeat.
°Change your mind.
°Sleep under your bed. Make love there.
°Squat. Get to know the ground you walk on.
°Take three steps forward and stay there.
°Catch on.
°Make popcorn.
°Whistle to the Moon while standing on your toes.
°Walk around the block. Smile.
°Nurse yourself awake.

April 27
11:23 am

Hazy, heavy, and hot. Three prayers to the air conditioner this morning:
Please. Please. Don't stop.

Mom and I just got back from our morning swim. We have the luxury
of using J's pool while they're away. Mom is strangely adamant about her
morning exercise these days. Like she's giving it her best, last shot. She's even
taken to an evening walk every night after *Jeopardy*. Walt doesn't make the
swim or the walk.

While swimming this morning she started to mention something
about menopause, with the conclusion that, "You have to have a strong mind,
a strong will to get through it." She peered at me like an old crone, her lips
pulled tight and her head tilted at me, chin tucked in. She was giving me

advice, standing on the edge of the pool kicking her legs while I doggy-paddled back and forth, trying to relax and exercise at the same time.

She said her doctor gave her only one piece of advice about menopause. He suggested that if she were feeling down in the dumps she should just get in the car and go for a ride. "Yeah, right," she laughs, lifting her head up. "I sure did drive fast to get away from your father."

I think there were days when she wanted to ride right into another world.

Writer Zora Neale Hurston once wrote, "Sometimes you have to go somewhere to find out who you are."

I guess it took a strong will for my mother to eventually turn the car around and drive back home.

I'm starting to think that menopause is the eighteen-wheeler that carries women from one state to another, across unfamiliar territory and back again, arriving at the end of an unpredictable expedition, standing taller and stronger for having unloaded her own baggage.

April 28
9:43 am

Sunday

Dreamed I was pregnant, again. Woke up wondering if there will come a day when right along with a heart transplant a middle-age woman can get a younger uterus and start all over again. Oh, my. Who would want to do that?

April 29
5:14 am

Monday

Took a trip to Miami for an art fix, leaving early Saturday morning. Before leaving home I decided to stop in a glass gallery in Boca and drop off my slides. I brought a couple of pieces to show them, just in case they were interested in taking on a new artist. The woman at the desk, Jo, was very polite in her perfect little black dress and tight, cropped blonde bob, but also very aloof in that snooty NYC art gallery way that makes me think I have dog shit on my shoes. I told myself on the two-hour ride down that it didn't matter what she said or anyone said about my art, I was just taking a shot in the dark. Nothing ventured; nothing gained. Just another thing to try and hustle. If it works; all the better. Another opportunity to sell something; get money; pay bills. Funny how all my inner coaching didn't soak through to my inside self. My heart started pounding the minute I approached the desk. "It doesn't matter. It doesn't matter," I kept telling myself. My tongue and lips suddenly swollen and feeling like I was just shot up with Novocain, could barely get my voice around an introduction.

Here I am, a woman who can sell anything, talk to anyone about anything, but when it comes to my own artwork I go crumbly and numb. I guess I wasn't expecting her to say Yes when I asked if she wanted me to bring a piece in from the car. And when she said, "This is strong work." I was silent, chastizing myself on the inside for not having a rap to go with my work. Like I should've talked more about myself, my work, the meaning of life, anything. But I didn't. I just stood there staring at my work like I didn't even know who it belonged to. I was a stranger to myself, staring at these very present ancestral heads and hoping my heart didn't suddenly stop. She said she'd keep my slides and show them to the owner.

I spent the rest of the drive south trying not to beat myself up for not shmoozing more and chatting myself up.

Remember to talk softly and kindly and lovingly to yourself.

We stayed on the "strip" in South Beach, renting a cheesy room for the night for $69. A nice sexy price. We immediately threw ourselves into the crowd walking the pedestrian mall, visiting art galleries, taking a tour of artists' studios, perusing the interior design shops all fresh with the smells of designer leather and all those chotchkes you like but wouldn't know what to do with once you got them home. It was hot and humid out, but I fared pretty well. We arrived later in the day and between the frequent dives into the air-conditioned shops we made our way to dinner at an Italian restaurant for pasta and goat cheese salad, getting buzzy with Cuban coffee and tiramisu.

On Sunday we got up early, or at least earlier than the party-goers who kept us up half the night banging doors and yelling, squealing, and romping through the hallways. We had a greasy egg breakfast at a sidewalk café, which we think may have been the place near where Gianni Versace was murdered. We then headed for the Miami Art Museum, where I continued to burp up eggs and fried potatoes while trying to digest someone else's art at the same time.

I was fascinated by a Yoruba beaded art show at the MAM that included a few contemporary pieces. All so sacred and dazzling. I especially loved this one display of ancient pieces called *ibori*. In the Yoruba tradition each child begins her journey in this world with a beaded object symbolizing the uniqueness and spirituality of her "inner head" or *ori inu*. All rituals and offerings are made to the *ibori* regarding the child and are meant to influence and shape the child's destiny. Conical in shape, each *ibori* is designed to remain upright and alert like the "inner head" it symbolizes. It is kept in a specially prepared "house of the head", which celebrates, hides, and protects it. On death, the person's "house of the head" is disassembled and scattered, to mark the departure and transformation of the spirit. To the Yoruba, ancestors are not dead. They are departed and continue to influence the lives of their descendants.

The *ibori* were elaborately beaded and decorated with cowrie shells, all looking like pyramid-shaped juicy fruit baskets. I love the idea of the inner head. Maybe that's where that strong will required to get through menopause is, that Mom keeps talking about. My inner menopausal head.

Also, a video piece by a British artist, Tracey Emin, really stuck with me. In this six-minute piece (thank goodness she kept it to an easily digestible length) called, "Why I Didn't Become A Dancer," she narrates her sexual experiences at a very early age while the fuzzy camera images show footage of her town; almost like a walking tour of what she might have encountered while roaming the streets. It ends with her in a well-lit room dancing to some disco music in hiking boots. She's also wearing cut off, ragged, jean shorts, and a red blouse...looking very normal, all the time facing the camera and smiling. It was very evocative and light, almost humorous, and at the same time heavy with emotions. There was something about her deeply personal experiences and the simplicity of the imagery that caught me. A sad glimpse of her life, all the while smiling backwards at it. The whole notion of surviving and dancing and finding courage lifted my spirits.

Of course being inspired by all the art we saw also meant that I was inspired to continue making art; something I haven't done in weeks. Gee. No wonder I'm feeling nutsy. We want to have a studio next summer somewhere near a city. I need access to a glass furnace, and we want to be able to go into the city in less than an hour. We need a place to live and a studio space. They can be one and the same and pretty humble. They say that if you tell five people what you want, I mean *really* what you want, you'll get it. I don't know if there are five people I'd brave telling. That seems so sad to me.

L leaves for NYC tomorrow. Another conference. I can't stand the thought of him leaving, even if I know (intellectually) that he'll be gone only a short time. I suddenly have this incredible abandonment thing that feels like someone scraped leftovers into my psyche from someone else's mind. It's just too deep and complicated to belong entirely to me. It's just that changes don't come easy to me now, even though I'm in the middle of the Big Change. They used to. I could take off in a second to go anywhere with anyone. Like get in a car with a strange guy and end up nowhere for days.

8:14 am

Monday morning still. Sun hiding behind filmy thin clouds. Not too humid. Slight wind out of the west. No seeum bugs biting hard. Ocean a sea-green steel with riffles running west. I've been laying low—very low, with a weary low back ache. Must have pulled it gardening, although my wise-cracker within says it's from sitting at the computer too long waiting for email. I waited a week before seeing the chiro. I don't know why I wait so long, because it always helps. Just figure it will go away on its own, I guess. Doing lots of pool therapy using our neighbor's pool while they're up north. It's been a treat at night to go over and just soak and kick. It's too small to do laps, so I'm not compelled to compete or push myself into some regimen. Confined by someone else's saner boundaries I simply soak and relax. I hate this push, push, push mentality. And after living with Mom I can very definitely point to its source. Or at least I know who else in my family has it. Nothing, no one, nowhere is ever fast enough, clean enough, good enough. Nothing is ever acceptable the way it is. Everything needs to be changed, fixed, made different. Argh. I hate when I fall into it.

Pema Chodron's ideas about loving kindness are ones I want to embody. I beat myself beyond repair and then drag my whipped body around for a few more miles, just to see if I can force a bit more blood, work, sweat out of it. All in an effort to fix, change, manipulate, control what already is and then martyr my efforts. So now I'm practicing Acceptance. I'm willing to let what is *be* what is. I don't want to immediately reject what I create just because I'm the one who did it. First Accept It. We'll see how this goes. The thing is I've always "aborted" in the past. Now that I'm giving birth to myself I just don't know how to do the follow-through. But I do know one thing. I'm not aborting this one. I'm not giving up on myself, no matter what. I'm following through on me. Besides, the alternative is uninteresting.

There is no such thing as groundlessness, I tell L at 6:30 in the morning, as if I'm giving a lecture in a dark room and can't see who's in the seats. Yeah, sure, shit happens. But that's not because we're groundless. It's because we don't understand groundedness and what being rooted (and eventually rotted) in the Earth really means. Groundedness simply means that shit happens. We live, grow, and die. That's the garden doing what it does: blossom, rot, and decay. The rot feeds the Earth soul. In the garden, the stinkier the better. More nutrients to feed the roots. When stinky stuff happens that just means get back to the ground beneath our feet. Breathe. Let the stink soak into our soul and feed what aches to be fed and nourish it. Right, honey?

Something's got my tongue and I can't stop. Enlightenment phooey. How about a little teaching on endarkenment? Learning to trust the unknown, the roots, the ground beneath our feet, the stuff that can't be seen or explained. How about letting go to total grounded dark being? How about that? Total acceptance by a huge Mama Blue that takes us spinning nearly 900 miles an hour in the space of a day and, holy shit, some days seems like a big bumpy ride all right. Feeling fully alive, connected to the flapping wings of a butterfly or the *keedo keedo keedo* of a cardinal in hot pursuit, or holding a tiny seed and knowing that in a few months, with the right stinky stuff pulsing through its little plant veins it will grow in the luscious dark ground and when it's ready to spring up it will be a ten-foot sunflower. Still living half of its life in the juicy dark ground and half in the lighted sky. Isn't this what it is to be living in the moment? What it means to breathe? Isn't being fully aware of the magic that surrounds us, lives in us, is us, no matter what the details of living and dying bring what it's all about?

Re-membering groundedness is where we can feel safe.

I look at L again. "Did you know that to the ancient Greeks, hell was considered moist and nourishing? Hey, let's go swimming."

So we tumble out and head to the ocean; our feet firmly planted on our bike pedals.

Here are some quotes from my new guru, Ma Zen:

On Julia Roberts: "That's the second time she's been on the front of *Good Housekeeping* magazine. What in heaven's name can she teach me about good housekeeping?"

On the priest after Sunday mass: "He just gave this talk on how bad material things were and here he goes sending the basket around again for a second collection. What's that all about?"

On her horoscope today that predicted a change in her domestic environment: "What the hell is a domestic environment, pray tell?"

DESCENT

May Day

It is so freakin' hot. Only six more months of ever-increasing heat and humidity. Called B this morning. 11 am my time. 8 am hers. She slept in. I tell her I think I'm losing it. I can feel L pulling away from me. I caught him looking at the new wrinkles forming on my cheeks. I'm looking like one of those dried apple hags that kids make on Hallowe'en and stick on the end of pencils and make scary noises with, all the while dancing around and poking them in your face and taunting, "She's gonna get you." Only I hear them chanting in medieval verse, "She's gonna *be* you." Over and over again until I'm chanting with them, marching mindlessly around the kitchen brewing dark-brown elixirs to balance my teetering hormones and tottering mind. "Where are the Baubos?" I whine, thinking it would be nice to have a sacred clown dance, a bawdy jig around the table, lifting her skirt and cracking lewd jokes about someone else's husband and the dick that got away. At this point I'd take a really bad Elvis impersonator. Anything to make me laugh and hoot and holler long enough to forget the things I want to forget and help me remember the things I'm forgetting. I had another breathing session yesterday. K told me to bring my bathing suit because it was time to do a "water" session. This conjured up a few too many biblical accounts of baptism and although I didn't ask exactly what we'd be doing I had an entire scene bubbling up in my mind of me bending over backwards, a direction, by the way, that I don't bend any more, in the pool, while a chorus of innocent bystanders sing off-key hymns about salvation and redemption. My stomach started to turn just thinking of it. But I braved my anxiety. On the hour-drive there I nearly turned around and went back, my stomach was trying to exit my body by way of my throat and breakfast is not so tasty on the way up as it is on the way down. I had to talk to myself in very simple sentences. *It's OK. You're gonna be fine. Everything is good*, which I knew, of course, was a downright lie. I felt like Anne Frank must have felt just before the knock on the door. Only I'm not so optimistic about people being really good.

As soon as I get to K's I immediately confess that I'm really anxious and almost didn't come. She said that meant that something wanted to be released; something old that I was ready to let go of but was scared to look at. Great. Not because I'm happy about letting go of more old crap but because therapists always say this just before they flush the toilet and wave bye bye with that sweet smirk on their faces, like they've got the inside scoop on your inside crud. But I trust K. She's a Goddess without much disguise. Except she reaches across the big tub, filled with water way too hot by my hot flash standards and grabs a snorkel, telling me I have to go underwater, lie on my side, and breathe through the snorkel. I've done a lot of strange things in my life in the name of healing. The shamans from hell who couldn't stop arguing about where each one of them should stand while I was lying naked with a ginger compress on my chest and they smudged me from head to toe until i thought I was going to choke to death. I've sat in sweat lodges feeling like I was going to shrivel up and disappear, watching the toughest-looking guys get carried out the flap after fainting. I've been prodded, poked, and puked. And now I'm being asked to snorkel for demons, face down in someone's bathtub with a sponge-covered clothespin on my nose and my fingers in my ears because I forgot my earplugs. The water, K assured me, best replicates the amniotic fluid of my mother's womb and would help with my "rebirthing" experience. Hadn't I mentioned that one of my goals in therapy is to grow up and away from my obsessively needy relationship with my mother?

Now I'm back at the beginning. "You're *re-birthing*," she reminded me. This was to unblock any trapped emotions. The snorkel, well, that's so I didn't drown while doing it. Unlike a lot of adults who have trouble getting their face fully submerged in water, I happen to like snorkeling. I'm even fairly excited about scuba diving. My first dive just thrilled me to no end. I jumped in, slowly sank and once I reached the tremendous depth of twenty feet, didn't want to move. I was so startled by the sound of my own breath that I fell into an instant trance and just figured I'd wait for the fish to come to me. I was happy just to sit on the ocean floor and twiddle my thumbs. The dive master was bewildered beyond reason. "I've never seen anyone do that," he said not so proudly.

So I started breathing underwater in K's bathtub, after complaining that I'm menopausal and the water is too hot, to which K replies with the firmness of a drill sergeant, "I'm menopausal too. This is the *right* temperature. Just get in. You'll be fine." I like that she's a take-charge kind of woman who doesn't namby pamby me and cave in to my stalling devices. I concentrate on my inhalation, just like I'm instructed. K says she'll tap me on the back if she needs to remind me to pick up the breathing pace. I'd learned my dive lesson well and immediately obeyed, taking faster in-breaths and leaving a shorter pause after the exhalation. At one point, after what seemed like a decade of snorkeling for demons, I heard K say, "Relax your jaw." But by then I was already thrashing my way to the surface. It occurred to me that I didn't want to be born, not this time, not even the first time. A very strong and completely uninvited feeling rushed over me (even though K says all feelings are invited when we enter into a therapy contract) as strong as a bulldozer pressing against my outstretched hands. "No, I don't want to go there." I heard myself saying, but not being able to actually speak, reminding me of all those bad dreams where I'm trying to scream for help and dial the phone at the same time because some slimy monster is about to break down the flimsy door that I just managed to lock in the nick of time and I can't find the numbers on the phone and when I do get through to someone it's the wrong number and when I open my mouth to scream a little worm wiggles out in a puff of dust, scaring me to exhaustion. By now I'm slumped against the bathtub, my hair clinging to my forehead in wet clumps that actually feel refreshing. I am snuggled in my mother's arms and crying. I do not want to go home to the house where the shadows huddle behind the doors. I am only days old and I know, can sense in my baby body that what lies ahead is a long dark road.

What I see, hidden in the corner, standing over by the refrigerator is a tall, dark shape of a man with striped overalls. He is carrying a wire mesh basket with three glass milk jars in it. He is quiet and smiling and no one else knows he's there, but me, the newborn who's supposed to feel safe and secure, but who knows that in the razor-sharp outline of that shadow there is a sad healing story that will take almost fifty years to unravel.

May 2
3:22 am

I am either way too silly, too hungry, or too hot and clammy. Then suddenly very, very cold. I scare myself every other day thinking I've contracted West Nile Virus by proxy. I don't leave the house any more in summer because my head is pounding with puffy sinuses. I stay in, perform adoring rituals to my air conditioner and poke my head into the freezer every once in a while for a cheap rush. Of course, there's sad and angry too. But not necessarily in that order. The half-dozen behemoths of emotion that stand at the top of the driveway between me and a nice little happy house demand enormous payoffs before I can slip by and make it to the front door. Emotional extortion is more like it. If I do manage to sneak by they scramble to block my way, tumbling head over heels like drunken moose, throwing their big muscled hind quarters against each other to be first in line to get to me before I reach the door knob and make one-half turn to safety. Grief, the big lanky emotional moose, caught up with me this morning, nabbed me with a hip thrust to the heart. I didn't see it coming. Well, maybe I did. I've been dragging myself around for days, checking in on Walt, staring intently at the blankets when I opened the bedroom door to check in on him in the morning, watching to see if they're still lifting and falling, or still.

L and I snuck out for about an hour last night to get Mom a watch. She doesn't like to be alone with Walt these days. She gets all skittish and quirky, pouting with her head slumped to her chest. B says I must feel real guilty just *trying* to have fun. But it's not exactly guilt that I feel. My heart aches when I see her revert to her four-year-old self and the obviously very old idea that she can get what she wants if she feigns a cracked hip or a heart attack. I have to prepare her for about three hours to get her in the right frame of mind to be able to accept that we will go out and, yes, we will come back. Then she asks me every few minutes, "What time did you say you were going out?"

She remembers the names of all the dead people in her family, the words to every song from 1945, the days and times she goes to Bingo, and the fact that she takes one aspirin every other day. She even retains water. But somewhere between five minutes ago and now, my mother's mind opens like the jaws of hell and ignites the fine momentary memory. She gets to sounding like one of those cheesy wall-mounted plastic fish that sings, as you walk by, over and over again, *Take me to the river*. My mother's other run-on line as she stares vacantly at her watch is, "And what time will you be back?"

She's little and growing littler and all I want to do is hug her so hard that whatever got so twisted in her ever since Death has set up camp next to Walt's bed will unravel and then rewire itself into a tight new bundle of wires strong enough to hold up the bridge to wholeness and the solid ground of living real estate that once was My Mom.

It dawned on me: she's worn out her watch from watching it too much.

We are plunging ahead with a trip to the store, leaving her with her night-time family and our free respite TV relief workers, Alex, Pat and Vanna, and Emeril.

We will go and we will come back and we will try to smile and touch each other softly, somewhere in between here and there.

May 3
4:21 am

Just before going to sleep at night, L and I play a fun game in the dark. Call it a devouringly boring date night. We call it, Ask and Tell. Tonight I started the questioning first:

What don't you believe in?
Donald Rumsfeld.
What do you believe in?
National Health Care
What don't you believe in?
John Ashcroft
What do you believe in?
Art
What don't you believe in?
Religion
What do you believe in?
Reading
What don't you believe in?
The Pope
What do you believe in?
Gnomes
What don't you believe in?
Mowing the lawn
What do you believe in?
Trees

I am silent. The thought just burst into my mind: I am waiting for him to say something that he hasn't said yet. Then ask abruptly, catching him off guard, "Do you believe in me?" He looks at me with one of those Where the hell did that come from? looks. Now I'm the one feeling about four years old and pouty. I think our marriage is falling apart because I'm growing hair on my upper lip and fermenting cottage cheese on my thighs, and the invisible, emotional part of me is reverting to infantile.

"You?" L says with a curious tilt of his head like I've just thrown a horseshoe at the basketball hoop. "Of course I believe in you." He is not that convincing.

I am so needy it hurts the skin resting on my teeth.

The questioning halts. We make love slowly, our tongues thrashing urgently in each other's mouth.

May 5
9:12 am

Sunday

I'm not sure if I know what spirituality means, really. Even though I've written four books on goddesses, art, and healing. I know that when I look at those ancient clay sculptures of big, round, naked women offering up their breasts like ice cream sundaes in sacred communion, standing tall and proud wearing temples on their heads for crowns and fruit for breasts, others (several thousand to be exact) holding snakes and looking really, really stoned and those cosmic in-the-know, haughty bird women holding happy, holy bird babies, and even those scary Kali images, where she's dancing on the nasty blue monster, skulls draped around her neck like a Hawaiian lei, her tongue pointing directly at everyone, a bloody head in her hand, I find myself transported to this place in my heart that feels weirdly related to them all, spacious and inspiring. This feeling is unlike any other I get, except when I'm in Nature, which from all that research I did is exactly what "Goddess" is all about. She is gentle Mother and raging lunatic. She is Sun and Moon and every star in the sky. She is the Ocean and the Rivers and the ever-turning, ever-unfolding cycles of seed, blossom, and root (and rot). She is the creative cycle of life. This big coming home feeling that wells up in me when I dance in circle with women, perform a birthing ritual or drum my mind quiet just so happens to cancel out strong desires to punish myself with a swift step in the direction of the refrigerator or any other self-sabotaging trip, like calling myself nasty names, or running away with the lawn boy who mows and blows our neighbor's grass every Wednesday at 3 pm, but who's keeping track? That is, when I can remember that I am truly Nature's child.

So today I saw the Goddess in a short, round woman named C, who works behind the bakery counter at our local supermarket and who took the order for Mom's birthday cake. I was immediately intrigued by C's slow, even pace and concentration. Slow is not unusual here in the south, which my Yankee mother is very quick to point out and, yes, I was very glad my mother wasn't with me because she can't see the Goddess in herself or anyone else for that matter, but can't help but make very loud comments about everyone else's rear end who she feels is moving way too slow, or is in her very unjust world "just another foreigner." C was bending over a case of chocolate éclairs, organizing and pulling out what I'm assuming were the ones past their shelf life and stacking them on a gray plastic cart. Very carefully. She didn't hear me when I asked if she could help me with an order. I kind of startled her, actually. She jumped a little and then I noticed she was wearing a big old flesh-colored hearing aid the size of a baseball mitt.

I know I probably shouldn't do this, but I always do when I notice that someone is wearing a hearing aid, I raise my voice. Sometimes a little too obviously and feel like one of those people who automatically grabs a blind person's elbow and pulls them across the street, which I don't do. C took me around to the little cake-ordering station and, in spite of the fact that C was probably 65, she spoke in a husky girl voice, with a lisp, asking very very simple, no-nonsense questions. "What kind of frosting? What kind of cake? What kind of decorations? What color flowers?" C was very professional. None of this intrigued me as much as the two-inch silver cylinder dangling from her neck with a tiny crescent moon and pentagram embossed on the surface. The pendant seemed to dance all shivery and excited when C spoke, her little girl voice, her big goddess chest lifting and jiggling. So happy and thrilled to see that this ancient symbol had found a way into the first notch of the bible belt, I said excitedly reaching out my finger like Adam to God in the Sistine chapel, "Oh you have a…" But before I could finish my sentence C jumped in with, "Do you know who this is?" just as excited with my recognition. We stood speechless for a second; member of a secret society meeting in public for the first time.

"Yes, of course," I already had visions of C and me dancing the spiral dance on the next Full Moon. I quickly replied, lifting my head proudly to be able to say out loud in this very Republican county, "That's the Goddess."

To which C immediately snapped, "No it's not," rather insulted. She then picked up the little cylinder and bringing it to her lips laid a dreamy fast kiss on it saying quietly, her eyes darting back and forth to make sure no one was eavesdropping, "It's Louie."

"You're kidding? Louie?" This time my mind turned to the tiny chunks of bone and dust, dangling off C's neck. "What about the pentagram?" I was only slightly confused.

"Oh," she said looking down as if seeing it for the first time. "That? Oh, I don't know. A friend of mine gave this to me so I can have Louie next to my heart at all the times, where he belongs."

C quickly changed the subject and asked me if I wanted any numbers on my cake. "Yeah," I smile. "Make a big eighty-four."

"My Mom's eighty-six," she said with a smile. Then added rather sadly, "But she has dementia."

"Mine too," I said, just as sadly.

"She lives with me," C confided.

"Mine too," I whispered back.

C's eyes lit up. "Daughters, you and me." Then suddenly she dropped her head, getting back to business, her eyes now darting back and forth, acting like one of those dogs that's been beaten and even when you reach out your hand with a loving touch they cower. I turned around, wondering what caused

C to withdraw, and saw the store manager standing behind me hunched over and scowling like Quasimodo, his squinty eyes on C. She finished taking my order with a sudden straightening up that jarred loose our soul connection. She then walked away, looking back over her shoulder, giving one last glance to her boss and a little shy hand wave to me, lifting Louie once again to her lips.

May 6
3:17 am

Monday

I'm learning one little thing and it may even be a spiritual thing after all: In a lifetime it is possible to have hard, sad stories hidden in your heart, nestled up against light, joyful laughter. It's a kind of a Both/And way of being. I don't have to pick a fight with sadness all the time, trying to get it to be something else, cajoling it to change. And maybe the happy part of me has a very good paying day job entertaining sadness. And maybe sadness gives real, heartfelt meaning to happiness. Maybe my insides know how to get along better than I think and my job is to practice carrying around all the parts and get on with being a decent whole pachyderm, telling the whole truth and when I'm really hot and tired it's my job to find a nice shady pool and spray down the dust, and rest awhile.

> *Simple Acceptance.*
> *Both/And.*
> Or, as the old saying goes, You can't hide a piece of broccoli in a glass
of milk.

May 7
10:04 am

Tuesday

Got up early even though I didn't sleep much last night either. Low tide at 7:53. Decided to head out for a beach walk before it got too steamy. Feels like a wonderful day about to unfold, but don't know exactly why. Just a feeling. I need it: a good feeling *and* a good day. Counted thirteen turtle nests along the dune line, their determined paths leading from the ocean like tractor tires in the sand. Thirteen. The letter M: Moon. Mama. Mana. Matter. Metamorphosis. Me. Menopausal. A chicken-sized oystercatcher followed me the whole time screeching a piercing *Cle-ar, Cle-ar, Cle-ar,* eventually meeting up with her mate. I've seen this pair before; their long orange bills outlined against the blue sky like candy citrus sticks. Their mustard-colored eyes look like they belong to an anxious pedigree cat. The two eventually join a dense village of royal terns, all tidy in their dress whites. A half dozen gray and brown speckled plovers hang around the outskirts, bustling back and forth with the tide at a rip-snorting pace. I wonder if they have to take a little plover nap in the afternoon from all that energy expenditure chasing the edge of the tide, in and out all morning long.

The royals don't seem to mind all the company. They are such funny birds. They jostle around like overweight babies in a self-important fuss and bustle to get themselves all facing into the wind and then spend an inordinate amount of time staring at the sand with laser intensity, as if one of them has just lost an expensive heirloom emerald earring and they are all very focused on finding it. Every time they bend their heads downward, their jagged black crests pop up, making them look like they have instant Mohawks, becoming a bad-ass bird gang. As if operating from One Mind that issues a silent command, they suddenly take two tiny steps forward, then one backward, in perfect unison, like the June Taylor dancers practicing a new routine in the sand just to strengthen their ankles. The oystercatcher pair moves in a little closer. Perhaps they are lonely and want to get in on the treasure hunt. The royals are so busy looking for lost bird jewelry that they barely notice me approaching from the north. But then the command to fly is suddenly issued and the entire flock takes off so close in front of me that I can feel the rush of air across my face from so many feathers flapping at once. They fly out over the slow lapping waves, a popcorn bundle of clouds scudding overhead, then make a quick pitch back to shore with a wise-crack chorus of *Kak, Kak, Kak*, landing only a few feet ahead of me, all the while leaving the oystercatcher pair alone. The female oystercatcher turns a confused look at her mate as if to say, "Was it something we said?"

The two decide to play a different game, flying out over the dune, giving what looks like a soar and dive demo, eventually joining up with the terns farther down the beach. Each time I catch up to the feathered performers, they lift off and land again only a few feet ahead of me. I feel bonded in bird play; a human prop to practice an aerial maneuver. Suddenly aware of my heart beat and the soft wet sand beneath my feet, there is nothing in my mind, nothing but this moment, folded and curled into itself like so many waves against shore, leaning backward and pushing forward, forever. I remember a dream I had last night, triggering an unexpected longing; a small internal tug at my heart. I am at a dinner table with a group of strangers. Behind me is an Asian woman, maybe Thai or probably Chinese, who is seated on the floor doing Chinese brush work on rice paper. Her moves are deliberate, fluid, and pensive. Immediately I sense her spiritual essence and profound healing power. Across from her is perhaps a client waiting for a reading or a healing session. I tell the strangers that I can see into people's lives. An Asian man across from me asks me to "read" him. I pull up my hands and hold them out in front, palms facing outward to receive his psychic vibes. I tell him I see a stainless steel cook pot in his stomach. He laughs and tells me he's a chef. I'm attracted to his smile; slow, easy, and warm. I have an irresistible urge to touch his teeth. There's something about his teeth that pulls all my attention his way. I want to put my hands in his mouth and run my fingers over his molars. I feel warm and fuzzy all over and realize I really want to run my tongue over his teeth.

Suddenly the scene changes and I'm in a thrift store looking through little girl's dresses, all used and looking really stained all down the front. But the stains don't bother me because the man with the teeth is with me and I feel very comfortable, yet distracted. I can't seem to find what I'm looking for.

The turtle-nesting season started early this year. Do they know something we don't?

May 8
8:18 am

Wednesday

What prompted me to go the filing cabinet and grab a hold of my master's thesis from art school is beyond me. I read the cover:

Pretending that subtle energies do not exist does not change the fact of their existence. Learning about them, and how to work with them can greatly expand one's view of the world, and of the work that one is doing.
A Native American Credo for Health

Maybe all of life is simply remembering what I already know.

May 9
12:01 am

Thursday

I signed up for a pottery class. I'm taking it, not teaching it. I'm going to give Passion permission to flow through my hands and get back to playing with clay, my first love, prima mater. My first mother, Earth. I fell asleep reading Rumi. The last thing I remember is, "Love's secret is always lifting its head out from under the covers saying, 'Here I am!' "

4:33 pm

The only thing I need to remember right here, right now, is that it does not matter what is going on around me; my job is to listen to my own interior designer, my wise woman within, who knows exactly how to arrange my living spaces. Even though it looks like she's turned the house upside-down and in the middle of tearing off the roof she decided to go on vacation with the boy hottie who took the last nail out of the roof truss.

So, in the morning I'll take a few minutes to meditate (if I can sit still long enough) and see if anyone has cleaned the ricotta cheese off that baby girl who when I last saw her was dangling upside down between my thighs. Surely she needs an adult to pitch in and do some of the handiwork necessary to get on with living and breathing and being sad and happy, excited and bored, fully awake and half asleep.

My life is like a mood ring.

Picked up a couple of herb plants on my way home from acupuncture. Didn't have any intention of planting herbs when I woke up or even seconds before stopping at the garden center, for that matter. The car just turned into the parking lot before I even knew where I was going. I felt like I was steering one of those shopping carts with a mind of its own; one wheel frozen tight and unmoving, sending the others to spin in circles. No matter how hard I steer in one direction the wheels take me in another. Usually I end up standing in front of the imported chocolate, not knowing how I got there. So I find myself talking to the very friendly woman who runs the garden store and don't exactly know how it came to pass. I trust my engine within. Besides, Tara (yeah, I know, the Earth Goddess of Mercy and Compassion) has such a great smile. She talks about plants like they are people and when I buy one she acts as if I've adopted it for life. After only a few minutes, I felt my energy picking up just by talking with her, and touching the herbs and smelling their heady aromas. Decided to go with sage, thyme, and basil. My lemongrass needs a little company. She reminds me that the Moon is waxing: "Full moon in Scorpio in a couple of days," she chimes. "Good time to get your hands in the Earth," she adds. "Especially if you're dealing with emotional issues from the past. Remember, the roots start dancing when they hear thunder." I turn around abruptly to find out what else she knows about my roots, certain she's been peeking at my diary while I'm speaking to her zinnias. But she disappeared behind the fluorescent blooms of a crimson bougainvillea, smiling and chatting nonchalantly with another woman who looked to be about my age, also wearing a weathered, worried crease in her brow. Did I make a wrong turn and end up in California? Nobody talks like that in Florida. You'll hear complaints about stiffening arthritis pain, the rising price of prescription drugs, the falling barometric pressure, and where's the little coupon for double-photo prints at the drugstore. You do not hear poetic spiritual advice tossed around the petunias.

Which brings to mind another hard question: *Why am I living here when my real tribe lives on the other side of the mountains?* But that's another issue to be dealt with at another time, maybe when the Moon is waning and far from Scorpio, which always feels like a sexy Moon to me. I've got to remember to let my car make more daily decisions for me. Seems to know how to put a smile on my face. Letting go to the Whatever of Life feels good. Now if the Whatevers can come up with something interesting for dinner I'll be very very happy. Hope an idea pops up before I find myself standing in a tired stupor in front of the refrigerator with the door wide open and no place to go. It just seems freaky that after spending $127 dollars at the grocery store I can't find anything to eat.

Oh. I know. Toasted cheese sandwiches with sliced tomatoes and onions sounds good. Mom likes it and it's easy. And easy is good. Decided it's OK to have lunch for dinner. If everything is changing inside me, I'm changing the rules all around me.

May 10
8:44 am

Friday

I'd like to wash the bathroom floor today. I think it's a decent goal to set for myself. But I just don't see myself getting down on my knees for that purpose right now. If I did, though, I'd go at the funky corners with exuberance where little piles of rolled-up bug dirt, beach sand, and a few tumbleweed hairballs are building a stronghold for spiders and their unsuspecting prey. I think the spiders are actually taking up more real estate in the house than we are. They're everywhere; in the corners behind the couch, where the ceilings meet the wall, and in the cracks around the door. I have a hard time killing them, actually. My mother says it's bad luck to kill a spider. So I spend an inordinate amount of time running around with a plastic leftover container in one hand and a piece of stiff paper in the other, hoping to capture them and let them go outside. It all starts to feel kind of like a very bad waste of time, an intentional distraction, or a very bad movie. After all, it's not as if I don't have anything else to do in the whole wide world.

It occurs to me, too, that what I'm really letting go of is Walt. We had a mini-fight yesterday. I feel so ugly about fighting with a man who is losing his battle with cancer, because no matter how you look at it, there aren't any real triumphant winners here. I'm trying to convince myself that I'm really learning a lot about life and all that stuff that props me up like sticks against a sea wall, the waves rising and crashing by the minute. Thing is, I can't even remember what we fought about. Probably me trying to convince him for the umpteenth time this week that he's got to eat more or, or… And this is where he looks at me with those clear, sad, blue eyes apologizing for interrupting, but he can't help himself and manages in a struggled whisper, "Or what?"

We both know the answer.

I hold a can of liquid food up like manna from heaven and he shakes his head, holding his stomach. It's weird how I was so scared of that hose coming out of the hole in his stomach and now me and that snaky food tube that is Walt's lifeline are getting to know each other. Seems the closer Death gets to Walt's bedside the tighter I hold on and the faster Mom falls apart. She spends more time playing solitaire these days and looking lost. When I ask her if she's going to feed Walt she acts as if she doesn't know who I'm talking about. She gets that look on her face when she walks in and finds him sitting up in bed like a cat I used to have that forgot I existed the minute I walked out of the room, because when I came back in she'd pull her head back, open her eyes really wide and bolt down the hallway in one of those instantaneous feline freak-outs.

Actually, I don't think Mom is getting enough sleep. Walt is up all night tossing and turning and I can hear her yelling at him to "Just settle down." We're all so tired. I don't know who to worry about more: Me? Mom? Walt? L? Worry will not change any of the facts of living or dying. I know. Thank goodness I have an art exhibit coming up. I have something creative to focus on when I'm not chasing death around the bed. If I don't stand up and drag my dull thighs out into the studio to finish up the gilding on the little shaman hats then I may as well set the table and invite Flogging and Desperation to dinner. Their relatives Anxiety and Depression have been here for almost a year and they're getting jealous. I do feel very adult that my argument with Walt ended in a kind of truce. Instead of me trying to force him to eat, we decided that when he's ready to eat, he'll let me know. Asking for help is such a big deal for him. I laughed and reminded him that I spent too much time in New Jersey and I don't know how to deal with a Midwesterner. He smiled. I gave him a big hug and we both sighed. If that's all we have for each other, right now, then it's going to have to be enough.

May 11
11:58 pm
Saturday

Today has raced by with alarming speed. My mid-afternoon nap certainly took a chunk of it, I do admit. I've been nursing some leftover crap from a head cold. However, I do think the combined stresses (Mom's memory loss, Walt's increased pain, L's diminishing affections) along with hot flashes and anxiety (or is it anxiety and then a hot flash?) are shifting some junk around. I'm willing to let go of the old crud, hopefully not to make room for new crud. I really do want to use these changing years as a cleaning house practice. Yeah. It's a take-away game. And I haven't figured out what I want to bring in to the new space. Maybe nothing. I've listened to countless 'pausal women talk about "cleaning house" and getting rid of stuff that feels like it's bogging them down. I do feel I've been doing that for over a year now. Like all moving events, the most cumbersome stuff goes out last. My emotions, like an old refrigerator, will need some help getting out the door.

I've begun meditating every morning. It has helped my free-floating anxiety enormously. Did this anxiety suddenly appear, or is it like a storm system that sits off-shore building momentum until the waves are so big they take down the houses built too close to the beach? I don't remember feeling this antsy all the time. It took several days before I could actually sit in the chair without wiggling my foot during the breathing practice. I never had that foot wiggle before. In high school when the guys wiggled a leg nervously and uncontrollably I think it meant they were masturbating by proxy or something like that.

Menopause is starting to feel like I'm coming off a drug overdose. Estrogen withdrawal. I really do want to be positive. S seems to be floating like a feather on the breath of dawn now that she's "done with it." I feel like a crackpot. Where are the aunties and grannies; the council of wise women; the circle of elders to take my hand and pull me through? I want my mommy.

I've been doing some drumming and trance-dancing these days, too. Not every day, but when the tug is strong. I need my grounding "practice." I'm an old druggie from way back and that usually means a very spiritual person deep inside who took up with the wrong "spirits." Understandable. Never was presented with any meaningful rituals to turn to except cutting the lines, rolling the joints, and trying to get to that worm at the bottom of the bottle. So here I am pounding on my drum. "Gone haywire," the neighbors are probably whispering. "Knew there was something funny when she wouldn't put down a lawn."

May 12
3:31 am   Sunday

Maybe part of finding out who I am during these Changing Times is trying lots of situations and seeing what works and changing what doesn't. Life is kind of like one big buffet. I have to taste everything to see if I like it. What I don't like I scrape off my plate. What I like I go back for more. I keep going back to the garden.

I bought more new herbs: borage, chives, and dill. My tomatoes are doing well, as are the lettuce, snow peas, collards, and Brussels sprouts, which I'm hoping will do better when the rainy season starts. Peppers not so. Seems they need more of something that they're not getting here. Maybe I'm like the pepper plants. In the wrong place at the right time. Could also be the plant variety? It just sits there and then overnight disappears. I think the raccoons are having pepper fights at night.

Planted ferns, iris, and new yellow hibiscus, a "Miami" variety, near the house. Finally got the gingko in the ground just after she started turning autumn auburn and dropping her leaves. Amazing how genetically timed they are, even out of synch with the northern cold. She must count Moons, like me. Of course, we had to take out much of what we had planted there last year because I've changed my mind about what colors I want next to the house now. We've already moved the little orange tree three times. I just can't make up my mind where it should go. So far, starting at the front and going back we have oleander, bamboo, hibiscus, white bird, hibiscus, oleander, hibiscus, natal plum and then further up I got L a strawberry guava; supposed to be very cold-and salt-tolerant with edible fruit

I'm wanting more color in the yard. I keep propagating those native kalanchoe in the front. They're gray and spotted and have a bright-red bloom in the spring. I'm craving red. Must be a menopausal thing.

My new turtle mantra: "Slow, slow is the way I go." Keeps me close to the ground and humming. I'm really OK as long as I don't get into "rushing around" in rat pace and feeling scared.

E says I have to get off the adrenaline race. Says it makes my heart race and contributes to a low-energy slump. "OK," I tell her enthusiastically, "But how?"

Back to the buffet.

May 15
2:49 am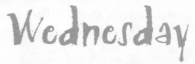

Pottery class is fab. I love that I'm not teaching and can concentrate on center-ing my own clay without having to run around to twenty students all screaming at the same time, "Me next. Me next." The class is mostly women, and mostly my age, with a couple of younger ones. There's a woman seventy-six who started working in clay only twelve years ago. She calls it her "escape" because her husband has Alzheimer's and she needs to get out of the house every once in a while. She says clay is her real home. I think I'm going to learn a lot from her.

There are two guys in our class, too. The one who is in his late twenties, maybe thirties at the most, caught my attention right away. His name is R. At first I thought he was weird and kind of shrugged it off. Just another art student. I figured he was stoned most of the time, but still I liked his energy and his wise-cracks that sort of sound like he's been reading the *Tao of Weed* and figuring out that life isn't what his parents told him it was. He's got a big blond Rasta knot for hair all piled on his head like a nest and tucked into one of those wool caps that the surfer dudes wear. He concentrates deeply on his work, making these hand-built pots that look like sea anemones stretching up to the sky, their mouths wide open and yawning. They're real fragile and look like they might fall over and break at any minute. But they don't. He pinches the clay in one hand and adds one small piece at a time, like he's making a quilt. He's tall and lanky and when he walks he kind of drags his foot. He's got a great smile. Did I say that already? And looks right into your soul when he catches you in the eyes. Sort of startles me a little. The first night he shuffled around and hugged us all before he left, saying something wonderful to each and every one of us, kidding about being "way beautiful" or "really cool," calling us "sisters" the whole time.

His eyes are bloodshot most of the time and squinty, like he's filtering out what he doesn't want to see with his eyelids. With the hat and surfer get-up I figured he was a neo-hippy pot-head. I figured I knew his number. This week he came in with his mother, smiling even wider than I'd seen him smile before. He held up his hands in a gesture of peaceful surrender and said in a quiet voice to the teacher, who he's obviously worked with for a while, "The brain tumor is gone." He'd just come from the doctor with the news. My heart just cracked open right there and fell onto the dusty floor.

Last night before leaving he walked up to me real slow, staring at me the whole time. He bent over and reached for my hand, all slathered in wet clay. Holding it like a butterfly he drew it up to his face and kissed it, saying, "I'm honored to know you." I didn't know what to say, but I stood up and wrapped my arms around him like he was my own son and I didn't ever want to see him hurt ever again. I'll tell you something. That kid has helped me get a grip on whining about hot flashes (at least for one night).

Life is just like that: One gift after another when you least expect it.

May 16
4:57 am
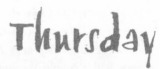

I'm trying not to count all the people I know who have cancer. Maybe it's because Walt is dying right in front of my eyes that I see misery everywhere and have to draw on every bit of strength I have not to collapse in a heap of empty clothes on the floor. Saw P on the beach this morning and she told me that two of her friends have colon cancer. R's friend just died of colon cancer, A just had surgery for uterine cancer, and T has a brain tumor. I don't believe in the God with blue eyes and a beard who sits in a throne in the clouds, but I'm very spiritual and I pray for people I don't even know because it gives me a vessel to contain my thinking when all I want to do is empty every drop of sadness in me. But then all I'll have is this echo bouncing back and forth inside me and I start pacing in a manic Annie Hall kind of way. I keep coming back to this simple hair-knotting ritual I've been doing for so long now I don't even remember how it started. Whenever my hairbrush needs cleaning I flip my mind into a trance and start slowly pulling the hair from the bristles, drawing out a long, fine rope of all the hair that used to be connected to me and is now on its own. When I've gotten all I can get, including those fuzz balls that hang in the bottom of the bristles, I wrap the hair rope on itself, repeating the same prayer: *Mother of All My Mothers, Please help wherever you can. I know you're big enough to wrap yourself around this world a billion times.*

Anais Nin once remarked that the dream is always running ahead of us and that to catch up to it and live for a moment in unison with it is the miracle.

I know that prayer and ritual work. It's my catching-up practice. If nothing else, i'm focused on something other than my own mismanaged board of directors. That can really get competitive: swatting at invisible flies. Tonight when cleaning my brush I added a little PS: *Miracle of All Miracles, If you've got a little magic left over in your mojo bag after helping the neediest cases first, can you please shrink my mother's hemorrhoids. Thank you.*

10:44 pm

Our house is obviously way too small for three adults with major neurotic problems and Death grinning a sneering lip-licking drool over the fourth. Mom and Walt's room is situated directly off the kitchen, with Walt's hospital bed pushed up against the wall that divides the two rooms. The kitchen table, which L made with leftover pine from a carpentry job he had in NYC renovating Bruce and Demi's penthouse (when they were Bruce and Demi and not Demi and Jason, or whatever her new boy hottie's name is) is pushed against the wall directly opposite Walt's bed. This is not good Feng Shui. Although the bad furniture arrangement makes for a great set design in a play that now defines my life, a *Waiting for Godot* re-make. Only we're Waiting for Walt.

There are days when sitting in a tranced-out stupor I zoom out of my daily reality and think of it as a theater production, just so I can get some temporary distance. I call this ongoing play (which feels a whole lot like work right now) "Kings In the Corner" because that's the name of the card game that Walt taught us and that now the three of us play at the kitchen table without him. The curtain opens and there's the hospital bed and the kitchen table back to back, a single wall between them. From the audience, the wall looks like a vertical black line; a colossal exclamation point without the period. It's obvious that the old man in the single bed is dying. The three, the old man's wife, her daughter and son-in-law are seated at the table having dinner. The old man starts a coughing fit, hanging over a waste can by his bed, spitting up long strands of brown mucus. The three try to eat, but when the old man coughs, the bed rumbles, the wall shakes, the kitchen table shifts, the plates rattle, the forks clink, the food slips and slides, and suddenly everyone is coughing. Hearing this, the old man finally settles back against the three or four pillows propping him upright and falls asleep while the three sit frozen with fatigue and grief, forks halfway to their mouths.

Act two: The three are seated at the table playing cards. The old man is awake, but barely. Seven cards are dealt to each player. The three talk in hushed whispers. The old man, who is hard of hearing, catches only a few words between labored breaths: "adult diapers," "no more radiation," "we have no idea." Four cards are placed face up in a cross. The rest of the deck is placed in the center of the cross. They never say death. Cards are played in descending order a la solitaire. The old man is relieved. Player to left begins by picking up from the deck. The old man reaches for the glass of ice on nightstand. Kings are placed in the corners. The three hear the bed squeak and daughter runs in to check on old man. Aces are low. Mother and son-in-law continue to play. There is no strategy. Old man drops glass of ice. Black Jack on red Queen. Nobody moves. First player to go out wins. Old man curses. Shit. Mother plays last card, Black King in the corner. Curtain drops to the sounds of old man snoring.

While shopping for adult diapers and another waterproof mattress pad I hear a song on the piped-in store sound system; an instrumental version of a very familiar tune. Rounding the corner I spy a new display of organic tomatoes and it occurs to me, as I reach across the bruised ones to get to the really nice ones, which haven't been squeezed or dropped off the back of a truck and hidden under the good ones, that I can't control the forces of life and death. I can barely control my bladder when I sneeze. Somehow I've managed to lock the tune into my head and I'm humming the wordless version all the way home. The words to the song come to me just as I pull into the driveway, next to Walt's hospice care nurse, who is making her weekly visit: *Let it be. Let it be. Let it be. Let it be. There will be an answer. Let it be.*

May 21
11:33 pm

Pottery class tonight. R peed his pants and apologized to the whole class. I don't think anyone would have even noticed because he wears big baggy pants and big baggy shirts that hang to his knees. But he said just in case we smelled anything funny, he wanted to let us know right up front. After spending half the night mopping the floor and changing Walt's bedding and bathing Walt because he knocked over his bed pan and didn't get his diapers on in time, I had only one comment for class, "Life is messy." Then I went back to centering the soft lump of clay on the wheel, letting the sensual feeling of wet earth, perfectly round and slippery, vibrate up my spine.

May 23
4:10 am

There are some things about coincidence that make my spine tingle. Like the time L and I were in Paris and on our last day decided to visit Chartres Cathedral to walk the labyrinth, the sacred eleven-circuit "maze" design laid into the stone pavement and filling the full width of the nave. It's about 40 feet across and was constructed in the Middle Ages around 1220. We arrived by train at the quaint village of Chartres and decided to first take a walking tour of the town, just to get our bearings, then visit the church just before catching the train back. However, when we started walking, a turn down a small alley put us on a side street that brought us smack dab in front of the cathedral. We turned and took another path back, thinking we must have made a wrong turn, only to end up walking down another narrow street that again emptied us into the courtyard facing the cathedral. Every turn had only one thing in mind for us. We had one of those stop, turn, and look at each other kind of moments followed by a shrug and a surrendered walk forward to the place you didn't expect you'd end up. It turned out to be a coincidence of deep emotional healing.

Upon entering the church we were immediately faced with one of those red velvet theatre stanchions, which seemed a bit out of place in my mind, and a sign to tourists indicating that visitors could walk the labyrinth between 12:30 and 1:30, emphatically noting that it was "forbidden" at other times. It was 2:00. I don't know what happens to me when I'm told I can't do something and every part of my rebellious trailer park being says "Go For It." I took a quick glance around and didn't see a single guard. I threw a defiant glance at L and said, "How are they going to stop us?" It wouldn't seem very spiritual in my mind to halt a pilgrim already embarked on a holy walk. The notion of having to go against the "established" rules to walk my spiritual path seemed all too fitting. So I brazenly stepped over the red velvet ropes and entered the very vaginal-shaped mandala moving slowly inward. I turned back and there was L close behind. I walked reverently, knowing that I am stepping over the memories of time and the footsteps of pilgrims and their prayers imbedded in stone beneath my feet. I'm seriously contemplating my connection to my Franco-Armenian ancestors, who surely passed this very way, when I double back around the first loop in the path, coming face to face with L, when just behind him I see two youngsters smiling and very serious, at the same time. Where they came from I don't know. They weren't in the church when we arrived. But there they were. One about age seven, the other maybe nine or ten. A boy and a girl walking close behind each other, the way school kids do on a class trip to a museum until someone fakes a fart and the whole group is roaring with laughter. I was waiting for the sound of a fake fart at any minute.

At each slow turn around the labyrinth path I'd catch L, a few feet behind me, and the kids comically close behind, looking like one of those Three Stooges skits, where the other two are marching along and Moe suddenly stops and Larry and Curly, who are very, very busy looking at their feet, collide into Moe, knocking all three of them down in a rousing pile of shrieks and roiling insults. The sight of my fellow clownish pilgrims caused me to spontaneously burst out laughing. My sudden outburst in the middle of the solemn silence that permeated every molecule of sacred air around us wasn't exactly the serious experience I was expecting. At this point, the boy trailed much farther behind the girl (his sister?), stepping off the designated path and then suddenly rushing to play catch up. Every few steps forward I'd get back my rhythm of solemnity and at each turn I'd see the comedy routine of L and the kids tight on his trail. I could barely concentrate on my own spiritual path, knowing what awaited me at each turn.

Aside from the comedy cathedral routine, somewhere in the back of my mind I kept thinking that at any moment some church official was going to step forward, shining silver whistle in hand, ready to blow it loud and screeching at any officious moment and request that we immediately vacate the premises because we had embarked on an illegal and forbidden spiritual walk. This awareness of being a "bad girl" for breaking the rules became an irritating distraction for the first half of the walk, until I suddenly realized (another informative metaphor) that breaking rules is just how I've lived my life. Just then I turned another bend and laughed to see the sitcom on parade behind me; the youngsters goofing on each other, L smiling the whole way. Well, I concluded, shaking off my entrenched and worrisome Catholic guilt, someone has to break the rules so others can join in. I arrived in the center of the labyrinth and this time when I turned around to face L, I gave him a big kiss. The kids joined us and then ran out, disappearing as quickly as they appeared.

Later, on the train ride back to Paris, I thought about the children I never had, would never have, and how this emptiness haunts me, following our relationship at every turn in my emotional life. I didn't talk about my feelings to L. On the walk back to the hotel room that night I picked two pink roses from a beautiful blossoming bush near Peace Park and, saying a prayer for letting go of what cannot be, I pressed them between the pages of my journal, blessing the past and the path before me. Many years ago a psychic once told me that L and I would have two "kids", but she said it would be a peculiar circumstance that would bring it to pass. I never thought about it much, but as I closed my diary on the fragrant pink rose it occurred to me that Mom and Walt were them: our circumstantial "kids."

I learned a few things about myself on the labyrinth walk at Chartres, and it wasn't at all what I expected: *Nothing is ever what it seems. Everything is exactly the way it needs to be. Having fun is good for the spirit.*

May 24
3:56 am

Friday

Went snorkeling today at the inlet. N, P, M, and T picked me up a 8 am; me standing by the side of the road with my bathing suit, sea socks, mask, snorkel, and dive gloves, slathered in sun screen and feeling like some *I Love Lucy* skit, with Lucy waiting for Ethel and gang. I have to admit I was terrified to think about walking out onto the jetty and "slipping", as N so nonchalantly called it, off the rocks into the ocean right where all the boats zoom in and out, men holding onto the steering wheel of their big-horse-power boats with one hand, a beer can with the other. I'm listening very carefully to N explain how we're going to stay close to the rocks and snorkel with the incoming tide and have a marvelous underwater experience while in my other mind, the one that's called Sheer Terror, I'm recalling every gory shark story, every desperate drowning accident, every gruesome motorboat collision with a swimmer that I've ever heard while reciting the astounding statistics that 50 percent of all boating accidents involve alcohol abuse. Just then some yahoo in a boat flies by and yells, "How 'bout a blow job?" N notices I'm frozen with fear and not able to descend onto the rocks, so she climbs back up, and talking to me in a nice soft mothering voice, reassures me that I'll be "fine, just fine" because she's done this a hundred times and we don't have to worry about a thing, as long as we stick together. She says the current is slow enough and we'll be able to just float along the inlet, which is a colossal gouge cut through the barrier island by those project-possessed Army Corps of Engineers, creating a channel where the river exits to the sea, thrashing water and swift currents included. And this, the exact spot where we, the happy menopausal mermaids, are to slip into the sea, navigate our way along the slimy dark-green rock walls of the inlet, passing under the inlet bridge (I think about Virginia Woolf's body wrapped around the cement posts, waiting for me in the murky shadows, her hair floating at me, reaching like seductive strands of slimy seaweed) for a fun day of underwater sight-seeing. What was I thinking? I'm not sure I believe in "past life" theories, but if I did, I was surely one of those people drowned at night in a handmade dinghy trying to escape an oppressive political regime. I do not trust big boats, men, or beer. I certainly don't trust the place where the three meet, which just so happens to be the exact place where I'm about to go swimming. N, who is the most trustworthy outdoorsy, athletic woman I know, a competitive surfer and elementary school teacher with the patience of a dog-trainer, tells us we have to go "NOW" so that we're not swept out to sea when the tide shifts, sucking the water out of the river, and us with it.

Standing on the edge of the sea wall staring into the ocean abyss I felt one of those fluctuating moments of keen self-understanding and spectacular self-idiocy coming over me. There are those times in my life when all my logical thinking shuts down and for the sake of either pleasing the crowd or sheer recklessness I leap where I have no business tip-toeing slowly. Hearing the word "NOW" flipped the toggle switch toward idiocy and I jumped into the ocean and popped up like a glass ball, joining my middle-aged adventurers already floating ahead of me. I looked back to see N smiling proudly before she jumped in after me. I was off all right. Feeling quite off my rocker in a state of animal panic. No turning back at this point and barely able to catch my breath I found myself swiftly moving with the current and so fascinated by the rocks racing past me that I nearly forgot that I was supposed to be looking at the floating world beneath me. Finally I managed to get the snorkel in my mouth and my face in the water at the same time. I caught sight of a school of round, black-and-white-striped fish darting left and right, dividing down the middle as I passed through them, looking just as frantic as I'm sure I looked to them. Still concerned about the boats motoring around me I passed into the shadowy gray water cast by tall concrete pilings, my muscles tight, my head uncontrollably bobbing in and out of the water, not at all relaxed enough to concentrate on the fascinating undersea world below my feet.

Just as I pressed my face into the water I saw a huge gray shape hunker down near the cement column to my left. Every part of me tensed up, my heart driven with adrenaline. I am a stranger here, I say to myself. I'm an intruder in the life of everything that lives here. I'm starting to beg for mercy when I realize that the haunting shadow is a mama manatee, a young calf snuggled up under her front flipper, nursing. I start back-pedaling against the current, but to no avail. I am caught in the forward movement. There was no hanging out or going back. The awesome sight lasted only a second. I looked around and saw my underwater gal pals smiling through their masks. They had seen mom and baby, too. Finally I start to relax in this oceanic pulse, the happiness on our faces carried through soundless salt water. Suddenly I hear P shriek and turn my head around quickly. Surely bloodthirsty jaws had nabbed her. I saw her struggling and lifted my head out of the water to see where we were. P had already ripped the mask off her face and was gasping with laughter. She had scared herself silly when the rope on the dive flag slid between her legs. She was relieved it was only her fear, after all. My face back down I catch a lone barracuda sliding beneath me slowly, eyeballing me and then darting away.

The incoming current was slowing down, the subtle force palpable against my skin. N said we had a few more minutes before slack tide. Then we could ride the current back out and grab the rocks at the place where we first jumped in. This seemed a little too much like a stunt from *Sea Hunt*. We passed children jumping off the rocks and a mother standing waist deep, watching her brood intently. A blue boat headed for us, the bow bearing down in the direction of my head. I swam to the side, hugging close to the rocks, yelling in my finest bravado, "Yo. Hey, Yo. Slow down." Suddenly the boater swerved and killed the engine, turning to enter the shallow wading pool area. The tide now pushed against me in the other direction. I suddenly felt a mild shift in the flow of the water and a resistance pushing against my body, where just moments before I was lifted along smoothly, silently. I had one of those cosmic drug rushes, realizing that I was firsthand feeling the tug of the Moon against my body, the shifting of the cosmic tides in weightless suspension, fully engaged in the blood and breath of an Earth Moon dance, pressing a profound harmonic YES! into all eternity.

Yes, for one brief moment I was going with the tide.

May 25
9:14 am
Saturday

It's raining and the sun is blasting. That's OK. I can't make up my mind either. I've just finished two chocolate chip cookies, followed by my new best-friend elixir, lemon balm. Does eating a stimulant followed by a sedative seem odd? No, not on a day like this, when everything I see looks like animals having sex.

At least from where I'm standing it does, inside the kitchen looking (peering?) out the sliding glass door. Two tan and wrinkled lizards are screwing on the patio lounge chair. And I mean screwing. With lazy eyes, all fiery and tranquil, their tails are wrapped around each other like bumpy mocha-colored leather cords creating one larger, flexible, clamping device with two heads in a stiff and silent (to me) stare for a few seconds and then they plink away, going in opposite directions. A butterfly the color of electric butterscotch is beating a swirling love dance with a look-a-like mate while a roving band of fat and furry bumble bees is working the hairy oracle, humping nectar out of every rainbow blossom in the backyard willing to give nurse. Another butterfly pair, sulfur-yellow with broad oval wings, comes into the picture, flitting and flirting and smooching and I'm sure I hear them singing, *Come on baby, light my fire...*

All the juicy stuff of life is happening right outside my window, belly to belly, face to face. Breathing In. Breathing Out. The first game ever played is still playing, driven by an endless round of reproduction mania: making face, winding the clock, rumping the greens, wiggling the navels, threading the needle, doing the rantum scantum, having a little of one with another. And all of it going on completely loose and easy in broad daylight in my own back-yard.

This is truly a breakfast of champions. Sexual tapas, heated sex treats catered by Nature. A delicate sparkle of ecstasy throbbing in every living thing.

I grab my new digital camera and try to catch it in technicolor. I want to hold on to this wondrous buzz of sensual beauty forever. Zone in. Be One with the buzz of life.

Or as long as the batteries last.

Turning around to close the screen door I am startled, aware of a little rush between my thighs, a ticklish tingle in my own sweet vulvic cabbage patch. Hmmm. If our bodies are no longer coded to create babies from the pulse of Moon blood tides, what is it that is calling my attention at this time, bringing my mind to meander to my fur pie, jelly box, and juicy jam pot, when the pheromones are no longer luring the boys home.

Orgasmic Ecstasy. Original Pleasure. Pure, plain and simple.

I have to have another chocolate chip cookie and think this one over. Uh oh. The stimulants are winning.

B calls while I'm trying to focus on this new-fangled mini viewfinder held at arm's length while zooming in on a pair of humping reptiles. I need my reading glasses for the damnedest things these days. I tell her I'm filming a new mini-series: Sex in the Sticks. "It's a low-concept reality show." B seems to think that unless the Queen bees are big-bosomed and wearing Manolo heels, it will have a limited viewing audience. B, just turned fifty-two, and single, informs me that she is taking salsa lessons with a young man named Autumn. "He's half my age, Nanc," she giggles. I tell her I used to go out with a guy named Summer, who had a sister named Rainbow. We laugh. "Nature babies."

It took me only half a day to find the journal where I wrote about my adventures with Summer.

Berkeley. 1972. I met Summer today while browsing for munchies in my favorite health-food store (where all the people are really very pale) on the corner of Ashby and Shattuck, just before catching the bus into another daylong photographic adventure walking around UC Berkeley and getting grab shots of people on the streets and shadows on the pavement, and whatever else catches my eye in the viewfinder. I love my light and breezy Berkeley days, "catching life." I love using my camera like a butterfly net; holding a piece of trembling, fluttering life for a perfect split second and then click, a memory made forever. Photography is so me. It sure suits my spirit, gathering little glimpses of life and filing them away, turning negatives into positives. Negatives into Positives. I like the way it sounds. Positive, negative, positive. A productive poem of greedy creativity. I feel rich with negatives! That's a funny way of thinking. But positive, really.

Oh. A glorious blue-sky day. The sweetest, brightest sunlight ever. I have absolutely nothing to do except to see what "comes up" while wandering and weaving, walking my way from one end of the city to another. An intuitive dance of listening, watching, waiting. I have only to feed my creative hunger and slip into the flow, the buzz, the whirl, the living highway of merging my skin with the world around me.

Zipping around the town is only half the magic, making love with sunlight and silver film one snap at time. I feel so alive here. The air so clear and so much light. Light is everyway. But I like the dark, too. At night, in the developing closet (isn't that just the coolest name for it? The Developing Closet. Sounds like a place for bad girls.) I love the darkroom, even if it's a little scary. I like being completely alone and silent and the clink chink when I pop the film can, the perfect and safe treasury of light images from my day's journey. In the dark I can hear my heart sing. In the dark, with my eyes wide open, I don't have to focus on anything.

I like how my fingers know what to do without my eyes giving instructions. Maybe my fingers have eyes, searching for the beginning tab to attach to the smooth metal spindle and then threading the snaky sprockets with one hand and rolling the spool counter clockwise with the other. Counter clockwise. I think I am a counter clockwise magician. But the real magic happens afterwards, watching the day's catch, like ghostly apparitions in black and white and gray, slowly emerge, reappearing in the hazy red light of the chemical tray; my darkroom womb. Sometimes I see something new, something I didn't see when I was taking the photo. A strange face staring at me from the corner of the photo. Or a leg caught in mid-stride hanging off the edge, the toe of the shoe stopped, never to move again, trapped in my world, forever on film.

A sweet young man caught me off guard today. I was looking for a yogurt that didn't have sugar, standing in front of the dairy case, reading a label and also looking for "active cultures", which Adele Davis says is the best kind. All of a sudden I saw out of the corner of my eye this really cute guy with a wrinkled white shirt, camel-colored corduroys, and hiking boots. He had a backpack woven with bright colors, maybe from Mexico or Guatemala. He just came right up to me like he's was looking for me and smiled and said, "Do you like stuffed peppers?" Just blurted it out. Not rude, but curious and cute. Sort of like he was all innocent and doing a research survey and traveling the world in hopes of finding an answer that would solve the mystery once and for all. Well, I told him the truth. "All depends." And he looked really puzzled, like I wasn't giving the right answer. And he wanted to know what depended on what. And I told him, "All depends on who's cooking them." I explained that my mom made the best stuffed peppers in the world. He said he was a vegetarian and one laugh led to another and then we were at his house, or rather the apartment he shared with four or five other people. It looked a lot like the place where I'm staying.

He did all the cooking, which was OK by me. It was actually a first. I've never met a guy who actually cooked me a meal. And then he pulled out chopsticks. I was sweating it because I'd never used them before. It wasn't easy picking up rice and small chunks of onions. It took me a while, but Summer showed me how to hold my fingers and where to rest the first stick before grabbing the other one. I practiced a little. He laughed, watching me pick up a morsel, only to drop it on the way to my mouth. He kept staring at my mouth. He's really gentle and sweet. And he kissed me when I finished eating. He has a front tooth that overlaps the other and his lips are delicious. He invited me to hitchhike to Vancouver with him to see some friends. I said, Why not? So we're leaving in just a couple of days. I love that hitchhiking costs nothing. I'll have to get more film. After dinner we made love. I didn't even do the dishes. I think he is young. It was all fast and happy for him. I mean really young. I didn't dare ask him. I feel so—well, so old; a divorcee at twenty-two. I figured I better teach him how to make me happy, too, or the trip to Canada is going to be hell for both of us. But not that hot. He was amazed that I didn't need or require him to have an orgasm. I told him it was his turn to learn finger placement. I think he felt left out, or some part of his male anatomy did anyway. But the good thing about him being young is he was ready to try again pretty fast, and we finally got our timing down. He smiles a lot and that makes me feel good. He's not pushy either. We took a shower and he scrubbed my back with a stiff sponge made from a squash.

Back from Vancouver. I'm not in love with Summer. He's definitely too young for me. And needy. I did get some great shots of our shoes, though, sitting side by side on a beach made of dark, round stones. Wrote a poem waiting for a ride over the Golden Gate Bridge.

I am in love
With a long seductive shadow
That creeps across the afternoon sky
And is related to me by Earth
In that rugged, scared place called my heart.

May 27
10:46 pm

Monday

The other day I planted three frangipani plants, geranium, rosemary, spearmint, lemongrass, amaryllis, and ferns. One of the women I met who lives down the street gave them to me. Our yard will be a jungle any day now. I also have a new red (oh that color red, again) banana plant, seven queen palms, and a tray of herbs including oregano, and basil, and nasturtium to plant. Gardening is my new meditation practice. I am partial to perennials.

It's still very bright and sunny during the day and I'm loath to burn in the midday heat, so I plant by Moonlight. I stand in the backyard, a barren beach of a yard, drawing circles and spirals in the sand, pacing off three paths that meet in the middle, a tri-via, a crossroads to symbolize my mid-life journey. In the middle of an arc on the flower spiral I'd look up at the waxing Aquarian Moon and howl. In the background I can hear the ocean roaring back at me.

So I'm laying out the backyard like so: a path leading off the back porch that meanders out to the crossroads; a place for the Menopause Queen to land, sit, administer her wisdom. One of those "If you build it she will come" kind of architectural invocations. Since these years here will be my Crone years, I want to give Her a prominent spot, or as landscapers call it, the *genus loci* or the spirit of the place. So I found my *genus loci* and She is Me, the Changing One.

One of the paths coming off this crossroad place veers to the left and goes to the four banana trees L and I planted last week, creating a wall of edibles along the back property line along with the loquat and lime.

The other pathway heads straight for the flowerbeds, which just so happen to be planted directly over the septic tank.

My herb garden is directly off the back porch. It's close to my kitchen so I can walk out and take what I need for cooking.

The front yard will have three citrus trees. L wants a grapefruit, Valencia orange, and I already bought a blood (red!) orange tree.

My mother says I should have married a farmer.

I think maybe it's the idea of putting down roots that intrigues me most.

JUNE

Saturday

I have to pay closer attention to subtle energies. After a little Feng Shui research I find out that the wealth corner of our house is smack dab in the middle of the bedroom. It doesn't take a Chinese spirit guide to figure out that what's going on, *or not going on,* in the bedroom, the tiniest room in the house, is not going to pay the bills. I can't change the configuration of our house, so I'll add a little red and gold (I have reservations about all this gold. A lot of raping, pillaging, and plundering in its god-forsaken name) to entice a little quick change.

It's obvious I have some de-cluttering to do here.

Decided to make a list of what's on, in, and under the nightstand. Or as L calls it: the "self-help pit" by the bed.

(Not in alphabetical order.)

° An amethyst crystal chunk from the centerpieces at our wedding.

° The Motherpeace Tarot Deck. I've had this since 1988.

° Medicine Cards. Bought these in 1989 after learning that my mother is one-quarter Native American. She can't tell me anything else about my ancestry.

° Progesterone Cream. P buys it wholesale and we decided to split a case.

° Lavender Massage Oil. I made this myself from the extra oil I drain from the top of the almond and sesame butter jars. (I can't digest peanut butter. I burp it all day long.) Added pure essential lavender oil for "Inner Peace." A little "Outer Peace" would be a good thing, too.

° 2 bottles of Bach Flower Remedies: Rock Water and Walnut. E says Rock Water will help my energy "flow" like water bubbling naturally from a spring deep within the body of the Earth Mother. She suggested walnut to help me create a "vibrational shield", preventing "enmeshment" with Walt's suffering and my mother's helplessness. She reminds me all the time that compassion is one thing, taking on someone else's spiritual path is another, and quite unhealthy. I sprinkle it generously around the house. She says to put a few drops in a spray bottle and spritz liberally day and night.

° Miniature statue of the benevolent Goddess Kuan Yin. My cousin CC brought this back from China. Kuan Yin's right hand is detachable, which I think is pure spiritual genius. CC says it's a portable "helping hand" readily available whenever needed. I really like that Kuan Yin's ears are long and droopy, stretching from the top of her forehead down to her chin. She apparently hears every word of suffering and transforms it into compassionate wisdom and understanding. Her porcelain-white face is perfectly and forever still, yet her robes are flowing away from her as if caught in a strong gust of wind. She's standing on a lily pad that sits on what looks to be a carousel of thrashing waves. I'm supposed to meditate on the ability to remain calm in the face of natural and inevitable changes.

° Photo of L and me taken while visiting Aunt Betty before her operation. It's early autumn. The leaves on the trees are showing a hint of gold, holding tight to summer's green and juicy fullness. We're standing on the frontyard of their house overlooking Crag Mountain and the beautiful Connecticut River Valley. I look young and happy, my curly hair blowing backward off my face. I'm staring straight into the camera, my right hand placed solidly on L's chest as in, He da man. As if I'm taking a solemn oath and stretched my hand beyond the confines of my own heart to rest confidently and comfortably on L; my hand, his heart. L's hair is long and in a pony tail. (That was just a year before I shaved his head.) He's smiling proudly, with a baseball cap that shades his face. Was it really nine years ago? I can barely remember how we got from there to here.

° A sumptuous Waterman pen L bought for my birthday sits on my new journal. It's so perfectly weighted and balances like a baton in my sometimes uncertain and doubtful hand. I hope someday to feel as poised and settled as this new pen feels in my hand. It's made of faux green malachite and trimmed in faux gold at the tip, top, and center. The word FRANCE is embossed on a black enamel ring between two gold bands where the two halves separate. He bought it the year I announced I was thinking of changing my name to Nancy France. I wanted to take on a new mother-centered moniker, from Frances. Using France also included the homeland of my paternal ancestry, but not so obviously. I felt like putting my mother in the foreground of my being. I didn't make this an official, legal change, but let the idea of yet another change hang around me until I could get used to it. I remember watching L beam as I opened the blue velvet pen case. I was a little confused, thinking at first he had bought me a bracelet, which would have been way out of character for me and this practical-minded man. I was reassured to find a pen snuggly strapped to a white satin lining. But not just any pen. He said he finally found the perfect pen for my pen name.

° A digital alarm clock. One of those traveling types that folds in half and conceals itself. I long ago got rid of any clock that made ticking noises that sounded out every second, announcing the passing of time in my ear when I'm trying to sleep and forget about just that. My mother says I have hearing like a hawk, in spite of repeated reminders that hawks are known to have keen eyesight, not necessarily hearing. She says it's because my ears are big, like my father's. Dad, Kuan Yin and me. I actually have very small ears.

I replace the photo of L and me, framed in purple amethyst chips, with a photo of us hugging in front of the Whitney Museum. It's got a wide gold-leaf frame with a big spiral swirl that moves across our heads like we're sharing one big Bam Bam hairdo.

We are changing. Together and separately. We are changing.

June 5
9:56 pm
Wednesday

Before going to bed tonight I'm going to prepare my bedside table with another magical potion so when I wake up in the middle of the night I'll have what I need without having to pad around the kitchen banging the cups and stubbing my toe on what I can't see. It's not that I'm looking forward to waking up at 3 am, but I'm getting myself in tune with this middle-of-the-night meeting with the Menopausal Queen. I drop a little motherwort tincture in a couple of tablespoons of apple cider vinegar. Mix a few drops of lavender essential oil in a base of sesame and almond for massaging my belly, forehead, and breasts. I like how the circular motion of moving around my belly button in the dark feels soothing and downright sensual.

Had a strange dream that still lingers. I am with a group of young women who are all primping and doing foo-foo, preparing for a kind of pageant or sexy dance performance for a group of reluctant men. Why they are reluctant I don't know. The performance is to take place in a pool; a poorly lit, somewhat mysterious, body of water near a pier. The men are all ages, young and old, and there is a black man in the group. I'm feeling awkward yet intrigued. An elderly man nearly falls into the pool and I reach out to help him. The girls are dressed for a topless show and they are to somehow lure the men forward into a different pool somewhere behind the stage. It seems there may have been a contest of some sort and these young women lost and now have to "offer up" their bodies as payback. I'm feeling disconnected from the women and decide to stay on the men's side. Then the women are hollering to me because it's my turn to get on my costume and get all gussied-up like them. Reluctantly I cross the line.

A young woman comes up to me and begins plucking the hair off my nipple, giggling, as if she's never seen anything like it before. I'm feeling odder and more uncomfortable as she continues to inspect my breasts while applying make-up. I'm just not interested in the "luring" game. I feel very insecure. She hands me a skimpy red apron that goes on over my head and ties at the waist on both sides. I feel oddly like my mother. Then I get into the pool and the black man (or is he Hispanic with dark skin?) comes at me. He reaches out and touches my hip and leg (I am naked under my costume) and recoils, scrunching up his face in horror, caught in his own private disappointment. "Oh, she's old," he gasps, turning to tell the others as he backs away. I feel terribly rejected. I hang my head and swim over to the edge of the pool, grabbing my thighs to see how he could tell by the touch that I was old. Oh, they're loose, I think to myself. Loose skin tells all. Suddenly a young man swims up to me and says, "Never a woman too old for me." I've lost all interest in dancing. The young man grabs my hand and we walk away together gathering turtles, picking them up and holding them in our arms to set them free on the other side of the pool.

June 6
8:21 am

If I get another Victoria's Secret catalog this week I'm going to scream. I'm writing a letter once and for all.

Dear Victoria (I hope you don't mind that I use the familiar. I've seen so much of you, and I mean so much of you lately, that I feel like I know your girls very intimately, so to speak). It's come to my attention that it's time you take me off your mailing list. It's no secret that I am not sixteen years old, or a size two, nor am I a double D, like your models who, by the way, my mother says all look like nymphomaniacs with too much leverage (her words not mine and I think she means cleavage not leverage, but she's 83 years old and sometimes gets words and meaning a little mixed up in her mind). She's also concerned that they're not eating enough, and says they

could use a nice home-cooked meal, not that she's offering to cook for the girls. She doesn't do much of that any more either. I do, however, want to know about that "Boyfriend Sleepshirt" that's on sale. It says it's the one that "you'll sleep with again and again." Does that mean the Sleepshirt or the boyfriend? And if it's supposed to mean the boyfriend, is that a hidden code for some conservative right-wing moral agenda, selling monogamy in a sexy lingerie? Because if it is, I think you're heading in the wrong marketing direction, barking up the wrong branch, so to speak. Anyway, just thought I'd let you know. PS. My mother thinks our neighbor, Mr Smith, might be more interested in your catalog and suggests you just change the address one digit. Sincerely,
The Menopause Queen

11:06 pm
Didn't do much for my birthday. Wasn't in the mood for a big shebang. Neither was Walt or Mom. L painted a beautiful birthday card for me; a vase of yellow daisies. Mom got me a six-pack of underwear. Since her last memory lapse we've taken away her driving privileges so she asked L to pick them up for her. I'll have to celebrate my 50th next year, when it feels better.

Spent some time alone down by the river contemplating UFOs, Unidentified Feelings and Obsessions. Didn't dwell. Changing my mind is getting easier these days. But not much, because I don't know what to change it into.

L and I took a walk on the beach after dinner, the stars twinkling bright and strong against the indigo underbelly of the night sky. A warm southerly breeze against our backs, we held hands the whole way. The rhythmic slapping of the waves on shore caught all my attention, forcing hard thoughts out and soothing feelings in. I can't even remember what we talked about. Actually, I don't think we talked much at all. Just before heading up the dune I caught sight of what looked like the dark-blue hood of my '69 VW bug floating up on shore. We stopped short in our tracks, not knowing what to expect. Lo and behold it was a loggerhead turtle come to nest; the first sighting of the season. I gasped and smiled at the same time. We stayed really still so as not to spook her. I encouraged her labored crawl with silent cheers of *Go girl go*. After what seemed like forever, in slow motion, she made it to the soft, dry sand against the dune line. With singular determination she began digging a hole with her back flipper feet, in circular motion, alternating right and left. We crawled on our hands and knees to get closer, sand flying in our faces. We settled down only a few feet away. She rested in between long stints of digging and I'm certain I heard her grunting every once in a while. Then she started laying her eggs, dropping perfectly round gooey ping-pong balls into the hole, all the while tears streaming down her beaked and leathery face. I read that sea turtles cry when they're nesting to prevent their eyes from drying out while on land. I thought I'd cry too if I had to carry that cargo around on alien territory just to perpetuate the species, and then swim a few million miles every year to do it all over again. After plop, plop, plopping about a hundred eggs into her sandy nest, she diligently covered them back up again, bringing sand back over the hole with her flippers in the other direction. Then, some internal switch flipped and with a heave she lifted herself back around to face the waves and lumbered down the beach, riding a wave into her own wet and fertile world.

We sat in silence, the stars breathing with us, the waves keeping time. Happy birthday to me. Thank you Mother Ocean.

June 9
3:18 am   Sunday

I've taken to wearing big earrings lately. Some of them look a lot like fishing lures and colorful lead weights. They pull on my ears and hang below my hair and make me aware of that line in my ear lobes that the specialists of earlobe lines says if you have one you're a dead ringer for heart disease. I've tried desperately to rub that line out of my ears and since that doesn't work, I decided I'd accent the big line with bigger earrings. Everyone who knows about this earlobe signifier will see it on me and feel really sorry for me and maybe be nice to me before I have the Big One. My father had a heart attack when he was fifty-four, but my friend J reminds me that he was a knock-down, drag-out drunk for most of his life. It wasn't the line in his ear that did it. So I'm into the big earrings and hope it's not some sort of primal substitute for flagging hormones. Like when there are no pheromones left to fire up my pussy power and lure a desirable mate, we attract in clever and immeasurable ways thinking we're being really artsy, but we're still holding out for a come-hither glance and mostly what we're getting is someone commenting about the fishing gear hanging off our heads.

I'm leaning toward the earrings as a sort of St Christopher medal.

When I was really young, way, way back in my early thirties, which seems like yesterday when I think about it for very long, I knew an older woman who seemed to me at the time to be soooo much older than I was. She was probably in her late fifties (not much older than I am now). I marveled at her sense of flare and flashy style. She always wore bright-red lipstick in a Lucy kind of arch above her top lip. Said she wouldn't leave the house without it. She sported her long silver-gray hair in a double wrap and piled on top of her head like a crown, looking like what Frida Kahlo would have looked like had she lived long enough for her hair to go gray. She wore sandals, summer, spring, autumn and on into the deep chill of winter, open-toed sandals, because she couldn't stand to have her soles trapped in animal skins. She only wore boots when it snowed and, even then, reluctantly. As soon as she got where she was going she'd pull off the boots and pad around barefoot, like a ballerina, lifting up onto her toes and twirling with her arms out to her side. I never saw her in pants either. She wore big, full skirts like the kind square dancers wear; all puffy with crinolines and extravagantly decorated with lace or bells or baubles. Bright pulsing hot pinks with deep-turquoise trim. Crimson red, black, and purple. Oh how she loved purple. And the earrings. Long and dangly and mesmerizing, which she bought at thrift stores and yard sales. "The bigger, the bolder, the better," she'd shake her head and you could hear her coming a mile away, bringing a breath of fresh air to cheer my day.

Betty went dancing on Thursday nights at the yoga studio in town. All alone. She'd been divorced for several years. Her husband, a professor at the college where I'd been teaching part-time (always an adjunct, never a professor) ran off with one of his students and left her with three kids to raise, which she did enthusiastically and creatively, I might add. She used to cover the living room walls with large sheets of newsprint and bring in the neighborhood kids for sessions of what she called Dream Drawings, letting them go at the walls with crayons and markers and marshmallows and macaroni, gluing and painting, singing and cheering like Auntie Mame on Ecstasy with words of rapturous encouragement, "Let yourself feel your dreams." All the while she'd be clapping her hands, calling out to no one in particular, but to everyone there, "Genius," "Brilliant," "Marvelous." She never took any of the dream drawings off the wall, but rather pinned up another blank sheet of paper right over the previous ones, creating a kind of hanging sculptural wall book.

I loved Betty with all my heart. I loved standing next to her and soaking up her vibes; wild, outrageous and who-gives-a-flying-fuck-what-other-people-think kind of attitude. I couldn't imagine dressing like her then, but I think about her a lot now when I stand in my closet and moan at yet another black pair of jeans staring in a dull drone back at me. I looked up to Betty because she was more than artsy and fun to be around, she was courageous. She was a survivor in more ways than one. She'd had a mastectomy at age 36 and outlived the doctor's prognosis by over twenty years. She used to say, "I'm a miracle," grabbing her one breast and giving it a little shake, "and I'm gonna spread my miracle around."

I haven't seen Betty in years. I'm sure she's still dancing somewhere on some night of the week, her arms open wide, smiling, laughing, and twirling in large dervish dream circles.

I think about Betty when I wear my big dangly earrings and get scared about those little freakin' lines in my earlobe. A few hours ago I went in to tuck Mom in and make sure Walt had all his medications lined up on his nightstand, and his watch was turned to face him so he could have a direct shot at it in the middle of the night and know what time it is at all hours, his nitroglycerin tab just to the right of the watch, and the box of tissues close enough so as not to make him reach and knock off the watch and the pill, when I noticed for the first time ever that my octogenarian mother, whose heart is as strong as any rocky mountain, has the same big long line in her earlobes as I do. After kissing them both good-night, like reruns of *Little House on the Prairie*: Goodnight Mom, Goodnight Nancy, Goodnight Walt, Goodnight Nancy, Goodnight L, Goodnight Walt, Goodnight Franny, I called P to let her know, with an exaggerated sense of enthusiasm, like Ethel bursting in on Lucy all squealing and girlish, that my earlobes are just like Mom's. After a second of trying to put two and two together P reminded me not to let the monkeys in the temple distract me from what's really going on in my heart.

I told her that maybe it would be better if I joined the monkeys. They look to be having much more fun than I am.

"You're grieving, Nanc," she said quietly. "There's no getting around it."

Rumi says that what seems to be changing around us is rather the speed of our bodies leaving this world.

I just want to slow down and enjoy the ride.

June 11
8:34 am

I did not wake up in the middle of the night last night! I slept in. Yesssssss. I love how this communion with my Menopausal Mind just keeps on giving me reasons to laugh at myself and move on, feeling lighter and more whole. I can hear that John Lennon song running through my head: *Whatever gets you through the night, is all right. Is all right.*

"Whatever" is knowing that the unexpected, in this case sleep, comes when you really need it. Thank you very much.

June 18
8:25 am

I like to think that I'm aware of some mysterious pulse or engaging hum that makes me feel connected to the roots and branches of very tall trees. I do love the ocean and the in and out flow that delivers clean white shells on shore like jewels worn smooth. I can still trip out on cosmic love juice when I'm in Nature. But one of my first, very big spiritual experiences was when I was working as a topless dancer. We were not called exotic dancers back then. In the club where I worked, which just so happened to be on the other side of the tracks in Fort Lauderdale, we went *topless* for five dances and every sixth dance had to go bottomless. Then we got down off the stage, and waited on customers. A perfect whore-to-housewife set-up, now that I look at it.

I was living with D at the time, who I later hitch-hiked with to Berkeley. D is now a big-shot editor with a porno rag out there somewhere. I went looking for him on the internet one night when I couldn't sleep and, sure enough, he's still doing what he always loved to do and which eventually drove us apart: taking pictures of nude women. Really young nude women. I'll never be able to run for Mrs Mid-life America and win because D can haul out an arsenal of compromising photos of me, which will not bode well for an all-American gal. I would like to have some of those photos, though, if only to appreciate my younger self, and a once primal drive that seems now to be all dried up.

D got me the job dancing, or at least the connection to the guy who did the hiring. D started out as a photo-journalist in college where we first met. He did a story assignment on the local *girls girls girls club* and after spending hours there came home all excited telling me how much money the dancers make in one night and why don't I go down and try out for a job because the guy who runs the joint, Ralph (such a perfectly bad name for a guy who runs a titty bar), is looking for some "wholesome and healthy-looking" new talent. Besides, after graduating we were getting ready to leave for the West Coast and the money would come in handy. I thought so, too. I had just finished reading Thoreau's *On Walden Pond*, being a hippie chick and all, and really liked the part that suggested that I beware of enterprises requiring new clothes. A job requiring no clothes was even better. At the precocious age of twenty-two I was starting to understand at least one thing about myself: like Thoreau, my new naturalist mentor, I didn't fit into the daily grind of working for a living. The idea of exchanging my time for someone else's dream was growing increasingly repugnant, in spite of the fact that I hadn't quite coalesced a dream of my own.

Since I had to eat, I decided that the best approach was to work the least amount of time for the most amount of money; an idea that keeps artists and aspiring actors fed, waiting tables while waiting for destiny to bring that big break.

Besides, I had been fired from my job as a cashier at the grocery store because I refused to wear a bra. I couldn't figure out how the manager knew that I was actually braless because I was not (and still am not) a big busty type. And besides that, the uniform jacket covered and hid what I did have. I think he was looking at me a little too closely. He was always smiling and trying to get my attention. Now the thought of going braless and getting paid for it seems like one of those big ironies of life. Destiny *was* smiling on me.

I got the job; the easiest and most honest interview I'd ever been on. On most, the guy is undressing me with his eyes all the while asking me about my hobbies and making little notes on my application. Ralph just came right out and asked me to take off my clothes and get on stage and dance. I'd been modeling for night classes at the local museum, so I was used to standing naked in front of people. Dancing would be a breeze and a whole lot easier than standing still and not being able to scratch an itch when I wanted to. Ralph played *Nutbush City Limits* and I danced wild and sexy on the small platform stage with a metal pole smack dab in the middle of it. What that was there for I would later find out, but I didn't dare touch it during my try-out dance. Architecturally it seemed like a poor placement for a ceiling support.

I'd never actually been in a titty bar, but heard enough about it to know what I was supposed to do. Ralph didn't seem to care what I did on stage. While I danced, he spent most of the time talking on the phone, smoking a short stubby burned-out cigar, laughing loudly, and only infrequently glancing up at me. Later on he told me that because he's around naked women all day long, he actually gets turned on when he sees a woman with her clothes on. I think that was a joke because he burst out laughing at himself every time he said it.

I had to borrow a pair of gray suede boots from my girlfriend because Ralph didn't want me wearing sandals on stage. Uh oh. The requiring new clothes theory was going out the window. Ralph tried to convince me that I had a promising career ahead of me. "You're a showgirl now, and you've got looks. You better make money while you can." I didn't believe anything Ralph said. He was a sad little guy who tried hard to be a daddy to his "girls." I liked him, enough. What I liked most was he didn't try to cop a feel or get me in a corner when I went in to get my paycheck, which wasn't a check but a skinny manila envelope stuffed with damp five- and ten-dollar bills that smelled like beer and stale cigarette smoke. I think I made four dollars an hour plus tips, which usually brought in over a hundred dollars a night, all total. At the time that was big money. I was saving every penny for my trip to California and never expected that spirit, Spirit, would cut my income short one night on a full Moon when I was PMS-ing long before there were words for that agitated state of heightened awareness that at earlier times in a village long long ago would have been used to sniff out danger, warn the clan of impending threat, lead the men in puberty rites.

I remember looking up at the Moon just before pulling open the side entrance to the "lounge," as Ralph liked to refer to his dancing establishment, and thinking *Oh Boy. All the nuts will be out tonight.* I stood maybe a second too long sniffing the damp night, letting the moody silver light work on that part of my being that sought out communion experiences by way of fashionably hallucinogenic pills called, at various times, Purple Haze, Orange Sunshine, and Window Pane, where memories of an immense and indescribable ecstasy of Oneness still lingered. I hadn't dropped acid in a long time and didn't want to. I hated the crash and the feeling that fought in my jaw like my teeth were cemented together and wouldn't unglue for hours. Speedy teeth. D and I didn't drink and didn't do drugs, at the time. We were high on art and life and self-portraits.

I'd been working for almost a month when it all came to a halt. It was my turn to dance and I felt bloated and crampy. The jukebox clicked on a slow tune, *Stairway to Heaven*, one of my fave songs, but certainly not a sexy dance tune. I kept waiting for that tiny turning point in my routine when the music takes over and I don't have to think about where my feet are going and the perfect moment to shake the hair off my shoulders and pucker up my lips for an innocent sexy come on. I'd gotten the hang, so to speak, of the pole and used it like the other dancers did, bumping and spinning and rubbing it like it was a long and slippery metal dick that ran all the way from heaven to hell and back again.

On the sixth dance I caught my underwear on the edge of my boots (which an admirer from the mideast offered to buy from me for $100) and almost fell over, if it weren't for the pole. (I wore white cotton underwear and didn't shave my armpits, which got me the nickname "Earth Girl.") I started to laugh a little, trying to pull myself back together, but the harder I tried, getting back together seemed further and further away, until it occurred to me that I just wasn't going to be able to get back to pretending I was a showgirl, as Ralph liked to call us. I stopped dancing and bent down to de-catch my panties, pretty matter of fact, like I was pulling gum off my heel, and when I straightened back up again something shifted in my mind and body, in the whole way I was feeling, and thinking, and seeing.

Time stood absolutely still and there I was standing completely naked in front of an audience of men, who looked as suddenly off-balance in their faces as I felt in my skin. A sense of wild calm came over me. What immediately followed I can't explain easily in words. It wasn't so much a feeling but an urgent sensation or impression that started to buzz and hum all around me like fireflies and bees meeting for the first time on a small pink rose. All at once, the space between the men sitting behind little round tables and the space on stage that came all the way up to my hair disappeared completely. There was no division between us. No *Them*, no *Me*. We became one big amoebic glob of humanity in a dull-lit room with gray circles of smoke suspended in stillness. They were breathing me. I was breathing them. No separation, no difference between us. And in the middle of the breathing in, breathing out, I had a terrified glimpse not only into the hunger and hurt in their lives, but the emptiness in my own. I couldn't contain it all and started to cry, tears rolling down my cheeks and dripping onto my bare breasts. I became aware of the music, like big puffy clouds moving in circles at the edges of time. The words of the song dancing in all the places I wasn't: *Yes, there are two paths you can go by, but in the long run. There's still time to change the road you're on.*

I stood frozen for what seemed like an eternity, but probably the entire experience lasted no more than a minute or two. When the music stopped I walked off the stage and out the front door. I stopped at the bar and grabbed my purse. I didn't say a word to anyone. No one tried to stop me, and I never looked back.

June 19
1:23 am   Wednesday

I like what K said the other night about forgiveness and how it doesn't mean that what happened and the things we used to do were OK or even acceptable. It just means that I'm making a conscious decision not to put my energy *there* anymore, forever draining it into the past. Time now, she says, to put my energy into the present and allow myself to feel joy in those places where I hid all that old shame and blame.

I think menopause is a rest stop. A place to re-fuel, get some nourishment for the road ahead, and empty the little pile of garbage that's been gathering on the floor behind the driver's seat.

I close my eyes, returning for a moment to the memory that gathered on the dance floor behind me. Like a mother tiger who knows how to collect her cubs at the first sniff of danger, I walk boldly backward into my past, and climb onto the stage where the free-flowing shadows of sadness call out for healing. Picking up her small white hand I guide the young woman who is me off the stage. There will be no more performances. No more games. No more pretending and pleasing. Making soft cooing sounds, and pulling her tight to my side so she knows she'll never be alone again, I wipe the tears from her hazel green eyes as we walk to a far, far away forest, where the filtering light from a golden afternoon sun warms our backs and guides our way. Stroking her long, shiny hair, I hear myself whispering from the sacred temple of a mother's wisdom, telling the young woman who still lives in the secret hollow of my heart that I love her dearly and I will always love her, no matter what went on a long time ago when she didn't know that it wasn't her job to try and give back to the world its lost soul.

June 22
(Did I miss Summer Solstice?   Saturday
Damn. Will have to do instant replay
tonight. Maybe another walk on the beach. Look for turtles.)
4:04 am

4 am is a bad guest. If it's here to stay, I better figure out how to entertain it. The nightshirt has to go. Sleeping naked feels so much better. One less distraction. I don't have to strip down in the middle of the night, shedding a damp rag clinging to my waist. This is a big change. I've worn a tee shirt or a cotton nightie since I can remember. My mother always made sure I wore panties to bed, too. *Like someone was going to do something in the middle of the night and I had to cover up my special-purpose parts so no one could see them.* I gave up the panties early on when I realized it was my mother's childhood memories she was trying to protect. Her father had molested her when she was a young girl. But the nightshirt stuck, maybe for good measure. Now it's sticking to me and I'm ditching it.

Yes. Naked at night. I like stretching my arms out over me and lowering them down to land directly on my soft muff. I like touching my bare skin, letting my sweat cool me. I like smoothing and petting and touching all of me without interference. See 4:12 am. This is all for you. I rub my belly in circles. I doodle on my tummy, sketching with my pointer finger and then erasing it with my open palm. How's that 4:17 am? My belly is an etch-a-sketch. All for you, you big lug of a hunk of passing time. Watch this 4:26: I'm opening my legs and doing Kegel exercises. Ha ha. You can't see me now. My muscles are twitching. Catch that 4:29. Hey 4:35, how about a little progressive muscle relaxation? Will you go for that? Beginning at my toes. Tighten. Loosen. To my calves and thighs. Tighten. Loosen. Getting bored yet 4:38? I am. Shoulders, your turn. Tighten up to my ears. Tight. Tight. Loosen. Face. How about this 4:42? Scrunch up like little prune face. Argh. Prune face? Hope it doesn't stick. Stick out my tongue. Try to touch my nose. OK. 4:44? Are you happy now? Had enough? I'm losing my mind over you. 4:56? We're almost there. The finish line in four minutes. What's the prize, anyway? Nothing? Nothing, you say? Hah. I'll think of something. I've got all night.

I really do have to keep my thoughts simple. I can't trust a two-way conversation in my head. My mind is a very tricky clown.

June 25
8:43 pm

Tuesday

Woke up with Wayne Newton in my head singing, *Danke Schoen, darling Danke schoen. Thank you for all the joy and pain.* Yesterday it was Kenny Rogers with, *Know when to hold 'em. Know when to fold 'em. Know when to walk away, when the deal is done.* My mental frequency is tuned to all the bad channels. I must be locked into the Las Vegas dial. Amazing how thoughts just keep running themselves around like gerbils on a wheel. Maybe there's a hidden message in this audio track? Nah. Not going there.

Making a cup of sage tea. P calls back. She had called earlier when I was doing yoga. Mom *for once* didn't interrupt me. For this I sing *Danke Schoen.* Her memory is shot like a slice of Swiss cheese and no matter how I impress upon her that yoga is not an interruptible event, she interrupts. I hear the phone ring, then I hear her creeping down the hall talking quietly into the receiver and then she knocks anyway to let me know I have a phone call and that she's going to tell them to call back. I go from Cobra Pose to Child's Pose in one short breath.

P says better to have Wayne Newton in your head than in your bed. She's farm-sitting for neighbors. A chicken died last night and Rosebud the cat is missing. How come these things happen when you're taking care of other people's pets? P is worried about Rosebud. She's too young to do that thing that cats do when they know they're dying: disappear into the wilderness. I think the animals get stressed when their companion people leave and are going through their own animal version of abandonment complex. I told her that's why farmers have that kind of calm indifference to their animals. They don't get all emotional because they know it's Darling Ducky one minute and *foie gras* the next. The life cycle doesn't come close to the heart on a farm because it's busy sitting on the plate. P says she'll never kill another farm animal. She's a vegetarian; a deeply compassionate being. I just love her for reminding me that our choices really make a difference in the world. *Do you know how much energy it takes to squeeze a hamburger out of a huge cow?* She rallies. With that we take off on a random rant, galloping like she-demons against the winds of agri-biz, pesticide poisoning, the fate of topsoil, mad cow disease *and boy aren't you glad you don't eat beef*, and how many rats she counted in the grain bin. She's walking in the garden as we speak; what's left of it. It's harvest time for the tomatoes. She's canning, and I am so grateful that there are women who still do this, especially women who are my friends. The fruits of her compassionate composting will end up on my kitchen table in just a few months, when she brings the miracles of seed and sun to me here, where growing tomatoes is like trying to sprout seeds in sugar.

I look forward to her return in just a few short months. I miss our walks on the beach and her couple-of-years-older-than-me *Been There* kind of wisdom. And as if that isn't a huge gift in and of itself, she and her huz are sober. Now if that isn't a big fat *Danke Schoen, darling* to the cosmic forces that give you good neighbors when you need them most, I don't know what is.

We hang up with hopes of finding Rosebud and I'm left craving the happy fatigue that growing vegetables brings.

We are sailing into summer. Soon it will be scorching hot, pitch-dank humid and vulnerable. Oh, and hurricane season is officially on us. My adrenaline pumps up a notch with every little spiral spinning off the coast of Africa.

June 28
11:34 am
Friday

Standing in Tree Pose this morning and staring out the window into the silent whirling world of butterflies, bees, hornets, little blue moths that look dizzy and lost, and lizards coupling like mute sex maniacs, an overwhelming sensation came to me, like a soft and velvety wash from the rooted places of my feet. Just when I was thinking of nothing *finally*, and standing really balanced and almost still it occurred to me that the Earth, at five billion years old, may also be going through menopause. It puts global warming in new perspective, along with a whole host of other moody weather patterns and unprecedented drought.

I almost fell over with the thought of it and had to go back into Child's Pose just to catch my breath.

June 29
3:01 am
Saturday

Waking up at 3 am really stinks. I'm tired of it already. Tired. Hah. I wish. How can I be fast asleep one minute and blasted wide awake the next? My shoulders are rubbed bristling pink from tossing and turning myself inside out against the heated sheets, hoping exhaustion will bring back a tiny little inch of sleep. I don't want to get up and read because I'll wake up too much and won't get back to bed before 6 am, which means I'll feel like shit warmed-over the rest of the day. *Shit warmed-over? Where does that idea come from?*

I'm soooooo grateful I don't have to go to work tomorrow. How do women do it who have young children, real paying jobs and a big mopey husband who won't do the laundry? I think I read somewhere that working women are still doing 90 percent of the housework? Why do we let that happen? I say let the housework go to hell. Or the guy who won't pony up to his share.

At least my timing was perfect to take this year off. I didn't really plan it to coincide with night sweats and sleeplessness. I simply needed a break from running myself into a frantic little circle making sure everyone else's needs got met before my own. I love my students, my college "kids" and miss them dearly. But not enough to put myself back in the classroom. At least not right now. I keep thinking about the idea for a Crone's Year Off. I read about it, but can't remember where. A mid-life sabbatical makes such supreme sense; time to locate the shape of who I really am after playing circus contortionist for the audience in my mind.

Lightning is flashing somewhere over the ocean. Walt is coughing, a deep, hollow rasp. I know he is awake. He sleeps during the day. He's been keeping Mom up at night, too. I'm starting to worry about her. Everything is falling apart at the seams. Maybe after the storm passes he'll settle down and I will, too. Thunder is too far behind the light. The rain won't come this far over the river. I think of these storms as the dry heaves. All noise, no rain. Where do the birds go at night? They are so polite to be quiet when I'm trying to sleep. I like being grateful about the little things. It gives me something, some little string to hold onto when everything else is all balled up and feeling endlessly hopeless. The Moon is waning. No shadows hanging on the ferns or the straggly coral pink hibiscus that stretches across the bedroom window like a crooked finger pointing west. M says she gets up and walks around the neighborhood until she can't drag her feet another inch. Then she goes home and collapses asleep on the couch. Sometimes she says she walks until the first glint of sunrise. She says, "Whatever it takes."

I wonder if she's out there now, walking off her brand of sweat-flash insomnia. She says you learn a lot about people in the dark. Last week she heard the new people on the corner fighting; a woman screaming, *Stay away from me. Don't you dare touch me. Get out of here.* M says she got scared and walked real fast when she heard her, not sure whether she ought to turn around and go the other way or stop and wait to see what happens next. She heard a door slam and then saw the car back out of the driveway real slow and then just stop with the brake lights lighting up the road in an eerie redness. The car didn't leave the driveway. It pulled back in just as slow and stopped about where it began, but whoever was in the car didn't get back out again. Or if they did, they made an effort to close the car door real quiet. M thinks maybe the driver saw her and tried to hide. At first, M says, she thought about calling the police, but figured by the time she got home it would be too late. She says next time she's going to bring her cell phone with her. Someone told me that the woman in that house went nuts after her last baby, and she never leaves the house any more. I can't remember who told me, but it sure makes me wonder about what goes on in that house during the day, let alone at night.

M told me about this Native American spiritual philosophy called Hanta Yo, which loosely translated means "get out of my way." It doesn't mean *that* exactly, but more or less refers to the belief that everyone has his or her own powerful relationship with spirit and it's really important not to interfere by taking someone's power away from them and doing things that they really have to do on their own.

Sometimes I get all mixed up with so many spiritual guidelines racing through my mind. Should M have called the police? I think I would have. But then again it sounds like it would have brought more trouble to an already troubled house. Hanto Yo comes into my head when I think about these things. Then I hear the voice of the Dalai Lama saying, "It is not enough to feel compassion. You must act."

I think I'll turn over one last time and jiffle myself into the Final Relaxation Pose. Whoever thought that calling this the Corpse Pose would help us relax wasn't thinking straight. I'll say a few prayers for the woman who lives on the corner. I'll concentrate on breathing. That's all I have to give right now. I barely have that. It's obvious I spent too much of my youth seducing men. I really should have learned how to seduce sleep. It would have been more useful at this age.

JULY

July 2

Tuesday

° Butterflies rule.
° Buy more chocolate. No need to hide it.

This is just a little something I woke up thinking about: My single girlfriends think that finding a mate is going to solve all their problems, while those of us hunkered down in the marital trench roll our eyes backwards and growl when we hear them whining about loneliness. Don't they read the statistics on divorce?

July 3
(Loathe the thought of another national

Wednesday

holiday coming up. Even if the concept is
one I can digest. Just not in the mood for patriotism
swarming with consumerist hype and hoopla and all those *Explosive Sales Events Going on In A Store Near You*. Stars and stripes and dollar signs all jumbled up together.)
3:12 am

You gave away your Pussy Power, she whispers. It's the Voice of my Menopausal Mind, Queen Mena. *You gave your Pussy Power to anyone who looked at you and smiled. And you called it freedom.* Huh, she says with a slap on her hip. *Real freedom isn't a one-night stand. It's a heartfelt commitment to love. But that's OK. We don't have to go into that right now. Back then, when you were twenty, you didn't have any teachers to help you understand that you are a divine child. You simply didn't know any better. You bought into the sex, drugs, and doing IT with every tom, and hairy dick because you thought it was the key to the doors of Cosmic Mystery.*

I try to intrude, interrupting by clearing my throat, "That's Tom, Dick, and Harry."

You know what I mean. And who can remember all their names anyway? The whole movement was probably another government plot to keep dangerous people, that is, people who think, distracted, numb, and dumb.

Well, actually, I kept track. I kept a list of everyone I had sex with.

That's the problem. You're remembering all the wrong things. Right now, we have to get your Pussy Power back so you can sleep at night. You see, every guy you ever had sex with left a piece of himself in you, in more ways than one, she howls. *You've got so many strands stuck inside you that you're all balled-up in there.* This pun makes her hold her belly and roar. *You're a walking carrier of left-over sex. Most of it bad. You've got prick and dick energy knotting you up from the inside out. You're a walking porcupine. Your energy, your sacred life force, your Shakti power, is getting stuck and stagnant in your lower chakras. That's why you're feeling blocked "down there." Your sexual energy is stuck in the past.*

Time for the Pussy Power Clearing, she howls as she lifts her cape-like SuperCrone and a fresh breeze blows across my face. *It's never too late to clear the psychic debris,* she squeals joyfully, as if discovering fire. *Remember,* she proclaims like a menstrual monarch on a crescent throne, *Pussy Power Rules.* Then whispers in a low breath, *But not if your Pussy can't breathe. And breathe she must.*

This healing meditation, she says in a teaching tone, *will take some time. Take all the time you need.* She informs me that no matter what else I learn during these changing times, I must thoroughly clear out the vibrational threads of all those old sexual encounters. *Well,* she snarks, *they weren't what you'd call relationships, were they?* She then takes a big breath, lifting her arms up with a loud inhalation, exhaling with a whistle. She starts singing glee-fully, spinning in circles around me: *Let your Pussy breathe, Let your Pussy breathe, your Pussy breathe,* sounding a lot like an old familiar tune, *Let the Sun shine, Let the Sun shine in, the Sun shine in.*

Pussy Power Healing Meditation as taught by Queen Mena
1. Make a list of all the men you ever had sex with. Contrary to popular politics, even if it was only oral, it was still sex. And you do want to clear your throat chakra, too. It's the center of creativity and speaking your personal truth. Pussy Power rules from head to toe.
2. If you can be outside for this meditation and be comfortable without being disturbed, then do it. Getting your feet on the ground is especially potent for this healing journey. But if you have to do it in an office chair at your desk, that's OK too. Where you are is perfect. Any time is appropriate.
3. Close your eyes and take a deep breath. Slow down your breathing, bringing your attention to your sweet and juicy, sacred vagina. As you inhale bring warm red and orange energy up from the ground into your vagina, like a soothing river. Bring to mind the person you wish to release from your Pussy. Then as you exhale let the Earth

energy take any and all of his (her) energy with your out-going breath. Let each breath be an exorcism of unwanted connections from the past. Breathe in, release and let go. Make sure you name who it is you're releasing. A cautionary note: Do not get caught in the emotional details of the past "encounter." This is very important because it will bind you even tighter. Simply speak the name and let it go back into the Earth. You don't have to think about where this energy is going after you release it. That's none of your business. Trust the Yoniverse. She can take care. You are freeing your energy for joyful living.

Now that's a celebration for freedom.

July 6
11:22 am

Saturday

I tell B about the Pussy Power Meditation. I've already cleared out about sixty dicks (oh my!). I don't go into describing it to B. Figure it would be counter-productive to conjure their names back up again after all the work it took to exorcise them out of my auric field. Except I can't help mentioning the guy with the micro-penis and the guy who I called Hardly because he had a per-petual, non-orgasmic hard-on no matter how long we did IT. I wasn't sure if I should count them. B says it wouldn't hurt to clear them out while I was at it. So I finished up with sixty-two. B says she'll do her personal "housecleaning" this week and get back with me.

12:02 am
Walt is disappearing daily, and now refuses to eat. He shakes his head defiantly, silently, like a child being asked if he wants some nice steamed spinach. I'm certain he would stick out his tongue if he hadn't grown-up a Lutheran in the Midwest. He is everything Lake Wobegon-ish living with us in the middle of a Fellini film. And I love him for his wisecracks and quiet wisdom that sneak up on me and soak in slowly. Funny how much Walt is teaching me. Two years ago at Christmas, before Walt got sick, and they both could drive, I enlisted him and Mom as my senior helpers in a creative cottage industry, making micro-waveable heating pads; those kind filled with rice that drape over sore and achy muscles like colorful little sandbags. I sent my aging elf-helpers out to pick up a 50-pound bag of white rice while I sewed together the dozen magenta-colored fleece and nylon bags I planned as gifts. (I carry a definite blue-collar, factory mentality gene in my blood and can't seem to make just one or two of some-

thing. I get a production and assembly line going and exhaust myself with the complex grandiosity of what could have been a simple, sweet idea.) Walt dragged the burlap bag of rice into the house, looking at me all the time with a dubious-but-kind-of-proud-of-my-work-ethic smile, punctuated by a Midwestern response to my jubilation over each accomplishment as I went along, "Well now, there ya go. One down, ten more to go."

My mother was happy as all get out to see me busy, busy, busy. (Where do you think you got all that busy-ness from?) And I *can* do things fast, buzzing from one side of the room to the other, just looking for things to accomplish, whipping up the little healing bags and piling them on the kitchen table for the next step, talking on the phone at the same time, arranging the pillows on the couch on my way from the living room to the kitchen, straightening a pile of magazines, books, and notepads sitting next to the phone, and gathering up dust balls and granola crumbs from the seam in the seat cushions of L's chair.

"What's your rush?" Walt inquired politely watching me spin and flit. "Slow down, take your time." Walter never moved faster than a very old turtle, which marveled and maddened me at the same time.

"I've spent too much time in New York City, Walt." I was trying to humor and defend at the same time while stuffing as much rice as possible through a hole the size of a thimble while Walt held the funnel and occasionally shook the rice down into the "lobster claw", as we called the U-shaped bags. "You know how we just like to get to where we're going as fast as possible."

"Where you going so fast?" He seemed confused at the whole notion of *fast*.

"I don't know Walt, just going."

"Hmph," Walt nodded several times, slowly, trying to absorb as much sense as possible from foreign, off-the-cuff humor, like so many wasted words. "I think you might be going nowhere, fast?"

I wonder if this year Walt will live to help me trim the tree.

July 12
3:14 am

Friday

I know Walt is going to die soon and all I want to do is run away. Or swim as fast and hard as I can with my eyes closed, like a kid who falls off the raft and races for shore, flapping the water and gulping and screaming, I'm going nowhere fast. That's for sure. So, this afternoon, I suggested that L and I take a ride up to the superstore for lovers. "Menopause research," I mention to him flatly as we climb through the stifling wall of heat waiting in the car. My sunglasses immediately steam up, but I leave them on anyway. There's a certain welcome comfort in temporary wet blindness. We drive in silence, the moldering air around me cooling too slowly, the a/c on full blast. I'm feeling weird inside and out; a swirling stew of mixed emotions with big chunks of tired, over-cooked potatoes bumping up against large strands of anxious, zombie noodles.

"Do you think it's disrespectful to be thinking about adult sex toys while Walt is dying?"

"Consider it survivalist entertainment in dire times of need," L says slowly, his own subtle style of breaststroke hitting the water with each dispirited syllable.

"I don't know how to wait anymore." I lift my arm across the emergency brake handle and rest it on L's leg. He drops his right hand on mine, saying nothing. "That's why it's called a mystery, I guess."

L nods, staring straight into the luminous heat waves rising up from the black road unfolding before us.

There is no mystery left untold at the sex store. I'm immediately impressed by glass cases lining a kind of foyer that greets you first thing inside the door, highlighting what look to be miniature Persian paintings. I'm grateful for the opportunity to slouch forward and peer at the art, hiding my face in the guise of aesthetic interest, while I lift my eyes, glancing around to see if I know anyone. At this point there's still time to slink back out unnoticed. But I don't. The frigid cold air inside is a welcome relief from the oppressive life-sucking heat outside. I'm already in love with their air-conditioning unit. Just walking from the car to the front door brought on a monumental sweat flood.

The store is almost empty except for a biker couple that walked in just ahead of us, holding hands. Seeing them I hastily grabbed L's hand. Oh, I give a little surprised gasp, realizing that the little paintings are actually an arrangement of Kama Sutra cards, with images of men and women wrapped in delicately pastel-flowered robes, their genitals completely exposed. Penis and vagina sketched in thin black pen marks with only a few fine and fuzzy strokes of gray pubic hair. Their eyes are distracted, staring blankly elsewhere, into the bushes, up at the sky, anywhere and everywhere, except at each other.

Passionless. Robotic. Penis stuck in cunt. Standing, sitting, crouching, swinging from a cherry tree, squatting next to a bird cage, lovers' ankles tied to a bamboo (spoon?). All parts frozen stiff in sex. Time totally still.

And still I get a little rush of excitement staring back.

I have always had a fascination with the retail side of sex. J says it's the fact that both my Moon and rising sign are in Scorpio. "Tendency toward sex and the occult," she told me one day while looking at my astrological chart, her eyebrows raised in one of those Holy Shit discovery moments.

A tallish young man with blond stringy hair stands behind the cash register and welcomes us as we step in. "Greeters," I whisper to L. "Just like Wal-Mart."

"If there's anything I can help you with, just let me know," he grins suggestively, eyeing us up and down.

Not on your life.

"Did you know that Grammy Smith washed Vincent Price's silk underwear one summer when she lived near the theatre in Lakewood and took in laundry?" I mention to L coming around the corner where the butt plugs meet the gigantic double-headed pink dildos, wondering where loose, unbidden thoughts come from, bobbing to the surface like depth charges in the middle of an oceanic storm. I wince at the mountainous stack of plastic "black jacks" sitting next to their pink brethren. I wonder, do these sell *that* well? Picking up the big injection-molded device and bringing it to my nose to see just how plasticy it smells (a habit of smelling everything that may or may not enter my body is a very old habit), I start fearing that the editing mechanism between thinking and speaking (and sniffing) is weakening with age.

I am becoming the woman I am meant to be; my mother.

"How's it smell?" L asks with a grin.

"Vince Price's underwear?" I ask mindlessly, picking up dildos and sniffing them one after the other like a French sommelier with corks. "She never mentioned it."

"Doesn't seem right, does it?"

"That she did laundry?" I move on, pass the butt plugs on my way over to the wall of vibrators. "She had to. She had seven kids and a drunk who couldn't keep a job."

"That's not right either." L is watching me and touching nothing. "I was thinking more along the lines of sex and death."

"You mean like how sex and death are natural *and* inevitable." I'm now eavesdropping on the biker couple talking with the cashier about lubricants, my mind sliding across the vast field of sexual paraphernalia. "And neither one of them should be 'toyed' with? Just left alone to nature's own devices?" I ask, keeping one ear on someone else's world just a few feet away.

"Yeah. Exactly."

I'm trying not to stare, but the cashier is squeezing tiny sample tubes of goop onto the woman's wrist the way a mother tests the temperature of a baby bottle. She rubs her wrists together and then pushes the slippery stuff around with the middle finger of her right hand, examining viscosity. Her biker guy, wearing a brimless black leather hat (isn't he sweltering?) seems nervously interested in the facts on lubrication. He nods and shifts his weight, ratcheting back and forth from one leg to the other. I intuitively know exactly what he's going to do next. And he does it on cue, as if responding to my thoughts. Bending at the waist, he sticks his nose close to his riding partner's wrist, and sniffs (Yes! Sniffs!) the sex jelly like a dog to a crotch. Standing back up, if not a little straighter, he gives her the thumbs-up signal.

"Yeah, it's *my* favorite," the stringy-haired salesman admits gleefully to the woman, who I notice is not as young as I first thought when I caught sight of the couple from behind. She is actually, probably, close to my age, but very—well, tight in the riding pants, so to speak. "It most perfectly duplicates a woman's natural body fluids."

What does he know about a woman's bodily fluids? This I simply cannot imagine. L and I are now standing shoulder to shoulder, a slack-jawed audience facing the slippery show. We quickly turn away when the woman spots us staring, nearly tripping over each other like clowns in a circus act. And just as quickly slip through the same door we came in, the cashier calling behind us from the lubitorium at the counter, "Have a rousing good day" in a slightly salacious manner, if I do say so myself.

At home, after getting Mom fed and making sure Walt is comfortable, we take a walk on the beach. Turtle season is at its peak. The mating pairs will soon be heading for who knows where in the eternal round of reptilian love. Along a secluded area of the beach, I hear the ocean calling out to us, yearning for skin. I grab L's hand and suggestively grin, "Let's take a dip." Without hesitation we shed our clothes and slip into the warm ocean water just as the sun is setting. We float and roll, diving and rising like dolphins at play, sharing an urgent truth. Weightless in the shimmering softness of liquid bliss, I am free and fearless. As far from death as we can get, I slide up next to L and wrap my legs around his waist. Arching backwards and lifting my breasts now floating up like instant miniature islands, twin sisters born in a vast blue-green sea, I let my arms dangle outstretched beside me, trusting my weight to the waves and the strength of L's hands holding me tightly around the waist. I lift my head and we kiss tenderly, hungrily, our lips slippery, salty and smooth. L nibbles at my nipples, licking his lips, making yum yum sounds. As he slips into me with a long sigh, a tingling tremble rushes up my spine. I notice the thin brim of a platinum Moon rising over his shoulder, skirting through a bank of cantaloupe-colored clouds. Earth. Water. Fire within.

Breathing In. Breathing Out.

The force of each wave pushes us together and just as gently tugs to pull us apart; all in perfect pulse and timing. I surrender to this natural ecstasy and familiar recital of human mating, wet and breathy and rhythmic. The hot dampness of our bodies merging with the heavy Florida air.

There is no better lubrication than the sea.

July 17
3:21 am

Wednesday

It will never get cooler here. It is so friggin' hot. Who am I trying to convince? Temperatures are still slogging between the low- to mid-nineties with infinite dense humidity. My New England body yearns for dry, breezy, autumnal relief. The startling dream that woke me up in the middle of a New Jersey winter and brought me to the torrid tropics just a few years ago is starting to feel like a nightmare. I admit I feel very small complaining about the weather. But I am uncomfortable. My menopausal body cannot tolerate the unending heat, inside and out. I can't pretend not to exist.

Walt's pain relief, six sticky chemical patches, arrived by special courier in a little brown wrapper. A hefty dose of drugs is sitting next to me, very next to me.

"I'd like to buy a vowel, please," a hyper voice yells from the other room, the "nursery" as L and I affectionately (and wearily) call it these days; the room where our two aging "kids" are unwinding their lives. Mom is watching TV. Walt is watching Mom. He never takes his eyes off her when she sits in the rocker next to his bed. She is his "lovely bride", as he so affectionately calls her.

Yes, a vowel would be nice; a long, open instinctive sound rising up and lifting me to a faraway peaceful island, where I can forget about dying, death, and diseases waiting for me in the next TV commercial, where pharmaceuticals are sold like candy, and aging parents are happily and actively wearing their adult diapers with a smile. Adult diapers do not bring smiles to our faces here, in the reality show that is our lives. Dying is all pus, puke, poop, and mucus. No wonder the spiritual side of this natural process is emphasized. Something has to keep our minds busy while our hearts bleed.

It's obvious. I am suffering from Full Moon whiplash, even though we are only days past the dark of the Moon, New Moon. I'm edgy, with a vague trace of desire rustling in my thighs and no energy to share it. I can barely sit still for a minute. My ass hurts; my wrists ache. I even look pregnant. Not an ounce of concentration in my mind. Yesterday, I couldn't for the life of me remember the visiting nurse's name, even though she's been here every other day for Walt. Words, please don't fail me now. Tried getting into a new book and it felt like I was shoveling wet sand. I put the recycling in the freezer. Mom had a good laugh at that one.

My menopausal mind is like a teenage slinky sitting anxiously at the top of the stairs. I have what I am now certain of is an attention surplus disorder. Talking to the delivery man who brought Walt's meds this afternoon, who failed to get my overly ambitious attention hammered down in a few seconds of chit chat, I started wandering, wondering with kinky curiosity, what color underwear he's wearing, if any? What he looks like naked with a towel wrapped around his waist? What the top of his head would look like with his lips on my nipple and his finger diddling my fiddle? Has his wife ever used a dildo? (I notice a wedding band on his finger.) How long does it take him to come? Does he roll his eyes backwards when he does? Has his wife *ever* had an orgasm? Does she use her hand? Does he?

It's obvious my life is happening between my ears; a wildly meandering mind distracted by the ridiculous. I'd welcome a wide-open vowel right about now. Somebody, please, give me an O.

"Vowels are worth nothing," Pat happily reminds his TV game pal.

DARVON 1976

My father is dying. A bottle of unopened Darvon in the cupboard, where Mom keeps the few remaining pieces of her wedding glass set, the "Wheat" collection, including several stemmed pieces, both brandy-snifter size, and larger, wider-rimmed champagne glasses. Only odd numbers remain. Three of this, five of that. Our house never saw a bottle of champagne. I knew it was special only by the TV ads around the holidays and weddings. When I finally did get a taste of the bubbly stuff I didn't think it was any big deal. It made me sneeze. Next to the mostly tobacco-yellowed stemware lived the hi-ball glasses that my brother sent home from Germany when he was stationed there in the army. Frankfurt or Hamburg. I can't remember.

I was eleven when he "signed up" to see the world. I do remember marveling at foreign towns that sounded like my favorite Saturday-night foods and wondering if those towns ate anything other than what their names implied. On one side of each glass, in an original set of six, is a brightly colored decal decoration lighting a big European city: *Madrid* (red), *Paris* (turquoise blue), *Rome* (green), *London* (orange), *Amsterdam* (yellow), *Athens* (white). At age twenty-four, when I returned home from California to help take care of my dying father I did notice, reaching into the cupboard, past the wedding stemware, how perfectly the little brown prescription bottle fit snugly just under the edge of *Paris*. I wrapped my fingers around the amber-colored plastic and read the warning labels. No, I wouldn't lift my father's pain meds, not then, anyway. It would be another year, a few months after my father died, before I'd be popping pills and thinking nothing of it.

July 21
3:23 am

Sunday

I've been crying for days, possibly years. Not continuously, no. If I did that everyone would know how I feel. No, I cry in private. I cry at night, in the bathroom when I'm very alone. I cry when my husband is sleeping, when he's working. I cry when I read the newspaper, when I watch TV (which is rare, thank goodness), read a book, listen to a stupid, sad song.

All these exterior devices are really opportunities in disguise.

I can empty my sadness in the guise of someone else's. I'd like to think there will come a time when I will be empty of it. The past. When I will no longer have to cry over something that happened long before I was born. Or the tears that come from longing for something that may never arrive.

Just this morning I was reading about Bonnie Blair's triumphant success at Lillehammer when she won her fifth gold medal. Winning a gold medal isn't what made me cry. That our names are the same doesn't touch me. It's how she crossed the finish line and immediately scaled a wall of people sitting in the bleachers to throw her arms around her mother and fall into her wide-open lap. Yes, this breaks me up. This scene of mother–daughter love that comes to me from black words on a white page makes me cry. The fact of her winning breaks me up, too. Anyone else's triumphs set me off.

It's not only grief or mourning but courageous winning that chokes the soft spaces in my soul.

July 24
3:54 am

Wednesday

I'm not very good at any of this daughter stuff. I think I'm so tough. But I'm not. I'm a confused pigeon. Mom was terribly sick with some bronchial cold-related thing this week. I want to scream, cry, rage at her. I don't. I take her to the doctor and demand antibiotics. I demand Zithromax. It's the only one my stomach can handle and since I inherited my mother's stomach I make sure she doesn't leave that office until she's got the script in hand. She's gotten antibiotics before and can't take them. Her mouth gets sore, vaginitis, "the itch down there" as she calls it. My mother defers all her power to the doctor so she won't tell him, ask him for something else. She just lets him be a demi-doctor god. And this makes me furious. And I'm running through my mind how many women healers, witches, nurses, midwives had to die in blazing fires and get crushed under piles of stones so this guy can wear the letters Dr. before his name. So he looks at her and asks a question and I answer. We're

like a ventriloquist dummy duo. She opens her mouth and my voice comes
out. He won't even look at me, this Mr. Big Shot Dr. never introduces himself
to me. Why don't I speak up? Why don't I call him on his rudeness? I don't. I
just keep telling him the same thing over and over. She can't take most antibiotics. Try Zithromax. It works for me. I notice some handout thing pinned up
on the wall about Jesus or something and now I think he's a right-wing
Christian and that really burns me up. I won't leave, though, until he listens to
her lungs. And I realize I'm deferring my power to him, too.

Shit.

Just Breathe.

She'll get the medicine and we'll be outta here soon.

She doesn't have pneumonia. I'm relieved. Pneumonia was my real
concern. Lungs are her weak link to a 911 call. Saying thank you like a little
girl, mother just about crawls from the doctor's office. I have to slow down for
her because she can't walk fast. Emphysema. I'm mad at her again for not
taking care of herself. She smoked for 65 years and just recently quit (under
duress of my threats: quit or else). I wait impatiently for her, standing near the
car, my face tightened around a hard stare. Every cell in my body says walk
next to her, hold her, help her. I hate it when I withdraw, punish, and hold
back. Getting in the car she is silent as we pull onto A1A, heading south to the
pharmacy. She knows I'm mad at her. She knows me. She knows more about
me than I do. I think about diapers. My diapers. She changed me when I was
stinky and sick and pukey and filled with sickness. She stayed home from work
to care for me. She rubbed my back and took my temperature, standing over
me in bed holding a cool cloth to soothe my fever. I see her staring down at
me. She does her mothering best, but she is not tender. Maybe she is mad at
me for keeping her home. My mother wants to go to work. Has to work. She
likes to be anywhere but home. Working to forget is how she has survived. We
drive along for a few moments and she says quietly with that Gotcha tone in
her voice, "I'm a tough old bird, aren't I?"

Yeah, Mom, you sure are. You outsmarted 'em this time.

Jean Shinoda Bolen talks about how we get these inevitable "soul
assignments" in life and the only choice we have when offered a challenge
that touches us on a soul level is how we will respond. I like the idea of
responding…not reacting. A kind of soul responsibility.

I make a pot of chicken soup when we get home. I give her a long
hug. I don't say anything. These hugs are uncomfortable for her. I feel her
tighten up. I don't care if they are. I need to hug her. This I do for me. Yes. I
am another her. She doesn't know how to take care of me and I don't know
how to take care of her. We just stumble along bumping our heads, touching
our hearts, and hoping the love shines through. She's feeling better now and

I'm happy. And I'm back in the garden cleaning up the dried weeds and stalks that snap under foot.

Just another day in the jungle. Roots blossom, harvest seeds.

July 31
4:39 am

Wednesday

Haven't written in days. I read that Stephen King writes every day except his birthday and Christmas Day. This is just my opinion, but I really think someone has to tell him to stop. Take a look around. Leave home. Travel. Talk to strangers. Play with his kids. Get a grip on something other than the world inside his own head. Take it from me it's not the best place to find yourself day in, day out. And we could do without another Stephen King novel, in my estimation. Even though I'm probably the only person in the world who hasn't read even one. (Although, I loved Jack Nicholson in *The Shining* and how he went up to his room every day in the guise of typing up some really important manuscript and the only thing he wrote over and over again was, *All work and no play makes Jack a dull boy*.). Seems I already live in scary places in my mind. I don't need to get on a paperback bus to take me there. Then again, King says if he doesn't write at least two hours a day, he's suicidal. This, I can understand.

AUGUST

August 3
9:12 am

Saturday

I figure tonight I'll make myself stay up until midnight hoping I can short-circuit the 4 am estrogen nose-dive that bolts me up out of bed, heart racing and mind not too far behind. I'm taking 1500 mg of Evening Primrose Oil and walking at least 45 minutes a day, pounding the sand barefoot and deliriously grateful that it's only 88 degrees and not 92, which it's been all week. It's a mid-summer reprieve. As brief as it will be, I'll take it. But what are a few degrees here and there. I'm starting to despise the Sun and understand perfectly well why my ancestors who lived in the Mediterranean region worshipped the Moon. Seems to be just another irony of life that I moved here because I needed the Sun and now find myself snarling and hissing at it like Lon Chaney in *The Werewolf*, peering out from under the collar of my coat pulled up across my face. Or was that Dracula?

L is in New York again for yet another interview. That's three so far this month, and I haven't had a moment to myself since he left. I'm craving solitude like a toothache craving Novocain. I don't know how single mothers do it. I'm surprised there aren't more dead kids lying around lawns all over suburbia. I made a very big mistake today. I mentioned to my mother after being interrupted seven hundred thousand times while trying to finish up the gold-leafing on the new sculpture pieces, that we'd have to work "something" out so I can have a few moments to get my sculpture finished for the museum show, which just so happens to be too soon to mention. She looked at me as if I forgot to tell her that I was an artist and it was all new to her and how could I have left her out of my life. Instead she says very quietly, "You're getting tired of me, aren't you?" She was so sad and scared thinking that "something" probably meant I was going to dump her off in one of those nursing homes where you're tied to the bed and fed mushy, white food, just so I can devote my life to some stupid piece of sculpture. I almost broke into tears because it did seem actually very stupid to make a cold piece of glass more important than the most enduring, beautiful being right in front of my eyes. I have to remember that I can't include her brain in on my thinking. It's torture enough for me to be in my brain trying to find solutions. I have to instead come up with the answers and then let her in on the fun things I have lined up for her while I'm wasting my time in selfish pursuit of meaning. What I really need to be doing is remembering that there's nothing more important than love and see if I can keep it in mind when every part of me wants to wrestle her to the floor with a roll of duct tape.

So I finally snuck off to the bookstore and made another mistake that scared the crap out of me. When I came out of the store, I lost the car. Just totally stood there like a transparent boulder, only a few steps out the door, totally dumbstruck. It wasn't so much that I couldn't remember where I parked. I couldn't remember where I was. The parking lot didn't look the least bit familiar and I wasn't sure where I was supposed to be. I froze, Terror (with a capital T) huge and hungry, breathing down my back. Fighting for time and hoping something would flood my memory with recognition I had a vision of me walking around the parking lot for hours, mumbling and pulling on door handles until somebody came along, grabbing my elbow and leading me directly into the back of a patrol car, all the while slipping my arms into a strange white jacket that ties in the front.

Frankly, I blame the whole parking lot brain fart on the fact that I spent over an hour in the bookstore reading *Be Here Now*. Rather, re-reading it. It was all that talk of cosmic oneness and thirty-hour hallucinatory drug trips that buzzed me out. Not to mention the fact that on the way past the Women's Studies section, before meandering blurry-eyed to the cashier, I caught sight of a rather thick book entitled *cunt*. Yes, with a small c, which rather intrigued me. Not the title, but that it wasn't capitalized. I squatted down to flip through it and considered it pretty strong language for this very Republican-voting district that I can't believe I live in. So I bought *cunt*, and the latest *Harry Potter* book, even though I haven't read the first four (or is it five?) yet. I figure my choices confirm the fact that humans are fully capable of desiring contradictory things all at the same time. And, flashbacks are real.

August 4
4:12 am

Sunday

B called this morning, waking me from a dull stupor. Tells me she bought new bed treatments. "Bed treatments?" I ask, trying not to sound too domestically dumb. "Is that a menopausal code word for vaginal lubrication?" She goes on excitedly to let me know that she's spent $500 on a new green and gold brocade duvet cover with golden tassels, matching pillow shams, dust ruffle (for ruffling dust?), and matching sheets. While she's telling me all this I'm hoping she didn't do this for her new lover, because all I know about interior design I learned from *Designing for the Sexes* and from what I've gleaned from this, my extensive TV research has shown is that men hate, just hate, frills and ruffles in the bedroom, unless of course they're hanging off a red satin crotchless negligee the size of a postage stamp. Forget the golden tassels, unless their only purpose is to tickle their male appointments. But B is so happy and I'm so happy for her, even though I don't know a pillow sham from a game show. We celebrate her sensual bedroom makeover with loud and lewd hoots and a You Go Girl lusty cheer.

I hang up wondering why I didn't get the girlie-girl gene.

August 5   Monday

I never thought I'd end up in the hospital. Had no idea that when L and I left to go out to dinner at our favorite beachside taco joint that he'd be racing me to the emergency room, my palms flat out and pressed against my crazy chest thinking I'm having a heart attack. Nope. Never dreamed it would happen to me. But it did. Don't even know what brought it on, but after eating I got up to pee and on the way back from the bathroom felt a rush of anxiety that nearly tore off the top of my head. My heart went into disco fever, doing flip-flops like a jumping bean on mescaline, my mind racing right alongside it. I thought for sure it was reruns of Fred Sanford having "The big one." My face must have looked very upsetting to L because he jumped up and ran over to me as I wobbled my way back to our table. "I think you better take me to the hospital," I managed to squeak, and in a flash we were racing across the bridge. By this time my arms are getting all tingly numb and I'm running a rough draft of an obituary in my head. At the same time I'm trying to comfort L, apologizing for being such a hypochondriac and it's probably nothing and I'm over-reacting and better go through the yellow light because brain damage might set in if they don't get to me with life support in the next few seconds. Climbing out of the car into the eerie light of the emergency room, I was quickly wheeled into a bed, plugged into an EKG apparatus, by a twenty-something EMT technician, who just so happened to look like every guy who ever pumped my gas when I lived in New Jersey and it was illegal to pump your own, and who lifted my breasts to paste on the sticky electrodes like he was lifting a loaf of sourdough bread ready for the oven. I am not modest by any means, but it was all happening too fast and in slow motion all at the same time. A young aide with a Brooklyn accent, who looked too much like Fabio and knew it, went over my chart and then began prepping me for an IV saying in that familiar New York twang, "Wow, you can't be fifty? Are you sure?"

I nodded a small, shy yes.

"You really hold your age. You look so much younger. You know that (he actually said dat)?

 I manage a slow shrug.

"Yeah. You look forty, maybe."

I think my heart started pounding harder. Or maybe it slowed down. In any case I was starting to feel a bit more relaxed when the doctor stepped in and glanced at the printout from the EKG and gave me a thumbs up, saying he'd be right back in to talk to me, which made me feel a little better, until I heard the snap of latex gloves and an older gentleman, who had been wheeled into the emergency room next to me with stomach pains getting a rectal exam answering all the questions about the shape, color, and frequency of his bowel movements. Halfway between a cough and a laugh he joked, "Geez, doc, you get to a certain age and there's only one hole in your body anybody's interested in."

I couldn't help but laugh with the doctor.

The cardiologist on call convinced me to stay in the hospital overnight to test my enzymes. Even though there was no indication of a heart attack he wanted to make sure with a full work-up, telling me that women have different symptoms and he knew that I'd feel better going the full route. I sent L home to tuck in Mom and Walt. I made him promise he wouldn't tell them my whereabouts until the morning. "They barely sleep as it is. This will keep them pacing all night long." He agreed. "I love you," I mouthed as he patted my feet on his way out the door.

"Me too," he mimed back.

I didn't get an ounce of sleep in the hospital, with bloodletting every few hours and more EKG testing in which my breasts were handled more than any loaf of sourdough in San Francisco. The night nurse in the cardiac care unit was truly caring and compassionate. We talked about being hippies and hitchhiking across country and later she confessed to never telling her kids about her wild past, laughing all the while sucking blood out of my arm into a little pink syringe, shaking it with great drama, and whisking it away to the lab.

In the morning I was wheeled up to diagnostics for a stress test, again, hooked up to another heart monitor and asked to walk briskly on a treadmill, after which it was determined that my heart was in top condition. "Well, what is it, then?" I asked the cardiologist, who said he'd done a half dozen stress tests already that morning and it was only 10 am. I was wondering if they were all menopausal women.

"You'll have to talk to your primary care physician. Make a follow-up as soon as you get released."

I was happy when I checked out of the hospital with all my parts still intact. Not one person mentioned menopause, panic attack, anxiety, or basically anything about what I may have experienced. They only told me what I didn't have. And for that, I was happy in my heart.

August 7
3:56 am

Wednesday

Life is weird, if nothing else. Tonight on my way back from the bathroom, in the short space of two footsteps toward the bedroom I get this idea from out of the shadows of a hallway reality that maybe I'm related to Hildegard of Bingen, the eleventh-century mystic, abbess, artist, and composer, who suffered a terrible illness until in her mid-forties she awoke from a powerful visionary dream and devoted her life to art and healing, painting these wild eco-visions of pulsing green goodness at the center of all creation. I think she was way ahead of her time with the Earth-friendly approach to spirituality. And then I think, Well, it is possible, isn't it, that I am related to her? Except that like me, she didn't have children, so I'd have to be a long and distant cousin. Who knows where my ancestry leads backwards. Sad to say, I can name only two maternal grandmothers before me: Florence and Vesta, and I only knew Florence. Since Hildegard lived about 900 years ago that means we're about 45 grandmothers removed, give or take a few. Maybe I have one cell of Hildegard's vision pulsing through my veins, a single glint of her courage still shining through me, like flashlight-splashed shadows glimmering against the garden at night. I wish I had a blood map, a map of the world that traces my bloodline backwards in time, so I can see where I come from. This genealogical tracing is about all I like about the Mormons.

Actually, this thought about carrying Hildegard's genetic vision was born from a sideways glance, a reflection of myself in the mirror while undressing for bed. Slipping my tee shirt off, my arms lifted above my head, the neck of the tee cropping my face in a tight circle, the white cotton pulled in around my forehead, just in front of my ears, and under and behind my chin, I looked like a nun, my habit concealing my hair, ears, and neck. Startled by so much of my hair hidden, and so much of my face exposed, I didn't know who was staring back at me. I scared myself, gasping a little. I didn't recognize the weathered gaze of the woman in the mirror. Where did she come from? I am surely not *her*. A witch in the forest? A washerwoman on her way to the gallows for being nice to a black cat? A bag lady? My arms fell to my sides and I leaned a little closer to the mirror, my hands clutching the counter top, looking like some psychologically arresting scene from an Ingmar Bergman film. Dame Edna, are you in there, too?

No. This round and aging face is not a stranger. Not a figment or film.

Not a rehearsal. The woman in the mirror is someone I know very well. She is simply, merely me.

In every moment, whether you are aware of it or not, you are making choices either away from or toward your authentic self. Get a grip, Hildy. Aging is authentic. And while you're at it, give up any illusions about control. It's a requirement for waking up to the rest of your life.

August 11
(This would have been my father's 89th birthday.  Will plant a small tree in honor of his legacy: me.)
12:33 am

L is in Pittsburgh on another, different, job interview. I'm hungry as all get out. I traipse into the kitchen like the old finical (yes, it's a word) bitch hound that I am. I spread almond butter and strawberry jam on two rice cakes; my midnight snack. Standing absent-mindedly at the kitchen sink, and staring blankly into the open darkness of the leafy backyard, I tune into the noises of night. There will be waves tomorrow if the current ocean swell lasts another twelve hours. I know this without any visual clues. I can hear the train whistle coming across the river as if it's passing down the street in front of the house. Unfortunately L will miss another day of surf. But I will enjoy the palpable buzz in the neighborhood when the "surf's up" and everyone who surfs and those who love to watch are "stoked" and wave-crazed. When we first moved here I made up a little ditty, a mnemonic device to help me remember what the surfers know about the wind and wave conditions:

Winds out of the west, the ocean is the best.
Winds out of the east, the ocean is a beast.

I carry my crumbly snack with me back down the hallway toward my office, leaving a trail behind me in the dark. Like the witch in the fairytales, I will be picking up the crumbs in only a few short hours, trying to find my way back into the kitchen in the morning. I fall into the reading chair in my office and resort to an old relaxing habit, flipping through the thesaurus. OK. I'm a word-geek. I find enormous comfort in words. Maybe someone else's words might be able to give me a few more clues than I have right now. In Rodale's *The Synonym Finder* there are umpteen synonyms for "old man" and not even a listing for "old woman." I'm actually surprised at this, thinking there are so many words tossed at old women. I do find an entry for "old womanish" interestingly enough, meaning *finical* (finical?) *hard or difficult or impossible to please, straight-laced, hidebound* (as in forest dog?) *stiff-necked, fuddy-duddy*. Digging deeper I see "old age." The last synonym listed is *weakness*.

I can easily scream, but don't, out of fear of waking Walt and Mom.

"That figures," my mother would say, in her starchy (finical, *exacting and fussy*) Yankee way, responding to the fact that her daughter is looking for the meaning of life and old age in synonyms, without much success. "You just can't depend on anyone else, these days." And she'd turn around and go back to sleep, snoring in seconds.

Obviously, I am looking in all the wrong places.

I grab Barbara Walker's *The Woman's Encyclopedia of Myths and Secrets* and open it like a game of book divination. Whatever shows up has meaning and guidance. Dog. That's the entry I divine. Included in the six pages for Dog, I read that a black dog was more commonly suspicious as a witch's familiar than even a black cat, and that some women in England, convicted as witches, were hung if seen fondling their dogs who, it was believed, were the devil in disguise. *Dogs, like other carrion eaters including vultures, wolves, and jackals, were connected with funerary rites, guarding the gates to the underworld, and the realm of the dead. In myth and legend dogs always accompany goddesses, as midwives to the dying.*

My chihuahuas within have new meaning.

My maternal ancestors hail from the British Isles. It is more likely that I am genetically linked to the woman who was hung for fondling fido.

The rice cakes have settled. Hunger wakes me up at night, along with the words to a k. d. lang song:

"*Even through the darkest phase*
Be it thick or thin
Always someone marches brave
Here beneath my skin"

August 13
2:22 pm

Tuesday

The hospice social worker just left. We spent almost an hour sitting together in the steaming heat of the backyard clearing in my menopausal garden. I feel very close to M. We are spirit sisters, on the edge of ushering another soul into the dense forest. "Yes," she begins reaching out to hold my hand. "Walter is dying." She doesn't call him Walt. She uses his full name, as if making him whole again. I tell her that I'm concerned about the depth of his denial. She listens intently, nodding. Hospice workers must get hours of training in the fine art of listening. She is soft-spoken and caring like no other "nurse" I've met. When I am done with my rattling litany of all the ways that I see how he's dealing with his death, or isn't, she tells me, in a reserved and comforting way, that Walter is more aware of his dying than he lets on. "He's really quite in tune," she offers, "even though he doesn't talk about it." With her depth of awareness, I am jealous. She knows more about him than I do. How could she? I have spent every waking hour (and many a sleeping dream) taking care of him. And now a stranger at death's door tells me she knows more than I do about the man who is dying in my house.

I must not let my ego-ridden emotions get in the way (even though it's taken me years to develop one), must not complicate something so pure and simple coming through us. Something strong and soft and wise wanting to be heard.

M knows more about dying than I do. This is obvious.

In the golden light of the afternoon, sunbeams streaming through the long oval leaves of the Indian almond tree hanging limply overhead, already showing signs of summer fatigue, the ziz ziz ziz cicada chorus bristling in the background, I look into M's eyes, now staring and waiting for me. "Maybe I'm uncomfortable with my own denial," I confess. "I didn't get this chance when my dad died." She nods again. "I was too young, too dumb, too drunk." More knowing looks. The certain terror of growing old has plunked itself right in the middle of my heart, next to the sadness of things gone by. "I'm scared," is all I can manage from my lips. M touches my head, stroking my hair. I fall into her arms, now open and offering me a wide and gentle hug. "What a job you have," I whisper through my tears.

"It's the most rewarding job in the world."

"More than watching babies be born?"

"Endings are all about beginnings."

2:11 am

It is true that whatever you need to learn just keeps coming around banging on the door until you're willing to open it up and listen to what it's offering up. I think Walt's dying right here in front of me is giving me a chance to love him without conditions and rules, and tell him just how much I do love him every inch of the way, wide awake and conscious, without running away or hiding. This opportunity to be fully present, moment by moment, is the greatest gift of all. Death is a larger-than-life Teacher.

M says the truth will set you free. It may set you on fire first, but eventually it will make you soar. And the rest of k.d lang's song buzzes through me:

maybe a great
magnet pulls all
souls towards truth.

August 18
3:13 am

I asked Mom to play a hand of cards; "Kings In The Corner", her favorite (easy) game. She looked lost this afternoon after coming home from church. Even though it's a bit more uncomfortable to play on the bed so we can be with Walt, our tiny discomfort is nothing, really, and we both know it. There was a time when he used to join us at the kitchen table for a few hands of the card game he taught us all how to play, but now he is too weak, ravaged by the demon drugs, the insidious tenacity of this cruel and devouring disease and the obvious fatigue of fighting back. He is half-asleep now; his eyelids are tiny slits, a half comfortable look on his face.

While shuffling the cards I twist around to look over my shoulder and catch him staring at me, blankly but intensely. He catches my eye and quickly closes back down in a half-here expression. I think sometimes that he pretends to be asleep so he doesn't have to pretend to be feeling good.

I deal out the seven cards of our aimless, scoreless game; a version of solitaire for multiple players. Walt's face seems more peaceful today, a brighter white glow hovering just around his already silvery-white hair. Earlier I caught a narrowed, squinty look on his face. Looking closer I smelled terror in his eyes. If this is my reflection looking back at me, I am not doing a good job as the dog at the crossroads. I have my not-so-skinny-ass tail between my scared and shaking legs and can't midwife anyone to the "other side" of anything if I'm going to bring fear into the room every time I come offering a wet towel for his neck.

I am an apprentice in training, I tell myself. Never been here before, in this way. I don't have to have the answers.

Tonight, the card game is slow. Mom is having difficulty concentrating. "These are some small, odd cards we've been dealt here," she says speaking mostly to herself. I don't reply. Emeril is speaking from the corner of the room. Walt's hospital bed only a few feet from food he can't smell, touch, or taste. With swift, self-assuredness and a flare for the dramatic, Emeril torches the white meringue atop a lemon custard pie with a propane flame until it is singed caramel brown and sweating sweet and shiny round beads of egg sugar. The lobster pies, with flaky, butter crusts that he's been preparing so painstakingly are placed in the oven and immediately he pulls the future pies, pies-that-*will-be*-when-they're-done, from another oven. A sleight-of-hand trick I'd like to accomplish.

A flush of self-consciousness crawls across my forehead. I sense Walt staring at me and catch him, again. This is starting to feel like a game I don't want to play. Does he have some inside scoop, some near-death knowledge about life that he isn't telling us? How did this quiet, Midwestern man come to live with us anyway?

I turn around just in time to hear Mom sigh and squeal all at once. "There," she lifts her hands up like she's being arrested. "I'm out."

I look back at Walt, opening my mouth to say something light, silly, entertaining; the cosmic clown and coyote that is my way. Can you believe that, Walt, she beat me again? She went out on me in the middle of the lemon curd.

But Walt is asleep, and I say nothing. The light on his bedside table is beaming across his handsome thin and pale face; a single glistening tear is streaming slowly down his cheek.

August 22
4:14 am

Thursday

Of course I love my husband. We've been together for almost twenty years. Besides, we're artists, we speak the same language. Well, except when it comes to you know what. These days I'm feeling like a sex mute. "I can't help it," I tell him adoringly. "It's just not in me tonight. My hormones are shifting."

"I can't help it either," he pleads. "Mine are too. And they're moving in your direction."

"Can we make a date for, say, another night?" I'm serious about this. While standing in the grocery line I read that if you make an appointment, yes, an appointment, for sex and then mark it on your calendar you can prepare yourself ahead of time. Like a dentist's appointment, maybe?

"Like when?" He is eager to get it in writing.

"I'll let you know." I reach out tenderly to touch his slumping shoulder. I tell him that if he decides to dump me for a younger woman can he please give me a couple years' notice. "Are you kidding?" He looks at me like I'm crazy. "And go through menopause twice?" Maybe he hadn't thought it through. He's not into cars. Trading in every five years wouldn't occur to him. I love him for that.

Right about then the phone rings and I decide not to answer it. After all, if I'm too tired to do *the nasty* (as M calls it), I dare not jump on the phone even though all the while my wildly intuitive mind is stretching to get a fix on who it might be. L lifts his brow, waiting to see if I'm going to make a break for it. My wonderfully patient huz knows how much I love to talk on the phone more than anything else in the world, giggling, howling, and whispering with my menopausal tribe. After the echo of the last ring clears the air, and while looking woefully in the direction of his male member, he says in a quiet and hopeful voice:

"Do you think if I could make it ring, you'd want to answer it more often?"

August 23
2:43 pm
Friday

I'm sitting in the office of AS Diagnostics, waiting for Mom. She's having a pelvic ultrasound, a repeat test of one she had in June, which she can't remember. It's one of those bladder tests where she had to drink 32 ounces, yes one full quart, of water an hour before the exam. I didn't think we were going to make it on the drive over. Even when she has nothing in her she feels like she has to pee, bad. She's here because she has recurring bladder infections. The doctor is looking for signs of "something else." What my mother has, no doctor will find on any scope. She's just plain old pissed off. Walt is barely holding on by a thread, and she's traumatized after a year of taking care of him. We all are. He's in the hospital, again. He's frail and dehydrated. We gave it all we had and took him into the emergency room yesterday morning after falling out of bed. He called last night at 11 pm, only an hour after we got home from the hospital. We had just gone to bed and, falling quickly into a safe sleep knowing that I wouldn't be getting up in the middle of the night like a zombie-nurse to help Walt to the bathroom, I heard the phone ring like it was in a bunker far, far away with no energy to lift my body from my soft bed. At about 1 am on a wobbly trek to the bathroom I checked the answering machine. I was thinking the hospital may have called to give us the final news. But there wasn't a message, only a loud clanging noise and a woman's voice in the far background. I knew it was Walt and I imagined a nurse coming into his room as he dropped the receiver, weak and exasperated, trying to contact us.

He called again at 8 am. He's scared. He says he has to "sign the papers." He thinks he's supposed to be out by 11 am today, a thin panic in his whisper. He is being transferred to the VA hospital at some point this week, but the day hasn't been determined. More paperwork. More waiting. A geriatric nurse friend of mine said the other day, "Nancy, I've learned one thing about this big Mystery: No one dies when you want them to."

"Don't worry, Walt." I try to console him. I feel like shit because we can't take care of Walt any longer in our home. I feel like a hospice failure. He needs more than we can give him. We are spent. And still I have room to house his feelings: Abandoned. Pushed aside. Left to die with strangers.

We can't take Walt back into the house because Mom is going crazy and we are wiped out with exhaustion. I count in the back of my mind: over a year since Walt was diagnosed with cancer. Thirteen months of lingering in between here and there.

"I'm going to a veteran's nursing home," Walt said on the phone, reminding himself and me at the same time. "I guess that's the way it has to be." I can hear a hint of resolve and disappointment. We sigh at the same time.

A nurse comes out of the back room, where the technicians work their diagnostic machinations and where my mother is probably still holding a quart and moaning. "Mrs Hatchit," she calls looking around. I look behind me. No one responds. I wouldn't have responded either. I'd have changed my name a long time ago.

"Yes. Walter. It's the only way it can be right now." My chest tightens. "Mom isn't doing well, and you need special care right now."

"I'm worried about her," he manages to confess, his voice trailing off.

"I am, too." I respond sadly. "I love you, Walt."

"I love you, too," he says in between a labored breath. My heart cracking open because this man, who is nearly a stranger to me, has said three big words my own father could never say.

"Take care of her for me," he adds with concerned effort. His voice tells me he's closed his eyes and sunken into a sad resolve. I plunk down in the chair for only a second after hanging up. No time to cry. Mom has a quart of water to get down and a twenty-minute ride. I have five more phone calls to make before getting Mom to her next appointment: one to the VA admissions in Orlando, two to the VA clinic here, one to the social worker who never answers her phone. I'll leave my sixth message, raising my voice when I mention that this dear man nearly gave his life for our country in the Big War and this is how he's treated! One to the physician's assistant, who has tended Walt for the three years he's been with us, in hopes of getting him to bypass some of the red tape so we can get Walt into the Orlando VA hospice sooner than later, and finally a call to the funeral home, which I'm not looking forward to.

This is the first time I've ever had to make arrangement for a cremation.

Finally, Mom is released from the back room, bounding out like a smiling puppy. "OK," she chuckles, "let's go shopping." She has obviously forgotten or doesn't want to remember that her husband is sitting in a hospital bed, dying, in another part of town. My mother, lost in time and space, is starting to scare me more than watching Walt die.

August 24
3:16 pm

I feel like a plane circling the airport, not allowed to land. What is left of my mind is floating above a crackling storm stuck over my life's small village. I have umpteen projects sitting on my desk and no energy to lift a single piece of paper. Mom is sleeping, has been in bed all morning. Can't even take advantage of my free time. I've tried to call Walt, but no answer. L left this morning at 5 am, driving to a conference in Mobile, AL.

Finally I get through to the nurse's station after an arduous session of plucking chin hairs with my new magnifying glasses that make each weirdly wiry hair look like the root stock of an oak. I catch myself thinking just how relative everything really is. I also feel like a very bad person because it was a relief not to wake up and hear Walt coughing and wheezing.

No one is supposed to parent her elders alone.

The very officiously nice nurse says she'll wake up Walt and have him call back. He's sounding so proud of himself when I answer. He's walking a little. "I have strength," he mumbles through his gums. I am tearful at his strength of will, and angry about his denial because it keeps us from really getting to the heart of saying good-bye. But who am I to decide what Walt needs to do? The hospice nurse in the hospital has told him that if he gains some strength then he won't have to go into a nursing home. Why she's saying this I don't know. Wouldn't that be a miracle if Walt started walking, gaining weight and was able to join us at home and be with Mom? I am giddy with lightness just thinking about it.

I am dreaming.

I need a walk, or a pint of ice cream. There was a day when "I need a drink," would have worked. But that isn't a choice for me any more.

I turned off the light, tossing and turning myself into delirium, the words to an old Steve Miller tune ricocheting through my head: *Time keeps on slippin', slippin', slippin' into the future.*

Woke up a few minutes later, to an acrid burning smell wafting into the bedroom. I run into the kitchen to find my mother leaning over the sink, giggling and swatting at the rice-filled heating pad, hanging limply in her hand. She tried to warm it up in the toaster oven. She forgot that it goes in the microwave.

I made us both a cup of chamomile tea. Mom confessed over the flower-scented steam rising into her face, looking like an image from a Halloween movie, that she has tried hard to cry for Walt, but can't seem to shed a single tear.

"The tears will come, Mom." I tried to comfort her as best I could, patting the back of her hand, smoothing out the delicate, loose skin, staring into her beautiful blue eyes and having one of those surprising epiphanies that burst forth when you least expect them: Every man I've ever really loved had blue eyes.

I remember, too, another time not unlike this one, walking her down the hospital corridor when my father died some twenty-three years ago, my arm wrapped around her shoulder, her head like a tired, over-ripe fruit, hanging heavy on her chest.

I felt no wiser this time, sitting at the kitchen table, counting our losses again, like a river curling through a canyon.

She nodded, but it didn't seem connected to my affirmation of tears. She took a final sip of tea, and shuffled off to bed.

Why didn't the smoke alarm go off, I wondered?

August 26
11:25 am   Monday

My State of Mind:
° Hidden, even from me.
° When I do yoga I see a tight, wrinkled brow staring tensely back at me in the mirror. Oh how I want to "soften" my face, as the yoga instructor encourages us.
° Excited by new art exhibit at the museum, but no energy to move it forward.
° Worried about everything from deadly mosquitoes to terrorists.
° Multi-tasking all over the place.

After watching me race all over the house this morning trying to do the Monday Morning Marathon, catching up on laundry, phone calls to the hospital, the hospice nurse, Walt's brother, and Mom's urologist, my mother walked briskly into her room as if being dismissed from a very boring corporate board meeting. She starts talking to me from her room.

"Are you talking to me from your closet again?" I sound like a drill instructor screaming at her newly assigned recruits. "I can't hear you."

"I said, you're built just like your father."

"I am not. I'm built just like you."

"No, you're not. I have big boobs."

I have to restrain myself from running at Mach speed into her room and pushing her into the soft row of pants and sweaters and locking her in the closet.

I feel like the big bad wolf…up to my ass in alligators.

I burned the toast this morning. Can't do the laundry, talk on the phone, get ready for yoga and brush my teeth at the same time. Rushed to the store after scraping the charred parts off the edge of the toast to get Mom's new meds. A new very very very expensive drug for memory loss. Realized on the way back that I didn't have on any underwear. No bra. No panties. Just me and my lime-green mu mu. Felt strangely exhilarating in a random, mischievous way. Like driving without a seat belt. Good thing it wasn't windy. My fur pie secret would have been all over the parking lot. Those kids they get to wheel in the grocery carts would have been last seen careening for the highway with an otherworldly Edvard Munch *Scream* on their faces.

August 27
4:34 am

Had an errant erotic feeling in yoga, not unlike a sudden itch. Caught me a little off guard in the middle of Butterfly Pose, rising up like a flutter from my twazoo, my vaginal taco. A palpable tingle and hum. What a warm surprise. I flapped my legs in appreciation. As an idea, it's thrilling. All I want to do is eat, clean out my closets, and sleep. I am an animal, alas.

How *do* butterflies mate? What does a butterfly vagina look like? A butterfly penis? And if a butterfly flapping its wings can cause a hurricane off the coast of Liberia, what in heaven's name do I accomplish when I flap my thighs?

August 28
11:43 am

L and I are sitting on the couch looking like two empty bags of skin, our bony, dog-tired legs pushed out in front of us, our heads leaning back on the only support we've got at the moment; an old futon that we brought with us to Florida. I bought it almost a decade ago for the new house we were moving into and learned a very big lesson in home décor: Do not buy furniture for a house you haven't seen yet. When we arrived with our rented moving van and unloaded our new big-ass, sturdy and solid faux Stickley furniture, and pushed it into place, I gasped. It looked hideous. Too big, too bulky, and way too much dark wood for our light and airy home in the semi-tropics. The southwestern-style pattern on the futon cover reminded me of a cowboy I once saw at a tiki bar in Fort Lauderdale (years ago when I used to go into bars looking for cowboys) who was wearing a big old cowboy hat, cowboy boots, and Bermuda shorts. He was probably the only guy I didn't end up going home with.

I've changed the futon cover at least a half a dozen times since, but nothing fits because nothing that simply covers up, hides, or tries to camouflage the truth is ever going to work.

But in this very moment I am in love with whatever can open wide enough to hold me in one big whole piece and offer some soft and familiar comfort, even if it's old, even if it is a pile of cotton made in a faraway country that still practices suttee; throwing its widows into the funeral pyre along with their deceased husbands because without a man an old woman is useless to that society. My mother, who worked her whole life to make enough money to take care of four children while her husband pissed his paycheck down the toilet, is now on Medicare, which doesn't provide enough money to buy food, pay rent, and buy prescription medication from the same "fixed" monthly pittance. I feel a random rant cranking up. Don't go there, my wise voice cautions. I step away from myself and watch the way I can get politically distracted real fast looking for someone, something to blame, deserting my feelings, my inner world to try and get a nasty fix on something outside myself.

I wished I'd never bought the freakin' futon. I shake my head like a dog casting off rain. I cannot let myself get jerked around by my wired and whacked out emotions.

Right now I need mothering; Mothering.

L and I are holding hands, staring into the space behind our eyelids, where I feel I've been camping out these days, searching the fruitful darkness for moist and mossy–rich softness to press myself against and sigh. Alas, my mother is asleep, medicated, resting. I turn and ask L; my head cranked at an upward angle of curiosity, "Remind me again why we don't drink?" He grins and shakes his head. It seems like only yesterday that I turned to him with the reverse question. But it was a long time ago. Riding in a big old rickety pickup truck, I was a bit hung over and feeling all foggy and mad because I couldn't stand feeling like shit; all janky and disconnected, flashes of my drunken father racing through my mind, I suddenly asked, "Why are we drinking, anyway?" I didn't expect the reply L tossed out so easily. Obviously he hadn't grown-up in my mind. "I don't know. Let's quit," he says, like he's offering me manna from the goddess divine.

"OK," I choked. I was only half-serious. I saw myself sneaking sips and lying and trying to get through my fake promise and not feel like a cat burglar.

But it worked. No lies. No sips. No regrets.

Yup. A long time ago. I made a commitment to myself about something and I've stuck with it. And if that's all I have today, it's enough to feel good about.

    And in this very moment holding hands with the one I love feels like pure ambrosia, even if I'm sweating all over, and it's not from lust.

August 30
10:36 am

Friday

Just finished an intense yoga workout in the voiceless space of my own living room. What a luxury it is to be quiet and tune in to the sound of my own breath, stretching me from one long animal pose to another. On an inhalation between Cobra and Pigeon Pose (which I've begun to notice lately makes my twazoo tingle and which I'm enjoying, thank you very much little city bird), I saw the dark and hidden underside of all things, and it's clumped with dust balls, wagging webs, hollow bug bodies, dried skins and smeared worm trails. I nearly shrieked. My furniture needs a thorough dusting.

    Stick to what feels good. Let go of the rest. Prioritize, please.

RETURN

September 1
9:14 am

Sunday

Sitting quietly doesn't scare me so much these days. I think that watching Walt die has given me this gift. When I'm willing to tune into the world around me, the world has something to say, easing out the anxiety that runs in frantic loops around my mind. The robins are trilling happy bird ditties in a rich and rolling pitch: *Cheer up, Cheerily, Cheer up, Cheerily.* A dozen or so round and plump, red-bellied backyard visitors are splashing in the birdbath like dizzy kids in a wading pool. The mocking birds call back *Chack Chack Pretty Bird Chack Chack Pretty Bird* in between a gurgling *Clunk Thud Clunk Spwish* rising up from the motored orchestra of the fridge against the kitchen wall.

A small engine airplane putters and sputters overhead, sounding as if it may be taking its last breath, then revs up and throttles away. The palms are talking, too. Or is it the wind talking through the palms, scratching and *Wish Wish Wishing* against each other, big green leafy hands loose and brushing against the sky like windshield wipers on slow speed? A breeze picks up the wind chimes dangling over the flashy burgundy-and-yellow-spotted crotons, given to us by our new neighbors the first year we moved here. The *Tlink A Link* song of the chimes catches my heartbeat and resonates in a frilly high note. When I take time to participate in the harmonic symphony, even the electrified heavy-metal appliances have a song to sing. I am never alone, but always bound in an intricate and complex creative pulse. A symphony of winged electrons moving and linking everything to everything else.

I am never alone.

When I stop pressing against the swinging doorway that leads to my soul, something wondrous can walk in and sing right through me.

Everything is waiting for me to fall in love with it. Even the past.

September 2
3:21 am

Monday

Drove around this morning after dropping Mom off at the SC, feeling lost in my own neighborhood. The sky hangs tight and dense like a warped sheet of gray, wet wool. The air pressing against my skin. Too heavy, too dank, too close. It's been raining, spitting and sprinkling for a day and a half. My mind is a mad and saddened monkey, jumping, pounding, and howling in a small cage. I open the door, reach inside and hold her close to my heart.

Visiting Walt tonight at the VA hospice. It's such a long drive. He has been basically out of it every time we've gone to visit. He can barely hold his head up and doesn't talk much. He goes in and out of consciousness, waking up suddenly, mumbling about his mother. Mom keeps trying to give him water and convincing him that if he eats he'll be all right. I shake my head, glancing at L with a hopeless look. No matter what we say, my mother is locked in her own world of hopeful dreams. Hope sucks the present out of everything.

So did the bill from my overnight stay in the hospital, one helluva panic attack: $6,346.

September 4
9:32 am

Wednesday

L's turn to take Mom to the SC. At long last, I'm home alone. Paralyzed by my own freedom. The heat is oppressive and unseasonable. I haven't gone into the garden in weeks. Did a morning drawing first thing before breakfast, putting a snake in each of my footprint outlines, and coloring them gold with red stripes and polka dots. Ran outside briefly to upright a garden sculpture of the Aztec Goddess Tlazolteotl giving birth, a tiny human head bursting from her vulva, her infant's hands tucked in by the ears, ready for flight, or the doggy paddle. Undoubtedly a neighboring raccoon brushed against the Big Mama waddling toward a midnight snack of sea grapes and cabbage palm berries. My feet burn running across the patio. Does this count for a fire-walking experience?

Lunch at the health-food store. "Middle Eastern Chick Pea Soup." I feel very alone today and very useless. Yes. Intellectually I know I'm not. But the feelings are there no matter how much I talk to myself on cheery subjects like the best is yet to come and look at how much I have to share and I'm just now giving birth to myself in powerful new ways and it isn't a hot flash, it's my inner child playing with matches. I stare into the pool of curry-yellow soup with bright-orange carrot chunks circling around spinach, thin slices of cabbage and potatoes cooked long enough so that the edges are rounded and soft. I love soup, even if it's hot. Carmen Miranda once said she could be very happy as long as she had a bowl of homemade soup and a song to sing. Now there was a sacred clown-crone if ever there was one. A woman who could entertain while balancing fruit on her head.

I want to be happy. I want to dance and sing. I pray for peace with every bite, remembering the look of ferocious love on the face of the Aztec Goddess giving birth, howling her pain in silence and leaning backward against a big hard rock.

My body knows something that my mind will have to catch up on.

September 5
1:35 am

Thursday

Walked to the beach tonight with P and S; a soft open sky already glowing with streaks of orange mango sunset and raspberry cloud puffs. While walking and talking about this and that in the easy way we fall in a unified walking/talking rhythm, mostly "how's your day going" we came on a blue sea creature thingy washed up with the white foamy tide, looking like a blue-petaled daisy with a rutabaga slice for a center. It was slippery and when we bent down to look closely the tide flipped it over, pushing it further up onto the beach. It looked helpless and beautifully curious and cautiously toxic. We stood silent, crouching over the slippery, seductive stranger, our thoughts circling us. What do we do? Is it alive? Should we save it? Or let it dry up? Without speaking I pushed my fingers into the sand and scooped up the blue sea flower in both hands and offering it back to the sea I walked into the lapping soft waves and floated him (her?) back home with a tiny prayer for survival. We kept on walking, passed another, already dead. Memory works by association. The dead blue sea flower brings up death. P mentions an obituary she read in the Sunday newspaper that went something like: Harold R. Mason died of congestive pulmonary disease. He was married 41 breathtaking years to his wife, Martha Louise. *This time, we laugh at death.*

September 6
12:57 am

Friday

New Moon. Can't sleep. Hailed today. A thunderstorm blew in and large, pinging balls of ice came down on the roof bouncing on the patio and rolling onto the green grass. 78 degrees. G called and when I shrieked at the size of the ice balls bounding over the yard she said the frogs and locusts were next. I ran out and grabbed a few of the biggest chunks. They are very strange-looking, like ice tumors, cloudy transparent polyps, all bumpy and misshapen.

I gathered up a half dozen, getting pinged in the head dashing around the patio. Put them in the freezer to show L tonight.

September 7
2:30 am   Saturday

Still can't sleep. Mom had another episode (or "spell", as we've come to call these strange invasions) this morning. She crept out of her room slowly and looked really scared and pale and swallowing too much, asking where the other girl was, the "one who was eating ice cream with us." I knew she was falling into the crack of time. The swallowing thing gives it away. Even before she starts to speak I know we are in for another roller coaster ride on the edge of her memory. Every spell she's had is accompanied by this unusual swallowing that she does in the middle of a breath, a word, a sentence, like she can't talk and keep her tongue or saliva where it belongs all at the same time. We put her to bed and she woke up two hours later as if nothing happened. She slipped away from us for a few hours. She woke up wondering if she'd missed Bingo at the SC.

I love this little gray-haired mother of mine and can't stand to watch the fun parts of her getting fried to a crisp in front of my very eyes.

When she's hurting and hanging on for dear life it feels like the swollen Dreary River runs right through me. Everything seems meaningless, translucent, and hollow, her DNA vibrating a low, bellowing ache in my heart.

Keep breathing, keep breathing.

9:14 pm

Visited Walt. Mom stayed home. Nurses are amazed that he is still holding on. I held his hand and I'm certain he squeezed it when I told him Mom wasn't feeling well and couldn't come along. He lifted his head only once, then rolled over on his side, turning away from me.

September 9
11:23 am   Monday

Today is good, even though I didn't sleep one single z. (M once told me, "Nancy, the days are innocent. Neither good nor bad. Simply days, waiting for you to create them the way you want them.") The green grass is washed clear from yesterday's torrential downpour, throwing buckets of rain at the windows. Good. We need it. The Indian almond is already dropping its leaves, anticipating the predicted cold front moving down from the northwest. Where else? The porter weed, which pops up unexpectedly everywhere and any-where in the yard, is blooming deep-violet clusters on a dark and snaky spike. I love coming around the corner from where we park the car and walking up the sidewalk to find a surprise visitor, a new plant shooting up, like an old friend waiting at the door. The aloe, too, so soft and fat and juicy and yet so painfully sharp along the edges is sending new shoots straight up into my patch of blue sky. Orange tubular bells stretch hungrily for air, lifting them-selves like ballerinas on tiptoe. By this afternoon the bottom layers of blooms will be drooping.

Autumn in Florida is so subtle. Newcomers are blind to it and ask, "Do you miss the seasons?"

"No," I tell them, lying with my mouth shut. "If you pay attention you'll hear the seasons change right under your sweat glands." Sometimes it feels like there are only two seasons here: hot and hotter. But eventually the snowbirds return and the traffic is brutal and the ocean starts to roar with a nor'easter and the pelicans cast long shadows when they fly over the beach.

September 10
10:16 am   Tuesday

Joined two mail order book clubs just for the sex and erotica specials. J says my Scorpio rising is driving my bus. I think my bus is out of gas and needs a new transmission. *Secret Sexual Positions; Ancient Techniques For Modern Lovers* arrived finally. "The Yawning Position" from the Karma Sutra intrigues me because I think I've been doing this position all along. However it's "when she raises both of her legs, and places them on her lover's shoul-ders" that I realize what part of the body is supposed to be yawning. I'm tired just thinking about it. And how about the "Unite Congress" position "when a man enjoys two women at the same time, both of whom love him equally." (I think this has been going on in Congress for a very long time.) I wonder if he has any feelings, in his heart, that is, for the two women. Also got a copy of, *The Time of Our Lives; Women Write on Sex after 40*. It's longer than I could have possibly imagined.

September 12
4:31 am

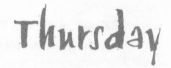

Daytripping:

7:30 am Drove to "Women Celebrating Women" breakfast at college. Met some new people. Scrambled eggs way too salty. Drive time=40 mins.

9:05 am Drop Mom off at SC. Drive time=40 mins.

10:19 am Drive to health-food store. Shop. Drive time=15 mins.

11:30 am Drive to pick up Mom at SC. Drive time=20 mins.

12:35 pm Drive Mom home. Drive time=35 mins.

Lunch No driving. How delicious to simply sit down and not be moving forward.

2:00 Drive to college. Sub for L's class (he's visiting his parents. His aunt is very ill.) Drive time=50 mins.

5:00 Drive back home. Drive time=50 mins.

Total Drive time=250 mins. Holy shit. That's 3.5 hours on the road today.

I could have gone to Miami. But what for?

10:04 pm

I'm sitting here reading a book (ho-hum) that was recently made into a big-budget (probably 150 million dollars or much, much more) Hollywood film already nominated for several Oscars (yawn, yawn), after having had a big scoop of vanilla ice scream and P's super-delicious date bars, and a decaf latte before that at a café while waiting to pick up my Mom at the SC. In the back of my mind the whole time since I woke up I'm thinking of a woman, several women, hundreds of women in a city half-way around the world that is about to be blown to smithereens by Americans. A woman who is huddling in a corner over her children or wondering about her little brother who was taken from the family just a few days ago, a woman who is probably comforting her elderly mother (just like me), all the while the ripple of unfathomable terror is about to tear down her spine, hundreds of tons of bombs about to destroy thousands of lives in the cradle of civilization, all in the name of eliminating terror. I feel split in a dozen pieces, screams and mean shit coming out of my mouth. How can anyone want to mass-murder an entire country of people in the name of peace? How many of us feel sick, sick to our stomachs about this over-zealous attack on a people already torn apart by political upheaval. Doesn't anyone see the absurd horror in killing for peace?

I remember a vague dream feeling: I am teaching an old lover how to fly. He is behind me, holding my hand and we are crossing a great opening, a grand canyon, a deep deep chasm. We are flying really high, our shoulders brushing the underside of the clouds. Even at this distance we can see into the center of Earth through the tiniest cracks. Suddenly I realize I'm heading for a wedding and my dress has a big stain on it. I finally ask the old lover to leave me alone so I can do what I have to do, although I don't know exactly what that is. He flies away and I land on the ground and start washing my dress in a river. The sun dances across the rippling surface, getting caught on the edges of thin waves. I scrub and scrub and finally lay down in the sun to rest.

11:51 pm

My cousin and godfather, Georgie (seems rude, disrespectful almost, to call a 71-year-old man by a boyhood nickname), died today; this morning at around 2 am. I hardly knew him, but all day yesterday I kept thinking that someone was about to call and let me know that he died. I waited, thinking I'd get an email from his sister. And then at 4 pm she emailed me the news. He was 21 when I was baptized. There are no photos of us together, of him holding me in one of those long, satin white baptismal gowns and a ruffled tight bonnet, looking like an aviator cap for infants. No smiles, no font, no priest. Not even my parents holding me. At least I haven't seen any in my Mom's archives of family albums, in the piles of black and white photos that Mom has recently begun poring over, alone, sitting on the edge of her bed, laughing and calling, "Hey, look at this one." All the time while I'm trying to read, sitting in the living room, where I have a clear view of her. No, I never really knew my god-father. Mom says he was a good boy. She doesn't say that about everyone. When I told Mom about Georgie, she was shocked, as if she hadn't known he was sick. I surprised myself at how matter of fact I sounded. I was hoping that my emotions, if I showed any, wouldn't leak out and spill all over her already fragile world. I realize that I may have come across as vacant or uncaring, in an attempt to empty myself for her sake. Becoming, out of necessity, fierce and protective has drained my drama reserves. Matter of fact is how I deliver the news of death. No room for emotional extras.

Emotions are merely signposts. Let them guide you, but keep them out of the driver's seat.

When I came back from my walk with P and J I realized I spent the whole time thinking about my Mom, alone with the news of death. I was hoping she'd slept a little. But I found her sitting at the computer, writing an email. I think she has discovered, not consciously, that writing helps, and may even heal the hurt. Tucking her in tonight she looked up at me with baby animal eyes and said, "You know, I don't feel that tired. I'm just not ready to log off right now." So she got back up and started writing a letter to a longtime friend. Instinctively she knows what she needs, even if she can't always remember what she wants.

September 13
4:21 am

Friday

I'm getting concerned that I have become so emotion-less. To be ruled and now abandoned by the same cruel master hurts, any way you look at it.

I think I expect too much. I want people to be better humans than they can be. Expect too much of myself, too. Gotta go easy on life. Because it's just life doing what life does. Coming and going and staying just long enough to teach me how to whistle and smile and digest cucumbers.

My life, my outsides, my insides are all mangled up in everyone else's. I feel things that don't belong to me. And what I need to feel I can't put my mind on. Something warm and old and familiar is living me, living through me. And I want to get to know the source of the hollow echo that bounces around my heart.

In Africa they say: If you tell the truth, you better have a horse by the door.

September 14
3:23 am

Saturday

Took Mom to the local historical museum on A1A. Saw the video on the treasure hunters searching for doubloons, pieces-of-eight, and the Queen's jewels, offshore from a galleon of eleven ships sunk in a July hurricane in 1715. All ships were carrying millions of dollars worth of booty, all for the Queen of Spain, who refused to consummate her marriage to the king until he paid her dowry. So he sent the fleet around the world pillaging for gold and precious jewels to present to the Queen. But, alas, all was lost and eventually the Spanish Empire crumbled. All for a fuck. Or to save sexual face, which isn't that uncommon, it seems.

Mom sat entirely engrossed for the full 45 minutes, nearly a life record. The new meds are really helping. She can concentrate on the moment. At this point I think she's doing better than I am!

Made potato and kale soup for lunch. The wind is blustery and I thought I'd never be saying this, but the heat of the soup feels good. Then off to the peace rally. Mom is in her wheelchair as we are marching almost a mile to the town hall. She has a smile on her face the whole time, flashing the peace sign to cars passing by who are flipping her the bird. A reporter sees the wheelchair and I can see his mind working overtime. Oh Good. Elderly in wheelchair will make good image. I want to jump in and answer the reporter's questions for her. I am a protective dragon daughter running out of estrogen.

I can get fierce. I don't want my mother to be embarrassed or, worse yet, dismissed. Don't want it to look like she is my prop and billboard for my own agenda either.

"Why are you here?" the pesky reporter asked in a somewhat patronizing voice. My mother is quiet, which the reporter interprets as confusion and starts to walk away. I want to throw my peace placard at the busy little dip-shit, who is now ignoring my mother in favor of some fast-talking rally promoter. "Peace," my mother calls after him loudly. "I want peace." My mother finds her stride and lets loose, alas. I sigh big relief. "No more wars. We've had enough." My mother seems angry and happy at the same time. The reporter likes her simple response and goes on to ask about her husband. Mom corrects her, "Husbands," she says lifting her head and adjusting herself forward. "Both in World War Two. My son too was in Vietnam." The reporter is scribbling madly. My mother enjoys all the attention. She did OK. I'm relieved. My mother is like Peter Sellers in the movie *Being There*. No matter what she says it sounds absolutely profound.

It was raining when we left.

Home long enough to change and then back out to the "All-Irish Revue" at the church; Ireland's version of The Ed Sullivan Show, on the road. Mom and I found two seats close to the front, but off to the side, with a good view of the small stage. I found myself laughing and clapping and feeling happy smack dab in the middle of a church auditorium. I looked across the aisle of faces; all old and formless and tan and wrinkled; Republican, retired, military. Wondered what dump truck dropped me in the parking lot by mistake. The woman to my left reeked of rancid perfume, Tabu maybe. I couldn't move any closer to my mother without sitting on her lap. All in all, the Irish step dancers brightened up my life. So young and energetic and passionate. I cried.

September 16
4:02 am

Monday

I'm wide-awake and itching "down there." I'm eating way too much sugar. It's the damned delicious cookies. Why can't I get a grip? I have so little will. Saw a shooting star and prayed for peace. Maybe start with patience.

I am human after all.

What if I just threw everything away? What if I just had nothing? I'm drowning in disorganization. My office closet is full of old cassette tapes, dusty books, file folders, photo albums, shoes, old magazines, texts for software programs I don't use any more, old business cards, an unopened box of floppy discs (we have no more floppy hard drive), framed photos I don't use, used envelopes waiting to be recycled, briefcases for my imaginary life as a business woman, a box of 4,000 pens and pencils, L's dress shirts, the scale. The Scale. (I want to throw that out first.) I will devote today to cleaning out my office closet. Well, maybe give myself the whole week. It takes more time to accomplish less these days. But who's comparing now to then. It will take what it takes and I'll enjoy the process.

Another Natural Law: Where there's loss there's gain.

Also, I have to stop buying clothes for my imaginary life. No more:
- Business suits
- Panty hose
- Ruffles, bows or "mock" anything
- Tailored "junior league" look
- Big evening-out outfits (never had one anyway.)
- Anything with fringe
- Pumps, heels, or any shoes that look good but hurt
- Tight pants (brought to you by the creators of cystitis)
- Thong underwear (so uncomfortable and itchy, but looks great on Italian women)
- Bras with wires or small pumps that inflate plastic bags (useful when flying?)
- Short shorts
- No big tees with rhinestones, sequins, or puffy appliqué cut-outs in abstract poodle shapes (will consider stars and crescent moons)

18 September
(Hip Hip Hurray. Cooler weather is just a month or two away.)
10:01 am

Got up and did yoga. It felt great to breathe so deeply and then let go completely. Breathing is so much easier when I'm aware of actually doing it. I can't believe how much I've been holding my breath. Meditating makes it so, well, obvious. I decided to take a walk on the beach afterwards. Never know what you're going to find. The ocean sure heaves up some wonders. Today, with the wind blowing out of the northeast it was a haul. On my walk north, I found an umbrella skeleton, the wire bones that are left after the fabric has turned inside out and rotted away. I carried it all the way home, dragging skinny lines in the sand behind me. There were all kinds of Styrofoam pieces scooting and hopping across the beach: pink nubbie thingies shaped like noodley small body parts. I bent over ten times to pick up white chunks of plastic chipped off a buoy, as if someone had chewed them up and spit them out. I kept thinking, these knee-bends have dual purpose: prayers to Earth and a new exercise routine that I didn't have to pay for at the gym. There were also flat white smooth pieces from a coffee cup left by the fishermen, who also manage to leave dead fish carcasses, decapitated fish heads, cigarette butts, and balls of fishing line strewn around their personal fishing spots. I was tempted to ask one of the men there to please take the smelly fish heads with him when he goes. I wonder what the hell some people are thinking. I suppose it never occurred to him that first of all, it looks really bad to the other fish, and second of all it really stinks after rotting in the hot Sun all afternoon, not to mention what it takes to get a pelican untangled from a run-in with loose fishing line. I chickened out about giving a lecture. I really didn't want to explain anything to a guy with a knife between his teeth fishing for something that smells like my vagina.

There were feathers big and small everywhere, too. Long thin quills with black-and-white streaks dotting the soft sand; pointing this way and that like clues on an old treasure map. That may seem like a happy image; all those feathers blowing around in the wind, but all along I kept thinking of the gannet bird (seabirds from Newfoundland) I saw two nights ago on my evening walk. I walked south that night. The winds were howling and the ocean waves were only about three feet high, but vicious, slamming one after the other onto shore, crashing forward with determined force. Not water I'd swim in, that's for sure.

I caught a glimpse of a dark spot just riding on the inside of the breakers, bobbing up and down in the foamy surf. As I got closer I knew it was a bird and I was hoping that it was fishing and getting ready to take off when I approached. But my gut said something else. The bird was hurt and trying desperately to duck dive under the waves and get out past the shore break, which was a relentless slam, one after the other. I couldn't stand to watch. I passed with prayers under my breath that this little gannet bird from a far off shore would eventually make her way home.

On the walk back, heading north, my heart skipped a happy note when I didn't see the shadowy gray bird on the shore. But it was only a few steps later that I saw her. Of course the winds had driven her north with the pounding waves. The tide was going out and she was lifted onto the sand in a heave that dropped her only about 15 feet in front of me. I focused all my attention on this scene and felt helpless to make a difference. I noticed that her right wing was broken, flapping loosely and uncontrollably. I didn't want to see that. It seemed so raw and unnatural. She looked at me, frantically spinning her head around and flopping forward. I don't think these birds can walk on land. I'll have to look that up in my bird book, but it seemed pretty obvious that this elegant gliding, diving seafaring bird was a stranger to a weight-bearing walk. By this time I'm nearly a wreck. I don't know what to do. I slowed up as I approached and she began jamming her long moss-green-colored beak into the wet sand and dragging herself forward, with all her might, like one of those images of a dying man in a desert. I winced at the effort of this bird to save herself. I walked a long half-circle around her and once passed I said another prayer.

This is Nature, the cycle of life. Nothing lives forever. Do not interfere.

So today I picked up one of the smallish feathers and carried it home behind my ear. I have a dream-catcher hanging in the frontyard dangling from a frangipani tree, which is just starting to bloom, all sweet pink and happy. I pushed the feather into the center of the woven web part. Just another reminder. Nothing lasts forever. I am learning to live in this beautiful, everlasting moment.

Breathing In. Breathing Out.

My mother sent me an email this morning.

She wrote, TIME FLIES. USE IT WISELY. (She uses all caps. Says it's the only way she can see what she says.)

Had a dream that Walt would not live another month. No images. Just the voice of another hot flash, the Queen.

September 20
8:34 am   Friday

I hear Mom fussing with her box of pills at the kitchen table. "Are you going to finish your painting today?" I ask like an overreaching teacher. She has begun a new career. At age 83 my mother has taken up with a brush and some whacky themes like "Biting Chalk," "The Potato With Eyes," and "These Are The Great Pantaloons." I gave her a little notebook and she writes down whatever comes to mind, keeping a list of dreams, childhood memories, or just what she ate for dinner. With a great deal of encouragement (badgering) she really does some wonderful, child-like art that makes everyone smile. "Those Damn Hairballs" is my favorite; a stick-figure cat with a big glob of you know what lying on the floor all surrounded in a brilliant neon blue background. We hung about a dozen of them in the living room and L even took one to NYC and showed it to a dealer, who was very interested. But we can't get her to get serious about it. And here we are, artists who spend every waking hour making stuff and can't get a dealer to look at us, let alone sell anything.

Got a letter from Social Security calculating my SS income based on yearly earnings since I began working in 1968. I got sick to my stomach. I suppose I can easily fall into a very bad depression because I haven't earned more than $13,670 a year since I was 16. I quickly came up with another attitude: *How brilliantly resourceful I am that I've gotten this far without working for someone else's dream.*

So there. I changed my mind and already feel better. Sort of.

Also helped to remember all those jobs I worked under-the-table for cash. Waitressing mostly. And the time I milked cows for a day, when I had to get up at 4 am and couldn't. The cows went on without me.

Took a look at the classifieds just in case. No listings for sculptor or Menopause Queen.

September 21
10:56 am   Saturday

A dove flew into the window that overlooks the pygmy forest of needle cactus in the frontyard. At the same time I heard a crash coming from my mother's room. In the middle of dusting her nightstand for the fourth time since yesterday, mother dropped the porcelain angel she's had since I was a little girl. It shattered into a field of white chips and slices with a dash of gold here and there. They spread like shrapnel, covering the bedroom floor. I'm not superstitious, but the bird flying into the window thing meaning that someone is going to die gives me the creeps. The day my dad died a crow crashed into our dining room window and we found Mr Chips, our pastel blue parakeet, dead in his cage, flipped over on his back like a roach, when we returned from the hospital. I remember staring into the cage, frozen at the sight of it, not knowing how to cry for either my father or Mr Chips.

Mom spent the whole morning complaining about a new red spot on her arms. She already has a million of these benign "age spots." Hell, I have them too.

"At least it won't be lonely." I am not sympathetic.

"Just wait. Age spots are waiting for you, too." This is her kind of wisdom. "Don't get old. It sucks. My fingernails are chipped and last night, look," she throws her arm out at me, "See here, it's swollen."

My head is about to blow off my shoulders. The light on the patio behind her is dancing across the newly planted basil, sage, and marjoram. It's finally cooled down a bit and all I want to do is play in the garden. A big black bubble of oozing viciousness is rising up from my gut. I'm going to throw the dishtowel over her head and pull it real tight around her neck.

"Get a life," I scream. "You're 83 years old. Something's got to give. So what, your ass hurts." I turn around and point to my own rear end. "I have a pain in my ass, too. Stop eating all that junk food you get at the Senior Center. You've got to take care of yourself, for Christ's sake."

Like a kicked puppy, my mother lifts herself from the table. She is now limping and dragging one leg behind the other, faking a buckled knee. I jerk toward her instantly to catch her. I am whiplashed into the cell marked, Shameful Daughter: Intolerant, Impatient, Unkind. I am my own jury, judge, and jailer.

"I need a nap," she whimpers.

I can't stop now. I'm on a roll and I hate myself even before I speak what I know I shouldn't. Don't do it, I hear from deep inside. You'll pay. A frantic inner voice and a crying child within tugging at my shirtsleeve is not enough inner wisdom to shut me up. The words are winding up like a professional baseball pitch, taking only a few seconds to work their way to my throat, pressing to fly.

"You just woke up." I yell.

"Just wait," she glances back pouting. And I am all at once on her heels and wrapped all over her. "I'm so sorry, Mom. I love you so much. Please forgive me." We stand in the doorway to her room, hugging and hurting.

P says I need a break. She'll take Mom out for a walk this afternoon so I can be alone. My girlfriends are getting me through hot flashes, mood swings, my aging mother, and a serious addiction to chocolate. Thank goodness for the small circle of menopausal women in my neighborhood.

September 25
(Somewhere along the line I
missed Equinox. Could use some
balance in all areas.)
4:44 am

Why can't I just shut my mouth, smile, be happy, and take my mother to church? No. Instead I have to grumble and groan, get up late, cause my mother to get anxious and start pacing. Then I hate myself and feel guilty because her feelings are hurt. Can guilt be an addiction?

The man sitting two pews ahead of us has no ears. How convenient is that? I make a mental note to make sure I lather up the tops of my ears with sun block.

My mother is totally in love with the priest, Father N. She loves him like she loved my father, the way any woman finds herself in love with a completely inaccessible man.

During our beach walk J and I talk about sex, and our slacking libidos.

"I just give him a Monica Lewinsky when I'm tired," she confides with an air of experienced knowledge. "That's all he wants anyway." She is resigned and a tad bit proud to have come to this insightful conclusion.

"I want a new couch," I confess.

September 29
9:54 pm
Sunday

Took my mother to the movies last night. It was her 52nd anniversary, or would have been had my father lived. L went surfing with the guys to Disney's fake wave tank so it was just me and Mom and memories. We saw *You've Got Mail* at one of those dollar theatres that shows movies long gone. I sort of liked it. A sappy kind of "poor woman victimized by rich man; rich man redeems himself by rescuing poor woman" plot line. Of course Tom Hanks is the quintessential rich guy and Meg Ryan the quirky, cute "girl" of his dreams. I did like the fact that Nora Ephron and her sister Delia co-wrote and produced it. Nora directed it. There were some low hits on the male species. I think it's the trend to just do the Harlequin thing on screen. Or was it always and I wasn't paying any attention?

Jean Stapleton plays a wise crone who says to Meg when she decides to close her bookstore because Hanks has opened up a big chain and sucked all the business away (which in fact is reality these days, isn't it?), "Good. I'm glad you're closing. It takes courage to let go and not know where you're going. You're a brave woman."

Anyway, Mom and I enjoyed the movie. I felt so very close and snuggly with her, sitting in forced, dark silence. Amazing that I came from her. Lived in her. This awesome birth thing never ceases to amaze me.

She's been really happy lately. Losing her memory has helped that, for sure. I think that if the only thing I do until the day she dies is make her happy, then I will have lived a good purpose. And maybe it's really that simple. Simpler than I ever imagined. *I look everywhere outside myself for purpose and maybe it's sitting here right next to me.* And that wouldn't be so bad after all. I have the ability to contribute to making one life better. (Well, aside from my own, that is.)

My philosophical reverie was broken by the only thing she said during the whole movie.

"That Tom Hanks sure is fat."

When we left the theater I held her arm and walked slowly with her up the incline exiting the room. "You OK, Mom?" She was limping and grunting.

"I'm like an old cat," she chuckled. "Takes a little longer to get up and get going than it used to."

She held on to my waist, her arm wrapped around me tightly. I felt a little electric buzz between us. Mother and Daughter. There were several of us coded Mother/Daughter pairs slowly leaving the theater. I wanted to gather us all together and talk about this passage in our lives; mothering our mothers and even if there's no cultural support, how do we lift ourselves up when it all looks downhill. Knowing I was not alone comforted me, on the inside. We kept on gimping until we were out. We reached a narrow red-brick path cutting across the grass to the car. We didn't let go, but laughed like girls trying to fit on the sidewalk made for one, pushing our hips together and wobbling.

We did it. We had fun together. We found joy in very small steps.

It takes courage to let go and not know where you're going.

On the way home while driving down A1A I nearly ran into a huge heap of a human slumped over a bucket by the side of the road. There was a bike bound and bundled with what looked like clothes and bags and blankets and loose ends sticking out everywhere and this shadow of a human sitting on one of those white plastic pails from a construction site or like the ones the fishermen use. It was dark and mostly what I caught were outlines, but familiar big-city-homeless outlines. I think he was passed out and just slumped where he sat, falling into the southbound lane. The whole scene scared me. Not that this was a homeless person, but that I nearly killed someone. I pulled into the fire station just south of the golf course and asked the volunteer there to call the sheriff. He seemed less alarmed than I did and he promised to call for help. I got back in the car and we drove home. After a few seconds of silence my mother said, "I think your father would have ended up like that if I hadn't stayed with him."

"Yup. I think you're right, Mom."

And maybe my mother had a single, simple purpose too. Not a huge, big one. But a small purpose; worthy and honorable. After all, those who care for the homeless are granted great praise.

Maybe it's just that simple.

September 30
3:23 am

Monday

The garden is pushing up nasturtiums, fennel, lettuce, and I just planted sunflowers. The tomatoes are now ripening and the basil is going in for a third round of flowers. If I clip them off I'm sure to get basil for weeks to come. Onions are everywhere, like soft spiky-green sculpture flopping all over the place. L and I planted five trees in the backyard on Saturday and it rained Sunday. Divine timing. We still have sea grapes to plant and several more trees in the frontyard. I never stop changing my mind about where to plant or re-plant. I like these transgressions of emotion, moving stuff around until it finds its home, just waiting and listening until the plant offers up a big, hearty YES to its new home. Or until I just get tired of digging.

I want to live on the edge
of a wild forest and
stir large vats of ripening love
gather wild greens and
sweep away the ragged
edges of fear.

OCTOBER

October 3
(First sighting of stink bugs in the
backyard. A 4-inch female carrying
a 2-inch male on her back.)
4:51 pm

Thursday

On the way to the store just a few hours ago I saw an elderly woman and man standing on the bike path on A1A. Their bikes were parked and they were facing west. She was wearing hot-pink shorts and a simple white T-shirt. Her hair soft and short and silver. He was bald. Both were stopped and still. I caught a glimpse of what they were doing; as good a glimpse as I could get doing 55 miles an hour and trying to keep the van on my side of the road. She was holding out her hand and an exquisitely lapis-blue bird was perched on her palm, dipping its head into what must have been a handful of food. I thought it might be a big ole jay, but thought maybe a scrub jay, a native bird on the endangered list. The image of her open hand and the bobbing blue bird nearly sucked my breath out the window. How long did it take her to just stop at that same spot every day and call out to the bird. And the two of them, or three of them rather, frozen on the bike path, immersed in some natural communion ritual. The bird was definitely not a domestic type. And in the middle of the path it seemed like there was no rehearsal at all.

She took the time to stop, call, and wait. And the bird came and ate.

Tonight I will call for my Soul bird. I will simply stretch my palm out to the golden-smelling sunset and pray for my story bird to nest and hatch me a big fat golden kiss. I will pray for my bird to bring a simple, direct healing story that turns the human heart around.

This is my wish. Let it be.

October 4
3:21 am

Friday

Bink. Wide awake. Dreaming I was staring into a larger-than-life-sized reptilian eye, half-closed and squinting in that sly, wrinkly and snaky way that reptiles do. Because I was so up close and personal and my entire focus was on the left eye directly in front of my nose I had no way of knowing the rest of the reptile. It was like looking through a microscope at a paint chip and trying to figure out what style house it came from. I think about what this eye-to-eye reptilian encounter might mean, and I know one thing for sure: sometimes I can focus on some little detail way too much and not see the bigger picture. Like getting red-hot divorce mad at L for dropping his socks just three feet from the laundry basket. Does dropping his dirty socks directly into the laundry somehow reflect badly on his manliness? As in, "Oh. He's such a girly guy; he actually puts his dirty laundry where it belongs. Tisk Tisk." I guess piling used socks in small droppings around the room is a manly act of courage.

So this is where my mind is at 3 am. And while I'm here I'm going to eyeball, obsess, fume, and stockpile all the other little things that right now feel like monsters in our marriage: hairs and little pee drops on the toilet seat (couldn't possibly be mine), shirts dropped on the couch, newspaper sections separated from main body of newspaper and strewn on top of various desks and tables throughout the house, three to five pairs of shoes piled at the front door, dishes piled in the sink (none of course are mine), and on and on. While I'm draining my mind loading the canon, my animal mate snores and snuffles, sleeping soundly next to me. Peering closer, I see he even has a slight smile on his face. Argh.

October 6
11:24 pm   Sunday

At breakfast this morning L and I discussed, briefly, the unnaturalness of monogamy. Actually I brought it up and then kicked myself for the rest of the day because doing so brought up other things that I don't want to think about. I started with, "There's new evidence that the consumption of five or more cups of tea a day wards off infection." And then launched right into, "Monogamy, although I've practiced if for as long as we've been together, as you know, is unnatural."

L says nothing, but nods his head in agreement. For this I'm really pissed. Why doesn't he disagree with me, hold his arms wide open and wrap them around me, his one and only honey pie?

"No animal is monogamous, you know?" I'm on a roll.

L nods. As the words tumble out of my mouth I can't catch my breath, "Am I talking us out of our marriage?"

"Are you?" I hate when he answers a question with a question, like I know the answer and he's giving me thinking time to come up with it myself so he doesn't have to commit to anything. It's actually amazing that this guy, who should have been a lawyer, signed the marriage license. My feet are taking me back and forth in front of the refrigerator. My mouth is taking me into a big stinky pit. I want to take it all back, every single word. I wish I'd never said it. I should have stayed in bed until later, much later. I pace faster, like a trapped mouse, looking for the cheesy little word crumbs I just spilled all over the floor. I don't want to say that what we're doing, have been doing for nearly twenty years, is unnatural, uncomfortable, or constricting. Really, I don't. I'm mad at myself and I'm mad at all men. "Is it all about sex? Is that what it boils down to? Tell me!" My voice is now accusatory and shrill (Oh how I hate shrill. It's what the newspapers say about female politicians when they want to diss them). "I want to know. Is it just a matter of sticking your wiener into something new whenever the urge comes up, which according to research is once every eight seconds, or is it eight times every second? Conquering another bitch? Roaming the woods, sniffing up trees, uncommitted and unencumbered?" I'm venomous and spitting.

"I hope not," L says. "You didn't sleep well last night, did you?" He wraps an arm around me, leaning his head on my shoulder. "And I think we ought to table this discussion for another time."

"How do you know I was up half the night?"

"I felt you staring at me."

I read somewhere that most of all human misery is caused by spending too much time trying to figure out how to get where we've never been.

It's not such a bad thing to feel anger. I told P that if you're not angry, you're not alive. How can anyone live in this world and not feel angry about one thing or another. It's only a feeling, a surge of burning ice washing up my spine and reddening my face, pounding against my heart. From any other angle, with the volume turned off, it could look like an orgasm. Maybe.

I will not let anger lubricate my transmission (if I can help it).

October 11
11:42 pm

Friday

Sitting on the beach this morning watching S, her two daughters, and her handsome twenty-something son with broad shoulders; a hunkasaurus with a swimmer's back. (Oh no. I feel like a creep even to myself. I'm ogling my friend's son. Menopausal mind fart?) Aside from thinking about his strong arms and the muscles all shiny and wet in the waves, I feel a little whimpering sadness in my belly. Something is missing in my life and I will never ever ever have what S has. No children. No grandchildren. No Grammy Nancy hugs and giggles. My arms are reaching and empty.

My mother is complaining about her hemorrhoids again. I want to wrap my arms around her and strangle the living shit out of her. It's so much easier for me to love her from a distance. Right now, New Zealand sounds good.

October 12
3:14 am

Saturday

Standing in front of the refrigerator. Door opened. Nothing to eat. Close the refrigerator door. Read the refrigerator magnet poetry instead:

    & purple shadow
    lick moon
    after scream out
    how?
    beat driving the crush
    do be next ly easy
    all top ly there
    felt some
    one must urge beauty
    produce play
    dream life
    eat hair less feet

9:43 pm
Called B. While chatting, caught a glimpse of my legs just below my knees. Screeched. My yelping scared B. She thought I saw a roach. No. That I can handle. From my knees to my ankles I am becoming a snake; a hairy bristling snake. I haven't shaved in weeks and my skin is white and flaky and neatly

organized in small white scaly squares that look like a microscopic river bed complete with sun-baked clay tiles turning up in the corners, looking like albino shin brownies. I can't get my mind off food. I need chocolate and make a dash to the fridge, digging up a misplaced chunk tucked behind the organic almonds. Cutting the imported dark richness with anticipation and exactitude I realize this kitchen ritual is vaguely familiar, accompanying the cutting of another mood-altering substance long, long ago.

I am now trafficking in the one commodity that's good for my soul; the truth.

October 14
4:21 am

Monday

Dream. In Tokyo. Leave hotel to meet L at outdoor café. Outdoor café?
Dreams are weird. Must be Paris. When I arrive he's affectionately sucking
(nibbling?) fingers of mysterious Japanese woman with blonde hair. One of his
students? I feel like I'm ready to blow my top, but don't. A kind of volcanic
dry heave sets in and I'm silently sobbing. I watch closely, staring, and start to
get turned on, like all the bad heat in my head is traveling south and turning
good. L finally sees me and I'm embarrassed, so I run away. L chases me,
yelling in Japanese.

Wake up wet and fuming like a sponge put through the microwave.
But decide not to get up right away. I hear Mom washing her breakfast bowl.
Always the same: shredded wheat and soy milk. Clang, clang. Bang, bang. She
doesn't drink milk. Lactose-intolerant. Crash, crash. Glass dropped on tile
floor? Or in cast-iron sink? Let it be the sink, I pray. Easier to clean.
Otherwise, we'll be cleaning up glass shards for weeks.

"Mom, are you OK?" I yell from my room.

"Oh that damned tile floor."

"Did you get hurt, Mom?"

"No. I'm not wearing a skirt. It's chilly out here."

"I said, did you get hurt? Are you all right?"

"What? Yes. Of course I turned the lights on. A glass fell out of my
hand."

I'm out of bed and on my way to the rescue. The third glass this
week.

"It's all over the floor." She is half embarrassed, half mad, looking up
at me with her tail between her legs.

It's glass shards for weeks. Time for plastic cups.

October 17
8:34 am

Thursday

Food-drug of choice: chocolate chips laced with Espresso coffee. Two ounces.
That's what I measured. I read somewhere that that's an acceptable amount of
chocolate for those concerned about overdoing it. I couldn't even wait till
noon, like that old drinker's maxim: "Not before noon, I don't." And there's
that cartoon where the hands of the clock in the background are perpetually
pointing to noon.

It seems like it should be later, not because I want it to be but because

I got up earlier than usual this morning. I'm sitting here at my computer updating my resume. I've decided to get back to teaching. Put my purpose out in the world. Get with young people and the other side of the life cycle.

The ritual blue-and-white porcelain bowl, a beautiful and delicate rice bowl with a happy cobalt blue flower design wiggling its way around the lip and belly, filled to the brim with chocolate chips, sits close to me on my desk. I can barely finish typing my resumé because I'm frantically reaching across to gobble up another little bite. I'll have to learn to type with one hand. I'm sad when I hit bottom. Like a blind drunk my eyes are half-focused on the dazzling computer screen, my left hand picking away at the keys, the fingers of my right hand stumbling over pens, open books, plastic CD cases, and an infinite pile of papers, all in a desperate effort to locate the hard, smooth, cool edge of the bowl and just one more delectable morphine-like morsel: my chocolate fix. Argh. They're gone. Lights are flashing. Bar's closed. Bottom's up. I never could nurse a drink. Funny. I used to drink to take the edge off. Now I use chocolate to put it back on. It makes my mind click. Clickety click. All hands on deck racing across the keys. Mind in a groove.

A big whopping hot flash just threw me back in my chair.

If I turn the temperature down any more it will snow in here.

October 18
12:13 pm

Friday

Grumpy as all get out this morning. Did not want to drive Mom to SC. Tried not to let it show all over my face like a big mope head when the most amazing magical thing happened that just about blew me out of the driver's seat. We were just a quarter of a mile up the road, my eyes half open, trancing out on those dazzling little road reflections that catch the sunlight and look like tiny stars imbedded in black tar, when suddenly out of the freakin' blue comes what looks like a tawny lioness loping across the Serengeti in that elegant, slow-motion gallop that makes everything we do with our human bodies look utterly clumsy and grotesque. At first I thought someone's dog had gotten loose, but shook my head. No way does any breed of dog have a feline tail that sweeps downward and curls back up into a perfect inward-rolling spiral. Certainly not a bob cat. Then it dawned on me. Did I see what I think I saw? Was that a Florida panther, rare, nearly extinct, and only about 53 left in the state, showing her holy, divine self to me and then like a streak disappear into the woods just north of our neighborhood, protected conservation lands (thank goodness or some cigar-toting developer would have her in a zoo already)? Yessssssssssss. Today I was blessed.

Ms. Mopey couldn't stop smiling all the way to the SC. And I didn't say a peep to anyone about it. I want to keep it all for myself; let the magic seep into my soul and fill me up before I share it.

Holy Mother Nature!

October 20
9:56 pm
Sunday

This morning the ocean is like a lake; all flat and quiet. Our neighbor saw a shark the other day when he was out on his surfboard. Sharks and all, I risk it. It feels worse to succumb to a Hollywood-manufactured fear and not go in. Maybe this is a case where I need a little fear as a cautionary agent. But I rationalize well in this instance. Great White sharks are virtually nonexistent on the east coast and what is here are a few big, or rather medium, old guys chasing bait fish in a lazy feeding frenzy. At least that's what I tell myself every single second I'm swimming.

October 21
4:19 am
Monday

P hikes into the Grand Canyon today with five other women in their mid-forties, except for the organizer's daughter, who is in her twenties. They met a week ago for lunch just to get to know each other before descending into the chasm. P says two are devout Christians; one chipper, one glum. The other is a butch biker chick with "America, Love It or Leave It" scrawled in magic marker on the back of her poncho. P didn't see this at the restaurant when they were heading out or she says she would have turned around and gone home. P's friend, who organized the hike, is an abortion doctor ready to retire. What a mix of menopausal women hiking into the wrinkles and crevices of earth. I tell her, "Better you than me." And I mean it. Already I feel like I'm in the big ditch looking up.

A male cardinal is swooping and darting through the Indian almond trees in the back. The vitex tree is in full bloom, looking a lot like lavender with compact, cone-shaped blossoms. The cardinal lands occasionally to pick at the little round black seeds, then spends as much time wiping his beak on the branch below his feet like someone sharpening a knife, first one side then the other. Yellow moths are flitting from one bloom to the next all around his head, carried on the breeze that's coming from the southeast today, bringing with it a heavy, spongy cloak of humidity. I can feel the weight of water in the air and want not to dread the weather. The sun is already too hot on my skin. S called. Low tide is around 4:30 or so. We're walking at 5 pm. I'll see if J wants to join us.

Walking saves me; soothes me. I am a walking junkie.

6:48 pm

I think S has totally lost her mind, and her memory. Halfway back from our walk she says she hardly remembers going through menopause, saying it was a few hot flashes and then nothing. "Hah! You're kidding," I yowl. "You did not have a One-Minute Menopause. You were a mental wreck most of the time. And you drove us nuts, too."

"Oh, really?" She screws up her face like I'm making it up.

"Yeah. Don't you remember how you just had to get out of the house, and how you walked your freakin' feet off up and down the beach, even at high tide?"

"Oh, that." A faint memory is triggered.

"Yeah. *That.*" I'm not going to stop now that I'm menopausal and hell-bent on telling my truth the same way she used to with me.

"Yeah. And how you worried yourself to a frenzy over the weather two months in advance, as if worrying about hurricanes could prevent them."

"Yeah. Well, I…"

"Yeah. And how you couldn't sleep, up at 3, 4, 5 every morning, wringing your hands and worrying about—well, just about everything."

"It was only…"

"You know it was a big change."

"Maybe menopause is like childbirth," S finally resigns herself in a confessional sigh. "You forget all about the pain once it's over."

We laugh. We have to.

October 23
3:02 am

Wednesday

Woke up thinking about a practice I learned in Chi Kung where you spend the whole session sending a root, a big tap root, down your legs through the soles (souls?) of your feet into the ground, getting firmly established, deeply rooted in the Earth. From this place of perfect union with the Mother of All Things we begin to take our first step in the practice of living. I visualize my root center and even though it feels all balled-up some days I have this sense that my roots are growing wider and stronger. I can't seem to keep quiet about what I'm going through these days. All these changes going on inside my body and staying silent about it is like having a Kundalini experience in the library.

The whole nation is filled with menopausal women and no one is talking about what's really going on. I don't call those ads on TV or in *all* the magazines for pharmaceutical antidotes really talking about what 40 million of us are going through. I'm so glad I have my diary. I can tell the truth, the whole truth and nothing but the truth (well, so what if it's my truth and it's distorted like light bending around a black hole). It's my story and some days that's all I have.

My story and a big, wide, bumpy root keeping me safely anchored in my own sap.

11:16 pm

My head feels like Hitler's hideaway and he's sadistically marching my nerves all over the courtyard, barking harsh orders, and snapping one of those little riding whips that cracks in the air like a mad teen slamming a front door. I take a few steps in one direction and I'm yanked on the leash of my own fear. I don't know whether to clean out the refrigerator or get in the car and drive to Las Vegas. I keep coming back to a line in a poem by Rumi that says we need to water the fruit trees not the thorns. But the thorns have grown so sharp and gnarly that I can't even get to the fruit trees any more. I need to bring a very big pair of snips with me when I go into the garden called Me.

Visited Walt today. The trip over was long and quiet, both ways. I don't have any more to give except prayers to end the suffering. It seems so trite and sad to hear myself say it.

How does Kavorkian get to be a criminal, and the bomb-dropping missions over small countries where mothers bury their war-torn babes, called heroic?

October 25
11:04 am

Friday

Yoga is slow-going this morning. Not that it's supposed to be anything else. I'm glad to be doing it alone, at home. Can skip over the hard parts and spend more time in Relaxation Pose, thinking about nothing, or trying to think about nothing. Nothing? My mind is a motor mouth. Runs on air. Why do I push myself in class? This is not yoga. It's me. I tell myself, repeatedly, It's OK to rest. Stop whenever I want to. Spirituality is not a race to see who comes out on top. The world will not collapse if I take a break (this is no consolation to my little ego). Better get started, otherwise yoga will turn into a nap. I start with Corpse Pose. I can see the frangipani tree just outside the window. Tight clusters of new pink flowers. So deliciously fragrant and heady. Will pick a few when done and float them in that little cobalt blue glass bowl. Place it in the bathroom. If I can remember what I was thinking when I'm done with yoga.

Thoughts just come and go. A few deep breaths and it's up and back and into Child's Pose. My head to the mat. Eyes closed. Think still. Still. Finally a deep breath and a long sigh. Wondering what S is doing this morning. Breathe. Tilt into Rabbit Pose.

Gentle on the head. Light in the mind.

S told me that when her daughter was in third grade she made her a Mother's Day card that spelled out M-O-T-H-E-R on the left side and next to each letter a little something beginning with that letter...An elementary acronym... "M—is for Marvelous Mom"... Back into Child Pose..."O—Others Are Worse." Smirk...Breathe...My art teacher in fifth grade was cool...So cheery...Probably only 23 at the time...She seemed so old at the time...Breathe ... Class of 69...Most are now on the brink of 50...Holy crap...Push up into Dog Looking Down...Oh, my thighs...Breathe...I can't imagine it really...Hold in Plank... a plank with a round butt?...Breathe...Arms are trembling...Pigeon Pose...Two tight hip joints talking to macaroni arms...Heard first boyfriend became a state trooper...Breathe...On all-fours into Cat Pose...Want to give a blood-curdling meow but won't...Breathe...Salad for dinner...Breathe...My crotch stinks...Hips back into Mecca Pose...Head on mat...Where did A end up? Dream about him sometimes...Breathe...Not in a good way...Stretch out for Locust... Always trying to sell me something...Breathe...Did the yoga tape just say, Lift legs and hips? At the same time? Not today, I don't.

Thunk. Thunk. Knife on table? Mother cutting pills. Rest. Relax. Breathe. With a butter knife? Breathe.

Breathe.

Done for today. Tomorrow will do standing poses. Maybe a handstand. Not a chance. Stop kidding yourself. Need a nap. Thoughts all mangled up like a junk drawer. Never got my butt off the mat. Never got my thoughts in neutral.

Tomorrow is another day.

October 28
3:09 am

Monday

Driving Mom to get a massage and Santana's *Smooth* comes on the radio. Mom is reminding me for the 400th time today that she wants to cash in her winning lottery ticket for two dollars. I'm all smiley and happy and agree to stop at 7–11 on the way home. I just loooooooove that song and start singing out loud. Mom is happy that I'm happy and starts tapping her foot, too. I remember first hearing *Smooth* on the radio and running out to buy it. "Right on, Santana. You go, mid-life guy." I played it all day long, getting up from whatever I was doing and hitting Track 5 until my finger stiffened. It was a cool autumn morning and I was making soup. L came in from the garage and found me dirty dancing in the kitchen with a huge knife in my hand. I grabbed his butt on the way by and pulled him into my arms. L looked terrified at first, like I was going to slice him up in some Loreena Bobbit menopausal fervor. He then saw that dreamy look in my eyes and got into the rhythm, bumping and grinding…sooooo smoooooth and easy around the middle of the kitchen floor. It got pretty hot pretty quick in the tight space between our hips. We made passionate, fast, and hungry love, leaning against the counter where I was chopping onions, celery, and garlic for a delicious (and that's not all) Carrot Ginger Soup.

Smooth and Spicy Carrot Ginger Soup
(For Getting the Juices Flowing)
Prepare this soup with a loose flowing robe or cotton dress. Do not wear underwear or bra. Let yourself feel free and sexy. Invite a very close friend for lunch.

Water-saute the following in a soup pot until onions are transparent:
(I never heat oil because it makes it rancid and indigestible. At least that's what I read. Use ½ inch of water instead and stir while cooking.)
1 cup chopped onions
3 stalks chopped celery
3 cloves minced garlic
2 tbsp curry powder
1 tsp garam marsala (or cinnamon)
1 tsp ground cumin
Add: *2 lb organic carrots, peeled and chopped*
dash of salt
4 cups water
Bring to boil and simmer for 10-15 minutes.
Let cool. Puree until smooth.
Add: *1 tbsp grated fresh ginger*

Serve hot with a dollop of yogurt and toasted cashews. Or, serve cold (but not right out of the refrigerator) topped with chopped pineapple or cucumber slices.

October 30
4:10 am

Wednesday

Still not asleep. Remembered something else: While waiting for Mom to get her massage. (Isn't it my turn next?) I see a young man pull up on a bike and stop right outside the big bay window that looks out onto the little main street. He peers into the window, sees me and smiles. He then takes off his green nylon backpack and drops it carefully on the ground. It looks to be heavy and loaded with who knows what. He then takes off a baggy blue tee shirt with the words "Chick Magnet" emblazoned across the front. I have to admit I'm getting a little excited; the lyrics and melody of *Smooth* still lingering in the recesses of my reptilian brain. I'm actually enjoying what looks to be one of those strip-o-grams that girlfriends send to girlfriends for an embarrassing surprise.

He's medium build and Florida-sunshine handsome, his chest and back are biscuit tan with a silky veneer of sweat glistening in the morning sun. He reaches down and pops a water bottle off the frame of his bike and starts guzzling water like there's no tomorrow. I can see his Adam's apple bobbing up and down with each swallow. I sit up a little straighter, feeling attractive and silly. I remember one day P and I were walking on the beach and a cute guy came by and I said, "It sure is nice to have young guys to look at, isn't it?" P just nodded. "What do you suppose they think of us?" I was hoping P would have some inside scoop, seeing as her son was about the same age as the guy who just passed. P didn't hesitate a moment before saying in a resolved and disappointed voice, "Nothing. Absolute nothing."

By now I'm settling into my chair and watching the boy-movie on the street and thinking P was really wrong because he looks again into the window and smiles, smoothing his hair with both hands and sucking in his belly. I ask the secretary if she knows this guy who's putting on a free show. "Oh," she says, "he can't see us. That's a one-way window."

On the way home we stopped at the store for carrots, ginger, and cashews. L was thrilled when he unloaded the groceries and quickly moved to the CD player, hitting track 5.

11:45 pm
Please, Great Spirit of Mercy and Fashion Faux Pas:
Please don't let me be an old woman trying to look like a teenager.
Do not let me wear a mini-skirt ever again.
Or if I feel I have to wear one, let it be a Halloween costume.

I fell asleep last night petting my pussy.

Hallowe'en
3:08 am

Bolted upright. Dreaming that Hanna (Who the hell is Hanna?) seduces L in a small apartment where I am living with three women in their mid-twenties. Hanna is also twenty-something. I feel like their grandmother. I catch L and Hanna in bed together. They are twisted and wrapped in bright-yellow sheets, trying to hide. I nearly burst out laughing because they look so ridiculous, like gigantic doggy chews. When L peers out from under the sheets to see if I'm gone, I get right in his face and say very calmly, "Bow Wow." I start grabbing all my stuff, but I don't know what to do with it. My arms are loaded with clothes and books and a chair. There are sacred objects (small figurines and intricately carved stone coins) hanging on the wall and I am trying to remember which ones I brought with me to the apartment. They all look so familiar. I can't decide which ones to take, so I take them all, grabbing at them like I'm in a Beat the Clock count down and I've got to get to the exit door before the bell rings. I keep dropping the littlest things and when I bend over to pick them up I drop something else. I'm really frantic. Suddenly I'm sitting on the toilet; all my stuff still in my arms. It feels like I'm pregnant and I'm pushing really hard to get the baby out, but nothing moves. I flush the toilet and it overflows, shit pouring out everywhere and I can't find the door.

12:21 pm

L is cheery and happy this morning and kisses me lovingly with a smile. Today I'll be chasing my tail all over the place. I better sit and take a few deep breaths before I leave the house. *Breathing In. Breathing Out.* I don't need to know what's going to happen today. I don't have to plan the outcomes. I just have to know what mental shit belongs to me and let go of the rest. Why do we seesaw our emotions? He's happy, I'm not. I'm happy, he's brooding.

    I dressed up as a witch (what else?) and had a blast handing out sweets to the kids and cackling real loud, "Trick or Treat my little chickadees."

    Felt good to get into a different costume.

    Halloween resolutions:
°So what if I'm getting a moustache.
°I won't fight fat anymore, not in my food, not on my bones.

    If Buddha can have a belly, why can't I?

    Last night before drifting off to sleep had a terrible sinking overview of my day with Mom, and wondered why I can't just be with her in a nice and loving way. Made her lunch: chicken salad sandwich (a little dry), not too much mayonnaise, leftover pasta salad on the side and a cup of sliced apples with yogurt (organic). Vacuumed the rug in her room, and swept up the sand around her walker. Won't let her buy ice cream, or any other "Sugar Free" products made with Aspartame. Don't like the food facts on that particular additive. Almost impossible to find anything for diabetics that doesn't have it in it. And then there's the chemical phenylalanine, which sounds like the decongestant medication. I'm wondering if these are the same and if so why would ice cream have a decongestant. I got her to use stevia, a naturally sweet herb with no impact on her blood sugar, and she likes it. She tells all the women at the SC about it and has turned the diabetics there onto her food "regime" that her mean daughter has put her on. I roll her hair after she takes a shower, running the comb through her thin, gray, wiry crop, receding along her wrinkly leather-brown forehead, speckled with moles. I yelled at her again for asking me three times when L was coming home. I just can't believe she can't get this straight. I've written his schedule on her calendar in red pen and circled it with a bright-yellow highlighter. Do I have to write it on the walls? You see. There I go again.

Breathing In. Breathing Out.

I'm a cold, mean witch. I do *for* her, yes, but not *with* her, connecting on a heart-to-heart level. I am a *do*-tiful daughter, doing and doing and doing. I spin all around her like a small tornado just to get all the chores, all the errands, all the everything done, but I rarely touch down. Rarely do we really connect where it counts, in our hearts. And this is what I want most of all. Not only with Mom, but L, too. Real intimacy. Real sharing. Sometimes I feel like she's in my way. When I drive her to the SC I don't talk to her much. I act like a bad boyfriend who has "deep and serious" things on his mind and can't be bothered to engage in a trivial conversation about the number of cars parked in front of the motel or how much garbage the neighbors have in front of their mailboxes for garbage day. I had a few boyfriends like that (but not for long) and felt so small and incompetent in their presence. It's true. Eventually we resemble our enemies.

Mom asked today *again* when passing the church, her church, "What do you suppose the priests do on their days off?" She is quite serious and curious.

"Boff young boys," I respond too quickly; amazed at even my own nasty wit, wishing I could retract it before the words have spilled out all over my karma.

"Huh?" She is a little confused at the word boff, I think.

"Oh, you mean the priests?" I am trying to redeem myself, backpedaling to beat the band.

"Yes. What do you suppose Father N is doing today? Do you suppose he gets a day off?"

"Well, he's probably visiting the elderly at a nursing home and rocking unwanted babies in the hospital."

"Oh. That's good."

I have to stop treating her like a pet dog.

11:56 pm

Mom and I took a walk after dinner. I try to get her out for a little exercise as often as possible. The nights are cool now and won't be for long when summer comes mushing its way across the equator and it will soon feel like all our clothes are made of soy cheese. But for now the evening breeze off the ocean is refreshing.

"You know you're not walking enough." I'm reprimanding her again.

"I'm doing the best I can."

"Stay on this side of the street." I yell every time she heads for the four-way stop, and I can feel a hot flash rushing up my belly and into my face. "Cars come around the corner way too fast. I don't want you to get flattened (at least not this time)."

And then she starts farting like a little motorboat and giggling like a girl.

"Mom, is that you?"

"I don't know what I ate that gives me so much gas."

"Mom, why do you think they call 'em Old Farts." She laughs and winks a sheepish and farty grin. Honestly, I do want to love her. I really do. When I'm making light, teasing her, I think I'm actually hurting her feelings in subtle, rude, and nasty ways. And all I really want is to hold her and hold on to her so she'll never go away, like I did when she tried to put me in kindergarten and I grabbed her ankles with my little hands and all the strength I had in my tight and terrified body, screaming, "Don't leave me, Mommy. Please, don't leave me."

Yes. I am mad at her. It's pretty obvious, even to a stranger. I am mourning in advance of her passing. I have to learn how to be with her without trying to fix her or make her into my perfect Goddess Mother. I want to have fun with her before she's gone, or I've gone mad. I've got to give up my grip. It's hurting us both. I have to surrender. But to what? When you've got nothing, nothing responds.

I just can't talk any more about the color of her poop or the pain in her hip or the red blotch on her arm or the mosquito in her room or how many times she gets up in the middle of the night to pee.

I'm a bad daughter, and I'm mean-spirited.

And I am tired.

I rock myself to sleep humming Bob Marley's happy reggae ditty: *Don't you worry, 'bout a thing, cuz every little thing is gonna be all right.*

NOVEMBER

November 1
11:57 pm

Walt died tonight at 8:25 pm. All Saints' Day. I don't want to get too cosmic-
ally woo-woo about Walt dying on this particular day because Walt was really
very practical, after all. What I really think is that he waited one more day so
Mom could get another pension check before she dives into widow's poverty.
He worried so much about her.

L is out of town. Another conference. I'm getting used to being alone
in our marriage.

At this point I don't know which emotion is vying for more attention:
relief or grief.

November 4
1:11 am

Mom has spent the last three days in bed. She hasn't once cried and just stares
out from under the covers like she's overdosed on Quaaludes. I can't even
entice her with ice cream.

Grieving has its own costume.

November 5
11:43 am

I can't believe how much chocolate I've eaten this morning. My head is spinning. I've given up booze, drugs, one-night stands, and wheat. I don't ever
want to think about giving up chocolate. In the middle of my self-induced,
delicious legal drug spin, a recurring thought has been poking its rodent head
around the corner, whipping its tail for attention. So here's the crazy little rat
thought that I need to just get out of my system: If I hadn't stopped at the toll
booth on my way to the nursing home to give directions to the guy whose car
broke down by the side of the road on his way to the airport and who didn't
know how to get back on the highway, I would have been with Walt when he

died. I would have been able to say good-bye in person. I really wanted to do that, be with him in the end. As it turned out I arrived three minutes too late. His body lay white and still warm, the attendants taking final readings for an official declaration of death. I don't know when or how it got so technical, but walking in on them like that made it seem like it was happening in a movie. "You old fart," I fumed at his very still face, his eyes half-shut. "You couldn't have waited another minute?" I sat with him for a while after the technicians left, covering him up with the blankets and tucking him like I always did when he was cold and couldn't reach down for the edge of the blanket. The Hispanic nurse, Rosie, who adopted Walt the minute he was admitted, calling him Baby and Doll and Honey, which he loved to no end, or as much as any shy and affection-avoiding Midwesterner can tolerate, was with him when he "passed over."

While I sat with Walt's body, talking real softly and telling him how much I loved him and how much Mom loved him and how much joy he gave Mom, even though they were only married for three years and how I will always be grateful that he didn't drink, like my real dad, Rosie kept popping her head in the door whispering, "Are you all right in here alone, honey?" Maybe she'd read one too many freaky ghost stories or house of the damned or was deep into her religion. Maybe she thought I was weird for wanting to talk to a dead man. But what I really needed was to be with Walt and tell him I was sorry that it didn't turn out the way we planned and that he and Mom, "the love of his life", never got a chance to—well, enjoy either their love or their lives together for very long.

I did my best, Walt, with the soul assignment given me.

I felt all brave and heroic talking to him, like he was going to turn to me and smile that sly, sweet smile. But he didn't move or cough or sigh or say a single word. I pulled myself away, packed up his pants, the sweat-shirt we brought him because he was always so cold and couldn't get warm no matter how many warmed-up sheets they piled on him, and the old-man leather slippers that looked like something Clark Gable wore with a smoking jacket and a pencil-thin moustache trying to seduce Myrna Loy, all the time mixing a martini and acting very devil-may-care. All things Walt never did or never was, at least not during the few years that I knew him.

Walt had a past I knew very little about except for the few photos he brought with him in a shoebox when he moved in with us. Photos of his farm-house, him on a tractor all proud and very blond and Lutheran, very hand-somely Swedish, hauling a trailer behind him filled with big bales of hay listing so far sideways that just looking at the photo made me want to lean against that crispy straw wall of grass just to keep it from tipping over. There are also the photos of the three foster-daughters he brought up who still kept in touch with him, writing and phoning every once in a while, more frequently when he got sick, calling him Daddy and telling him they loved him, but who never came to visit the whole time he lived with us. The one photo of a teenage boy with a Beatle hair cut who he adopted, but who got heavy into "dope" as Walt called it, grimacing and shaking his head like he still didn't know how it happened. Walt hadn't seen "the boy", who was probably now in his late forties, for years. All these photos and five boxes of pots and pans, clothes, and a few dime-store knickknacks that were packed in the attic when Walt arrived in his new Lincoln Town car and never got unpacked, including his deceased first wife's birth certificate, her divorce papers from a previous marriage and their tax returns for the past fifteen years, we'd have to go through again, sorting and shrugging and wondering how this stranger ended up coming to live with us so he could die with the only woman he said he ever really loved; his "beautiful bride," my mother.

I picked up the photo of my mother that he brought with him to the nursing home, the one he took on the day they got married. She is smiling like a girl, her hair permed tight like a pedigree poodle, happy to be with a man almost twice her height and width who in his old age still lopped his arm across her shoulder like a puppy and bent over and kissed her on the lips whenever they said good-night, embarrassing her to no end, shy like a teenager, and proud. I showed the photo to Walt one last time. "I'm so sorry," I managed before the tears started, streaming down my face.

Rosie must have been waiting outside the door. The minute she heard me crying, she ran in and threw her arms around me, holding me and rocking me like a big sister I never had. "You OK, baby," she kept saying in broken English, the most beautiful broken English I'd ever heard. "Everything all right. He such a good man." And then she told me one last thing that I think she thought would help me stop crying, but it only opened the floodgates wider. She said that I might want to know his last words because it was the first time in her life that a dying man ever said these words to her and she was really touched. I nodded and blew my nose and she continued talking. I noticed she wore a big gold cross with diamond chips at the four ends, where if Christ were hanging there they'd be imbedded in his forehead, hands, and feet. Hanging on the same tiny chain was her name in gold, Rosarita, written in fancy italics-style handwriting. Her name had gotten flipped, probably the hundredth time that day, from bending over bedpans and pulling old men up to eat their yellow jello and beige broth, and was lying on the cross backwards as if sleeping comfortably, facing the golden, crucified love of her life, another dead man.

As Rosie was talking she caught me staring at her neck and reached up half-self-consciously, half-apologetically to flip her name around the right way. Her beautifully manicured nails had a tiny gold cross painted on each one, a single tiny fake diamond glued to the center of the cross. She was getting all choked up as she was talking, quietly as if she didn't want Walt to know, the two of us, strange siblings, trying to console and comfort in those frozen empty moments when death has slipped in and stolen a piece of your life and you can't quite figure out how you'll ever eat or walk without wobbling or even begin to make the first phone call to let everyone know who needs to know. But Rosie kept on talking, filling up the space between us, saying that when she was changing his diaper and getting him cleaned up, he reminded her that his family was coming to visit, his wife and his wife's daughter, and he was going to wait for them. And she knew that we were on our way and that we'd better hurry. I told her that my mother wasn't able to come because, well, she just couldn't handle another husband dying. She nodded, understanding. She then blew her nose and got very, very quiet. She took a big breath, her chest rising up like a nervous soufflé then collapsing back onto itself. She said that just before Walt took his last breath, while she was pressing tight the last tab on the diaper, he looked into her eyes with the love of "Jesus himself" and whispered, "Thank you. Thank you so much."

I gave Rosie a big hug, never wanting to pull away and face the long drive home and Mom's broken heart when I walked in the door.

What I wanted was Walt's last words to be meant for me. But Rosie knew they were meant just for her.

November 6
3:39 *am*

Wednesday

I was hoping to get to sleep by midnight. Got into bed at 11:30. Finally finished *Waiting* by Ha Jin. Loved how everything and nothing happened so powerfully and so slowly. Turned off the light at midnight, even though I wasn't drowsy. Want to go to yoga class in the morning and need a good night's sleep. Don't want to be a zombie when I get there. I haven't been to yoga class in weeks (months?). At least I've been doing solo practice at home. But it's not the same. I get a chance to get out of the house, and the group energy is potent. Except for the guy who farts and snores during final relaxation. What is it about men in yoga class? Always grunting louder and taking up more space than any woman, as if no one else in the room matters. "Look at me, everyone. I am man. You woman. Hear me groan." I always start out with such good intentions, like inner peace and compassion and kindness, and then drift, wanting to stretch over and whack the back of his knee when he's standing perfectly straight in Tree Pose, just to see him buckle a little. Nothing really hurtful or vicious, just a little, "Oh I'm sorry. My Warrior Pose got out of control."

I'll be glad when my neighbors pack up and leave for the holidays up north. Not because I don't like them, they are quite charming, but because their air-conditioning unit is located only 20 feet from our bedroom wall. It's a monstrous and hideous contraption, all rusted and dangling with loose parts. It rattles and rumbles and drones in a loud, pulsing, grinding sound that I can feel vibrating from my skull to my breastbone. This cannot be good for my aura or my dreams or my sex life, in fact. I toss and turn and wait for it to kick off. Only three weeks before they shut it down, and counting. I hate air conditioning and I pray to mine every morning, hoping it doesn't suddenly shut down and leave me sweltering in the heat and humidity of another day. I do remember when I used to sweat hard and it never bothered me. At least I think that was the same me I am now.

The refrigerator has just clicked on, gurgling and sputtering and wheezing and right behind it, as if an early-morning electric symphony has just begun rehearsal, our own air conditioner joins in, sounding like an overhead vacuum cleaner. With a click and a fleep and whoosh the disharmony begins. To add insult to auditory injury I can hear the mosquito truck coming down the street to "treat" the area with some horrible poison that is probably killing off old people faster than medical malpractice.

Please, sleep, take me in your arms and rock me, rock me.

I think I hear Mom rustling around in the kitchen. The freezer door is opening, now closing. What the heck? The microwave door is opening? And closing? I can't believe it. My mother is micro-waving ice cream in the middle of the night. She's sneak-eating!

Nothing is still or quiet or peaceful, except Walt's ashes, sitting in a box in the garage. My mother seems to have forgotten that he died, and we don't remind her. She's finally getting a good night's sleep.

I love sleep.

November 11
10:09 am
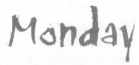

I'm sitting in the car in the parking lot of my favorite bookstore just minutes from the SC where I dropped Mom off for her Bingo and senior lunch. I wonder how many menopausal women are sitting in their cars, writing in their diaries right now? I read that 5,000 of us turn 50 every day in the US alone. A parking-lot, hot-flash jamboree for sure. J wonders if this might have an impact on global warming. I asked her politely not to blame us for one more thing, thank you very much.

I'll check out the thrift store, and the bookstore, and have a latte, decaf even, though it bothers my already irritated, irritable bowel syndrome. Or at least I think that's what bothering it.

L was supposed to take Mom to the SC today, but we got a call this morning from his mother letting us know that Aunt Sis died some time in the night. She had battled cancer for seven months. The suffering is over. I was asleep when the call came in, waking up in the middle of a ring. I knew it was bad news. The phone doesn't ring at 7 am these days for much else. L's favorite uncle, Bill, a tall man with an easy grin and good things to say about everyone, had died just two years before. I don't think Aunt Sis wanted to live much longer after that, even though she fought hard to stay alive, and got kinda nasty doing it. They'd spent nearly 60 years together. No children. When L and I are married 60 years we will be 92 and 98 respectively. Holy Cat Shit.

L spent the better part of the morning getting a flight to NJ for the funeral, first trying the internet, then the old-fashioned way; he picked up the phone and was immediately put on hold. Mom was pacing anxiously waiting for him. She hates being late, which means she'd miss the first few Bingo calls. L hadn't eaten or showered, so I offered to take Mom to the Senior Center for him, my lips mouthing on the way out the door, "You owe me." I wasn't referring to the drive favor and he knew it. While making love the night before, I didn't have an orgasm. I was too tired to work on it and L promised to make up for it "anytime."

I was happy to get out of the house, where Death had once again pressed against our hearts, squeezing itself through the phone line in the early morning hours.

Driving Mom to the SC I realize that someday I will be making a similar call to our family. I will not be driving Ms. Franny forever. Sitting alongside me in the car she's humming happily, stretching hard to read the license plate on the car in front of us as we pull up to the stop light on Ocean Avenue. She's obsessed with license plates, and the awesome fact that someone from Idaho or Colorado would actually be, right now, right here, sitting in a car near her in Florida. "That's Missouri," she says, dropping back against her seat with a sense of accomplishment. "Can you believe it? Missouri?"

"Yup," I barely rally. Misery. I can believe it. Misery loves company. That's where my mind is. One big ball of idioms. Even my authentic voice is starting to sound like a TV jingle.

Reach out and touch someone. Make healthy choices. Be all you can be.
I'm feeling sad today, even before the sad news arrived.

A jazzy Diana Krall tune comes on the radio and picks up my spirits, for a moment. My Mom and I jivin' together to the beat feels pretty darned good. A big sigh. Today is good, or at least right now. NOW. That's all I need is this moment. P reminds me that the silence following a parent's death is forever. Her Mom died three years ago. I remember how hard it was for P. I wrote her Mom a letter before she died and thanked her for giving me such a fabulous friend, her daughter. I cried when I wrote it. P said her mother cried when she read it. There I go thinking about death again.

"Look Mom," I point out her window. "A flock of pelicans heading home."

"Snow birds," she giggles. Then gets a serious look on her face like something just dawned on her that she didn't want to know. "I think they're going to New Jersey. I think they're going home."

After dropping Mom off at the SC, happy she has her own set of girl-friends to share laughs and stories about wayward kids and how times have changed, I head north on Route 1. On the way past a condo complex I see a man mowing dirt. No lawn, no green grass under the blades. What was once a huge green area of a frontyard, the nearly three-year drought has turned to shredded yellow straw, big clouds of dust billowing up around the man who sits, fixated on the dust in front of him as if mowing dirt is just another every-day job. Little bits of sticks and stones and dirty brown debris launching up all around his face in a hazy cloud. What's wrong with this picture? I ask myself, shaking my head and puzzled at my species.

Meredith Brooke comes on the radio and changes my mood again. Like a teenager on my first solo drive I crank up the volume and cruise, wishing L were by my side, his arm around me and leaning in real close. I drive on in thoughtful silence, then in a karaoke impulse stick my head out the window and sing as loud as I can into the thick, hot almost-Thanksgiving air: *I'm a bitch, I'm a lover, I'm a child, I'm a mother. I'm a sinner. I'm a saint. I do not feel ashamed…*

10:43 am
Farted my way through yoga class and fell asleep during final relaxation. Startled myself awake, snoring. Woke up thinking that I miss my red friend, my Moon Time, my flowers, Auntie Flo.

The Moon is always with you.

3:53 am
I'm alone with Mom for four days. As I pulled up at the SC to drop her off for Bingo, I noticed a pesticide truck parked in front of me. A young woman with blonde hair and a cheery face turned to us as we were getting out. I jumped on her before she had a chance to say good-morning.

I said, trying not to sound too accusatory, "You're not going to spray the inside of the senior center with pesticides, are you?"

"Well, yes. That's what my orders are." She pulls out a piece of folded paper all computer-printed and perfectly detailed. I immediately think her orders are coming from a right-wing Republican think tank; a new plan to eliminate senior social programs by eliminating seniors. A 21st century version of *Soylent Green*.

"You can't do that while the seniors are in there." I'm now out of the car and getting belligerent. What in hell's name is she thinking? Obviously nothing.

"But, that's my job. That's what I'm supposed to do."

"Not with my mother in there you're not."

"All right, all ready." She is irritated, too. "Is there anyone in there who has the authority to sign this paper that I couldn't do it?"

Authority? I thought to myself, mad as a hornet that some young tart was taking this bug-killing job way too seriously. How about plain old commonsense authority, I wanted to say. Spraying pesticides in a small room where elderly folks, most of them only a few nods away from their last breath, is idiotic. Doesn't anyone think any more?

"I'll find someone; don't go in there with that." I point at the round chrome pump canister of poison that she's so proudly carrying in her left hand; her right hand on the trigger of the nozzle attached to the rubber hose hanging down around her waist. She is dressed in green. Is that supposed to make me feel safe? Green. Like we don't kill grass. Seniors, well, we include them in the contract along with grubs, roaches, and rats.

Finally we get it straightened out, me telling the facilitator of the SC that she can't allow the spraying to take place as long as my mother is in the room. "It will kill her." OK, so I'm exaggerating and yesterday I probably would have volunteered my mother's presence wholeheartedly, kind of as a test sampler, and with a big smile. But today, I'm the Lioness and nobody is going to do harm to my kin. The facilitator agrees and looks at the young woman with the same look of disdainful disbelief as in, "Where's her brain at?" I love this woman who takes care of my Mom every Monday, Wednesday, and Friday, and makes her do arm lifts with a can of pork and beans in each hand, and tells me in a quiet voice when I begin to chastise my mother for taking four loaves of bread from the Free Bread table, "Don't fight her on this, Nancy. OK sugar, just let it go." Minnie is about my age; wise and strong. She hugs my Mom and takes care of the seniors who arrive at the SC three days a week for Bingo, a little (very little) exercise program, and a hot lunch, picking them up and driving them back and forth every week. Mom loves Minnie, too, and looks forward to seeing her wide-open, totally accepting smile.

The young girl (all of 20?), now nicknamed in my mind The

Exterminator, is happy to be able to get some of her mission accomplished and agrees to only spray the outside, holding up the still-folded piece of paper, informing us that she'll have to note it on her orders from corporate. She may as well have said, You're gonna get it. I'm gonna tell on you. Corporate Shmorporate, I want to yell. But don't. I kiss the top of Mom's head and follow the Anti-Nature Nazi back out the door. When outside I ask, "Doesn't that stuff scare you? It's so poisonous, you know. All of it cancer-causing." And this time I'm feeling sincere and almost a little concerned about this young woman, all freckle-faced and fertile.

"It pays the bills." She says without emotion, holding up the nozzle like a torch, aiming it at me aggressively. She then turns to spray the window frames near the door, and I bolt toward my car.

"That stuff can kill you." I manage to squeeze in before slamming the car door and feeling better inside the safety of my little sanitized bubble.

"At least I won't die in debt."

That is so un-American, I say to myself. I pull away shaking my head and wondering where I can spend the next 2 ½ hours before having to go back to the SC, and hoping the poison will be dry enough not to be air-borne by the time I get back.

I head over to the fabric store, acknowledging that I do in fact have a textile addiction. I for one have gone into deep debt for rugs, towels, sheets, and anything woven and sold on big bolts that hang on walls, or sold in a market place somewhere in another country. I blame this on my Armenian roots on my father's side. I was surely a traveling rug merchant in a former life. My mother says I'm more of a gypsy.

Called B while wandering the inner sanctums of the bargain fabric place just a few minutes from the SC. No answer, so I left a message. Talked very seriously with Alice, my customer service rep, who I was beginning to really cozy up to after first dismissing her for wearing a calico apron and a pair of scissors hooked to a piece of string and dangling off her waist. I'm feeling really guilty because I'm not home working on the finishing touches of the sculpture for the museum show, so it wouldn't matter what I was doing, I was falling into an emotional slump right in front of a beautiful Italian imported fabric with splashes of red and electric blue with black spirals and moss green dashes here and there. It was outrageously priced. I heard my tormentor within, *You should be doing more important things like making a living or at least contributing your fair share to the household finances.* That onerous voice can be so loud and obnoxious and unrelenting. *Look at you, wandering around with housewives and brocades looking for something external to soothe an internal mess. You think a little fabric covering is going to change your life, make you happy, forget about the fact that you're old and getting older every moment you waste here. And don't even think about taking home a fake bargello.*

My Tormentor within was interrupted by B calling back, "I hate futons," she screamed. "I don't care how you cover them they are just one big ugly lie."

"I know. I hate them too. I've bought a dozen covers over the past 8 years and nothing works. I want leather. I hate vacuuming the sofa. The dust mites are building skyscrapers with my very own dry, flaky skin."

"So give it up Nanc. Give yourself permission to get what you want."

"We're broke."

"Isn't feeling good an investment in your life?"

I love B for this. She is good for my leather-loving soul and firmly believes in the spiritual essence of renovation. "You're right. But…"

"But nothing," she interrupts, cutting my own excuses in half. "You know how good you'll feel walking into a beautiful room. It will make everything in that room light up. How do you feel now when you step into your living room?"

"Ugh. Not much lighting-up going on. The futon is all squashed and flat, like three stale blankets tossed over a towel rack."

"OK. Squashed and flat is not where you want to be, right?"

"Of course not."

"Case closed. I say go for it. We're not going to live forever you know."

"Don't remind me. I was just starting to feel good about red leather."

"I'd think twice about red." B cautions. "You may get tired of it real quick. Not to change the subject, but how's your Mom?"

I'm at the cash register with Alice, paying for a drab gold and brown fabric to throw over the futon chair. If I decide to go into debt for red leather L can always use the brown fabric as canvas material and paint over it. It was on sale, so not much strain on the budget there. Holding the phone with my shoulder I get in the car and marvel at my ability to talk, walk, and accomplish a financial transaction all at the same time.

"Great. She's on new meds and except for the fact that she's deleted a few files in her memory folder that we have to boot up after these spells that she has, she may live forever. I, on the other hand, may be ready for a padded cell by morning. Did I tell you I made up flash cards for her reminding her about her childhood. I edited out all the bad stuff."

Our connection was breaking up. I said a hasty good-bye to the crackling sounds on the other end and promised to call back later, hoping she heard me.

Mom took a nap as soon as we got home. I pulled out the fabric for the futon cover and it looks like shit. Way too drab. I knew this when I was buying it. I really need to pay attention to my guts. Of all the incredibly exciting colors and patterns, I chose mushroom brown. I've just created another black (brown) hole in the living room. L says I watch too much HGTV. He says we're ruining the Earth with all the home improvements and redecorating. Says there was a time when families were happy to have a home. Now, no one's happy with their home unless they spend every weekend, every penny, every Earthly resource improving it. I've decided he's one of those "good enough" guys. I'm not, obviously. Nothing is ever good enough. This I get from you know who: Mussolini, my mother.

Will get back to writing up artist's statement for exhibit. I'm sure I have at least a hundred of these tucked away in files everywhere. I change them all the time. Good to have something to start with though.

Pissed at my computer again. How adult is that? Paid $500 to upgrade the memory and have a CD writer installed and can't use it. For some reason my computer doesn't recognize itself or the new device or something like that. Got on the phone with the idiots (too young to know anything anyway) at the store. Decided to approach it like a grown-up.

"I'm having trouble with my computer. I just had some work done on it and can't figure out why it's not able to do what it's supposed to do."

"Please hold." Who would have ever thought that Led Zeppelin would be the music on hold. *And we're climbing a stairway to heaven.* Another voice comes on the phone and I repeat myself adding, "Can you please help me?" There, kinder, more polite. I'm getting more mature and professional by the minute.

"Just a second. I need to transfer you." OK, one more try and I'm going to scream. Already my chest is tightening. I'm calm. Breathe in. It's only the computer. Breathe out. At last another, new voice.

"Yes. This is Jason, can I help you?" This makes three times and if I hear him sucking on a pacifier I'm going to hang up. I straighten my slouch and pet my bitch within. "Sure, that's easy," he responds cheerfully, almost excitedly about my distress, as if his Einstein-mind has just discovered a new theory on relativity. "You need the software to go with the hardware."

"More software?" Now I'm steaming. "Why didn't someone tell me this when I was there?"

"I dunno. I guess whoever you talked with forgot."

"How much is the software."

"Hundred bucks."

"One hundred dollars?" I'm stunned, almost screaming back into the phone. "You're kidding?"

"I wouldn't kid you, ma'am." OK. Is this where I yell at the top of my lungs: Don't call me ma'am because you're not going to get me to spend a penny on anything if it begins with ma'am, OK kid? I have a pair of shoes older than you and they're smarter, too.

I hang up feeling perplexed. I don't know. Is it me? Can it be too much to ask for people to be competent with the simple things, like the jobs they were trained to do? All I want is something to work well and do what it's told when I want it. Or simply do what it's supposed to do.

B says I have to hire a wife.

November 20
2:12 am   Wednesday

It's been nine days since I wrote in my journal. Not that I've been sleeping that entire time. But I've managed a few seven-hour stints. What a difference it makes. Mom, L, and I went to Arizona to visit C, Mom's cousin. We flew out on a bit of a post-Walt-memorial whim and returned yesterday. I know one thing for sure: if I don't write on a daily basis my thoughts get all tangled up inside and it starts to feel like I've abandoned myself, run away from all the knotty and gnarled places that need attention. Then I start to feel like a small pony who can't find her way back to her herd.

You have choices. You can take care of yourself or not.

I made arrangements with C's son, J, my second cousin, who I've never met but who sounds really nice on the phone, to meet on Sunday; a kind of family reunion. Arriving on Friday we had a couple of days to get settled and take a look around. Friday afternoon we headed into a park just south of Phoenix, crawling and winding up mountain roads (Mom was scared to look down once we got to the top. She wouldn't get out of the car and hunkered down in the back seat like a wounded dog.) I marveled at the incredible color of dust and dryness that cracked and crumbled all around us. So many shades of brown. What a contrast to the juicy green jungle of my home in the semi-tropics! And what an even bigger surprise that this seemingly severe and barren land gives way to ragged living sticks and stately saguaro cactus that stand like old crones, spiritual sentinels in the glaring sun.

A few hours into the trip, we decided to stop in at the SMOCA (Scottsdale Museum of Contemporary Art) for the Ansel Adams show. Just as I'm relaxing and thinking I could live here, which is what I always do on vacation, want to move right into a strange place that is good only because it isn't where I now live, from the back seat my mother, who has been humming nervously and making lucid comments about the steep terrain, suddenly wants to know something I can't tell her. "Nancy," she begins real serious like and I pull my attention from my insides to her outsides, "Where's Aunt Ruth?" This, to any stranger, is a perfectly normal question.

To any person who hasn't spent 24/7 with my mother for over a year and a half, this seemingly innocent inquiry would certainly not generate the kind of hostility it does in me, and I immediately get a rancid rush of regret for ever thinking we could take our aging charge with us and actually enjoy a nice few days together. My mother's question has nothing to do with Aunt Ruth. It is a coded verbal clue that she has slipped out of present and fallen into the past, where all the dead relatives are living in her mind. L and I give each other a quick glance and wide-eyed nod that uh oh my mother is having another mysterious mental episode that four trips to the hospital and three follow-up visits to various medical professionals including a neurologist, a urologist, and a cardiologist can't seem to diagnose. Trapped in a strange city without the comforts of her own bed we are both tossed into a worried straight-ahead stare that looks like we are frozen in place and only the old woman in the back seat is alive, shifting and leaning and moving her lips to the only question caught in her craw, "Where's Aunt Ruth?"

I don't know what I was thinking when I decided to yell at her. Like frustrated parents without a time out, I wasn't thinking. I startled myself at the force of energy behind my words as I whipped around, flamed with hostility and screamed, "Mom, get a grip." Her eyes suddenly wide open, scared and darting all over me. "We're on vacation now. Snap out of this crazy shit." I was hoping that she'd buck up Yankee-style, like she always taught me. When she heard the scared part of me ranting in her direction, she froze, growing more anxious and looking like a deer jack-lighted on a lonely dark road. I felt like a shit for resorting to aggression when I pride myself on being a pacifist. I'm thinking, too, that I sound like all my friends who have kids and I feel so uncomfortable when they yell at them.

I hate my mother for falling apart on me, and instantly feel guilty (I can barely write the words). I know. I know. It's not her fault she's losing her mind and memory, I keep telling myself, hoping to neutralize the sludge of feelings now sitting on my lunch.

"What do you want to do?" L asks, mouthing the words without much sound coming out.

"I want to go the museum, damn it," I am pouting madly. Running interference with the few pleasures of my already ragged life really aggravates me. "Let's just pretend nothing is happening. It's the only thing we haven't tried." I am now strangely placid and calm.

"Sounds like a plan." L parks the car and I stay with Mom while he runs in and gets the wheelchair (thank you to the person who made this detail easily accessible so I don't have to deal with that today, too) and the tickets.

"Come on Mom," I've settled down and try not to patronize. "We're going to see some art."

"Art? Art?" she asks, a little confused about how we got from Aunt Ruth to Art, but switches quickly from inquiry to parroting. "Going to see Art? OK. Art. Yes, Art. Going to see Art."

In between gathering her sweater, her water bottle, and adjusting the foot rests on her wheelchair I give a hopeful look to L. Distraction, another good parenting trick, may work after all.

I suddenly felt exhausted with the edge of an anxiety attack barking in my belly. I've become undeservedly prey to panic. The hot flash that followed wasn't so bad. I can handle the pop-up beads of sweat that gather instantly like a moist facemask. It's the sudden dread, the feeling that everything is going to collapse around me that makes the whole experience feel like a bad LSD trip condensed to a nanosecond. I am becoming acutely aware of how much energy it takes to give away what I don't have. I haven't done yoga for three days and was feeling my muscles shorten around my lower back and shoulders. I tried a few Sun Salutations in the morning, but the carpet in the hotel made me cough when I lowered into Cobra Pose. I remember what Judy Chicago said in a video I used to show my students, a documentary of the making of her most magnificent homage to female-ness, "The Dinner Party." One of her assistants was whining in a group meeting about something not being right about the working atmosphere at the studio, to which Chicago stood up abruptly and interrupted in a bitch-howling blast, "It isn't right because it will never be right. There is no such thing as 'right.' Nothing in the world will ever be 'right'." Or something like that. And before Chicago sat back down she exclaimed with resounding finality, "Get used to it."

Sometimes it helps me to remember what Chicago said. That I need to "get used to" what I can't change. Instead of yoga I opted for a walk and enjoyed the refreshing, dry air of the morning, thinking about an ideal yoga space: no carpet, no curtains, no fabric, no knick-knacks, no incense, no candles, no perfumes, no pictures of gurus, masters or bearded white men in white robes. Simply this: a well-lit clean space (using non-toxic, fragrance-free cleaning solutions) with real wood floors, white or soft, pastel-colored walls, really healthy air quality, and no mirrors. No reminders of time. Also having a foyer or lobby, a place to take off shoes and leave personal belongings and personal baggage (emotional and mental) outside.

And while I'm walking I'm also trying not to think too much about ideals.

We made our way into the tall and contemporary open space of the museum and were suddenly surrounded by impressive and luminous black-and-white blow-ups of Yosemite's mountainous and forested landscapes, pulsing rushing rivers and ferns so verdant that I could almost smell the sweet dampness of the Earth beneath my feet. There, in a starkly odd and natural world of rectangular contrasts, devoid of color and nagging distractions, I quite suddenly and uncontrollably burst into tears, my fingers gripping the soft worn rubber of the wheelchair handles to steady myself. The harder I gripped, the faster the tears fell, sadness filling my whole body. L came over as if sensing from across the room that something was wrong. He said nothing at first, gently placing one arm around my shoulder, resting the other on the back of the wheelchair. He kissed my cheek lightly, licking lightly at my tears. After a long silent hug he whispered, "I know. I know."

"What's going on back there?" my mother called impatiently. After only a moment in the exhibit she grew deeply interested in the sensitively condensed world of high contrasts and glowing stillness staring back at us from looming rectangles. She asked L, who took over as chauffeur, to push her closer, pointing to the small white description card to the right of the craggy canyon just in front of us. She spent only a moment looking at the photo. She wanted the details. She wanted to know more: where the photo was taken, the date, the title, and anything else she could glean from the smaller rectangles that called her attention, reading out loud to herself like a first-grader. So engrossed was my mother in relishing something else to know, and paying all promise to the very moment she now found herself being pushed around in— the landscape of the new, she completely forgot about Aunt Ruth and the land of the dead. I found myself shifting calmly into the moment.

Moving from one room to the next she twisted around in her seat and, out of the blue, began telling us how uncomfortable her underwear had been on the plane ride out. "Those new underpants made me miserable," she said a little too loudly because she is hard of hearing and at this point doesn't really care too much what she says in public, or what other people think. I guess she figures she's got nothing to lose.

"How did you finally get comfortable?" I say, staring into the over-sized vessels in the second exhibit, carved of sumptuous maple and cherry woods. I am half paying attention and wondering, gratefully, how I missed out on that episode. "You seemed all right to me."

"I flushed 'em," she says, smiling proudly.

"You flushed your cotton underwear down the airplane toilet?" I said, barely holding a straight face, my hand jumping to cover my gaping mouth. L looks at me, holding his breath in disbelief, fighting back a burst of laughter.

"Yup," she turned back around, adjusting her fanny with a firm side-to-side wiggle. "I sure did." And like a queen in a ceremonial procession, pointed the way forward.

The ride to Sedona on Saturday at sunset was all rounded red boulders and ragged, weathered outcroppings in changing shades of golden amber and rich mesa reds that haunt and awe right down to the bone. I wanted to run into the desert, run wild, my arms reaching up to the Full Moon, rising like a slice of silver in the iridescent golden glow of the dusk. My wolf within wanted to leap and dance and scream and howl; echoes of my ancestors calling me home.

After an overpriced dinner at a restaurant trying too hard to be something that it wasn't, all three of us confessed that we would have preferred fish tacos, "Just like the ones you make at home, hon," my mother grinned, patting my hand with a far-off gaze.

November 22
2:34 am

Stopped at the health-food store. Picked up wild salmon, previously frozen. If you are what you eat, does this mean I'm a woman who runs with the cold fish? I'm looking for high protein, low carbs. At least, today I am. Last month I was a devout vegetarian and could have shaved my head and donned a saffron-colored robe. I have no principles any more. They come in one window and out the other. Every day is different. I can't stand the thought of killing small animals for the sake of a "diet." On the other hand, I hate food rules. If I eat what my ancestors ate, which seems simple enough, I'd be chewing on the pine tree outside my back door and trapping those cute brown rodents that hide in the rock pile next to it.

Mom pushed the cart around the store, reading the labels out loud. I walked about 20 paces in front, trying to smile with that pathetic, please understand what I go through every day, look on my face. She snagged two "Sugar Free" wafers in the bulk bins and popped them into her mouth, staring into the bin as if she were at a free buffet. I grabbed an entire box of wheat-free, dairy-free, chocolate chip cookies off the shelf. I have my weakness; that's all I can say. L says health-food cookies all taste like dirt. For him, it's pure butter or nothing. And in spite of our theory that when you eat in a Greek diner and you're a vegetarian, better get the grilled cheese and French fries because if you order the steamed veggie plate you will be very disappointed when what you get looks and tastes like steamed, corrugated cardboard, I have to buy health-food cookies (delicious, magical dirt). I can't do all that butter.

In the car, Mom mentions again that a woman at the SC is taking care of her son, who has brain cancer. I say again because every time I take her to the SC she tells me the story twice on the way up and at least three times on the way home. At the dinner table tonight she tells me again.

"Mom, I know this story." I'm trying to be very patient and my voice is calm. "You've told me twice today, OK. Don't you remember?"

"Well," she coughs a little distance between us. "Of course I do." She says this like I'm a monster for reminding her of something she already knows. I walk over and put my arms on her shoulders and ask her if for once we can just talk about something other than disease. She doesn't respond and turns away. It's obvious, in her mind, I'm taking away all the fun of life. Dinner will be a duel of rodent wills.

"How are the steamed carrots?" I peeled them, sliced them, and steamed them just al dente. They are organic. And I'm trying now to make friendly conversation and make up for my bad rat behavior.

"OK," she nearly whispers.

"How's the chard?" The red variety; her favorite. Chopped gently, consciously and placed lovingly into water that has reached a boil then left to sit for a minute or two. Greens don't like boiling water. They should be blanched slightly so the body can utilize the enzymes properly. Basically, eaten alive, which looks to be my fate tonight.

"OK." She doesn't look up or any way but at her fork.

"How's the salmon?" Poached for six minutes on each side, four sprigs of rosemary from the backyard to add a hint of the Francaise to the palate, and lightly coated with essence of Emeril. She just loves that guy.

"OK."

I can't tolerate the feelings that are rising up like battery acid in my belly. My therapy session is over a week away and all I want to do is cry right here, right now. I could have thrown a TV dinner at her and it wouldn't make a bit of difference. My mother is a mean shit. That's all there is to it. I'm trying to be a grown-up. I'm trying to remember those ads about "elderly parents" and how she's not doing this *to* me. She has a disease (admitting that she has a *disease* is hard to accept, let alone say out loud in writing.) Maybe if I sit here long enough and open my heart and imagine that all the goodness that ever was present in the world when people first discovered that Mothers were sacred will somehow show up between us and make up for my snot-nosed impatience, and maybe I will be able to look at her again without wanting to drizzle a little liquid rat poison in a fancy Jackson Pollack style on her plate and call it a nice Dijon reduction, "Just like a fancy restaurant, Mom."

I wait. Nothing. Then, in a little mousy voice she says, "Yup. This is good," looking up at me like a four-year-old who just found the cookie crumb in a fold in her arm. "Really good. Aren't you going to eat, dear?"

"Thanks, Mom," says Rat Daughter in reply, just loving the way her Mainer Mom says dear, *dee uh*, because that means she's back to basics and in love with me again. "I'll eat a little later. I ate a late lunch." She of course doesn't remember, and I'm not going to ask her if she remembers. Best not to remind her that she doesn't remember. I smile slowly. Her hair is all criss-crossed and poking out and I think of the Joyce Kilmer poem, decoupaged on a piece of shiny maple plank and hung above the kitchen table in the trailer, the only piece of poetry I grew up with…*a tree that may in summer wear, a nest of robins in her hair.*

Looking a little oily, my mother's silver-haired boughs are all flattened on one side from her nap. The turquoise cotton sundress that she wore to the SC this morning with the fish design on the front pocket flap that suddenly looks like a tiny bib, is now wrinkled and twisted around her waist. She's shrunk since she sat down at the table just a half-hour ago, looking a lot like Albert Einstein in drag. I reach across the table in my ratty sad way because I know there will come a time when I will give my right arm to have my mother sitting in the kitchen with me saying "OK" in a kindergarten way a hundred times over and no matter how hard I want her to be here with me in that future scene, it won't happen.

Someday she'll be gone forever.

In this very moment I want to be with her in a peaceful way so I won't have to deal with the unbearable burden of guilt, along with all the other mixed-up emotions that happen when daughters lose their mothers to death. I've read that regret (or is it bitterness?) corrodes the vessel it sits in. And I don't want heartburn again tonight from the emotional upheaval I've created at the kitchen table, where the temple mysteries known only to women are supposed to be shared.

Mom finally looks up and sees my hand resting next to her plate as if she's just spotted the hidden dinner roll. With a soft smile she lifts her wide and one time strong and solid hand and presses it gently, tentatively down on mine, staring silently into the space between us. We fit so perfectly, Mother and Daughter Rat paws, one overlapping the other like living leathery saucers.

If I could eat love I would do so with my tongue lapping loudly, because love was sitting right there, deliciously and patiently waiting on the table in front of us, and asking nothing in return.

November 27
9:13 am

Wednesday

O, my mother's companion sitter, comes tonight. She is a volunteer from Americorps, so thank you to that person, surely a daughter, who dreamed up this incredible organization that sends angels to the homes of elderly people so 24/7 caregivers like me can have four hours to do all those things that were once routine and suddenly become luxuries like: comb my hair, chew my food and go out, somewhere, anywhere and aggressively gnaw on my nails.

November 28
5:14 am

Thursday

Thanksgiving. We're keeping it simple. Staying home. No turkey. I can't stand the smell of roasting skin. The stench from the last bird I cooked, almost four years ago, is still living somewhere in the winter clothes tucked in the back of the closet. We'll have fish. And say our thanks quietly and then L and I will go for a walk to the beach and throw a rock in the ocean and silently make a wish.

Took me and my chihuahuas within for a long walk on the beach tonight alone. L wanted to work in his studio. Over-Reacts is resting comfortably, bedded down for the night, eyes twitching doggy dreams, quiet snuffles emanating from her little wet nose as she sleeps.

DECEMBER

December 2
9:10 am

Monday

Called S to see if she wants to team up and make a home-cooked meal for H and Y, the couple on her street that just had twins. Said OK. She'll make crab cakes and fresh mango salsa. I'll make tossed salad with balsamic dressing, steamed veggies, and garlic toast with a fresh fruit salad. Called H and Y to schedule the delivery time.

"Anytime, is good for us," said H, sounding like a weary new dad. "We'll either be eating, changing diapers, or sleeping."

"Keeping it simple, huh?" I don't know how far to push the humor here. We're neighbors, not close friends.

"Not too many choices at this point." He said quite good-natured considering he probably hadn't had a good night's sleep in three weeks.

"How are those little darlings?" I'm smiling and thrilled to be connecting with the birthing side of the life cycle.

"They are wonderful. We're so lucky." I could tell without seeing his face that H was smiling too. "Hey, thanks so much. This will be great. Y will be thrilled." He sounded relieved that help was on its way.

3:14 pm

The sky is gray and fat and puffy with afternoon clouds that put the smell of rain in the already-heavy humid air. I can hear a rumble in the distance, and my head is already feeling the pressure of a weather system about to break loose this side of the river. The five-street community where we live, all named after birds, is pretty tight when it comes to helping out our neighbors in need. Food is what we do best for each other. Two years ago a neighbor had a terrible accident and we divided up her two-week recuperation time between a group of eager volunteers and each one of us picked up a day's meals for her, bringing them to her door like merry maids of meals. I don't speak to many of my neighbors. I don't think we like each other all that much. Not that much in common, really. And we're all so busy with who knows what? Life, I guess. But food-in-a-fix is how and when we bond.

I took Mom to the SC this morning, but first made a mad dash to the store to pick up a few veggies for the salad and to check for fresh fruit in season. The pineapple was green and hard and I picked one up for later, hoping it would ripen before it rotted. It had a good three days to go. The papaya looked just right, almost ugly with big round spots and super soft flesh. Perfect. I grabbed a big honeydew and some raspberries. The yellow squash, although snugly wrapped in plastic, looked young and tender. I figured zucchini, yellow squash, grape tomatoes (organic), and sliced white onions would make a good mix for a lactating mom and her nursing twins. I left the onions in big chunks so she could pull them out if too gassy for the babies.

Standing at the sink, washing the veggies and trying to get as much done as possible before rushing off with my own wise toddler for her morning playgroup, I focused my energy on the amazing connection between the food in my hands and the not-so-long journey it would take to eventually become the blood and bones and ga ga baby sounds of H and Y's little girl and boy.

It's just one big delicious web of life, followed by a lot of stinky diapers and spit up.

I think about twins, the time-toaster popping up another memory.

Getting pregnant while I was in college was no surprise. My boyfriend J and I were fucking like rabbits and only half the time remembering to use birth control. We were together for almost three years and although "careful" we weren't always careful enough. I was the skinniest I'd ever been and while making love really got off on watching my hipbones, then visible, lift and thrust into J's tight, hairy, muscular torso, every sexual emotion running raw, careless, and close to the edge of sexual insanity.

When I got pregnant we were renting a huge, old and dilapidated house in Gainesville and growing marijuana, or "Gainesville Green" as the locals called it, in the three spare bedrooms that we locked from the inside so no visitor could accidentally open the bedroom door on the way to the bathroom. Access to our precious commodity was gained only from the back door and J had reinforced it with metal bars and heavy-duty locks. Hydroponics and the use of halogen lights, pollination, and hybridization completely controlled, made for zonker home-grown reefers. The tight, dense, and resinous buds were hashish-like and packed a wallop of a high, or at least that's what I was told. I didn't like pot. I stopped smoking years before I started growing it. Hated feeling stoned. I'd end up in bed with the covers pulled over my head after eating half a loaf of bread toasted with peanut butter and jelly, four glasses of milk as a chaser, and a few cookies just to fill in the blanks. I felt bloated and certain someone knew and heard everything that was going on in my racing mind. I made a good business partner in the marijuana business, but later when I started dealing white powder, my nose became very bad for business.

The only catch with growing marijuana in the house was the telltale signs of an extremely high electric bill, which could, in Florida, be disguised as an increased demand for air conditioning in the spring and summer months. While I was going to school full-time, taking art classes, J was a high-tech farmer. Living on student loans and big druggie dreams, we hustled a little dope to friends in south Florida, and an ex-boyfriend in Texas.

Mom had moved in with us right after Dad died. She got the bedroom off the kitchen and didn't give a second thought to cleaning the buds and weighing the bags. I don't think she really knew what we were doing. I think my mother was out of her mind early on. And so was I.

J was the kookiest guy I'd ever met. And I couldn't keep my hands off him. We did it everywhere. I was living in Fort Lauderdale in a very small apartment. Okay, it was a tool shed turned into a one-bedroom bungalow and no bathroom, but the rent was cheap. J was living in his car and thrilled to have a permanent parking place and a taller roof over his head. We used the landlady's bathroom. She was a forty-something artist trying to make ends meet after a nasty divorce. Right after I met J she convinced me to get my "ass back to college" (I had gotten a two-year degree from the community college there) and get the rest of my education or end up in a trailer park where I began. I was applying to colleges and we were both looking forward to leaving the area.

J, a nuclear physics drop-out from an ivy league college, was big into nutrition, eating mostly raw or sprouted food, which is how I ended up losing so much weight and feeling so sexy, not to mention that we were exhausting every calorie we ingested from *doing it* all the time, anywhere and every-where, including in the hammock stretched out on the patio between the tool shed and M's apartment, in the car parked on the side of the highway and in M's bathtub when she wasn't home, and quite often in the shower when she was home, thinking that she couldn't hear us because we couldn't hear her. I later found out from mutual friends that M was totally disgusted with me and my new wacko vegetarian boyfriend and made a point of leaving the house whenever we took a shower.

I remember one hotter than hot bump and grind session in particu-lar, not only because it felt so what-a-fucking-way-to-die good but because it's how I ended up pregnant with twins, or at least that's what the doctor said who had to do the abortion twice.

J was really quite devoted to me, early on (later on I figured out exactly what I was devoted to), picking me up from work every night and bringing me home. Getting out of the car after pulling into the parking lot where there was a side entrance to the bungalow, I stumbled on a small pebble (divine, orgasmic intervention one could say) or maybe it was a crack in the pavement. That is not what I remember about the incident. I do remember that I was wearing wooden clogs (just like the ones my students wear now!) and didn't quite have the finesse necessary to navigate a rocky path. Maybe my ankles were weak, or maybe it was that since falling madly in love with J, everything in my female being buckled whenever he was near. Seeing me stumble, J rushed (slithered?) to my side, reaching under my arm to help me back up. He kind of pressed me against the hood of the car at the same time, an old junker of a yacht-sized tub, painted yellow, that at one time sported a white vinyl roof that had blown off in a strong wind so J painted the rusting roof-brick red. It was so ugly. The car interior was also a hideous mess and the engine rarely started without J having to jump out, grab a broom handle from the back seat, pop the hood and whack the starter a few times to get it to kick in. If I weren't so dumb struck with J's handsome all-American (he was Canadian) good looks, alluring sense of mystery, and a shlong the size of Manhattan, the car alone would have been an indicator that I was going nowhere fast, unless you want to count the speed it took to go from zero to orgasmic bliss while writhing in the front seat. But I'd gone out with rich guys who owned hot little foreign jobs whose personalities and sex appeal weren't worth a dime. I was never attracted to the glitz. Basically I liked a guy with charm and charisma, usually an alcoholic or a druggee about to explode.

J didn't have a job when I met him, except for a part-time gig here and there working on boats, and he never got a full-time one the whole time we were together. He spent a lot of time trying to figure out how to beat the races; "the horses" he'd say while pulling a slow and sexy smile across his face, and glancing into his lap. You may as well have shot me up with Spanish fly. J was a sex drug drenching me from thigh to skinny thigh with love juice. He also had some very big ideas about writing software for diabetics (oh so ahead of his time). Along with his sexual prowess J had a scientific mind I couldn't keep up with. We lived on my income, which at various times included my job at a health-food store, and a short-lived stint as a cocktail waitress at a low-lit loser lounge near the airport after leaving the topless bar. And we lusted on love.

I often think about that night in the parking lot, which, good thing for us, was pretty secluded, nestled against the back wall of a huge marine taxidermy warehouse.

After J lifted me back to balance, I leaned against his car only half aware and much less concerned that the paint job that at one time must have been a shiny slick lemon yellow had now turned to dry dull dust and was brushing off on my new fuchsia pink wrap-around skirt that tied in the back and had an attached halter top. Made in India, it was 100 percent cotton, slightly transparent in direct light and very cool in the south Florida summers. I didn't wear underwear at the time, which made our impromptu encounters extremely easy, and which pleased J to no end. While helping me back up to a full standing position, J continued to reach his arm around my back and while slowly slipping his hands down along my hips, which even when I was the skinniest I've ever been I thought were HUGE, and looking me in the eyes and pressing his tongue into my mouth says in a slow and breathy voice, "You really want me to fuck you, don't you? Right here, right now?" Well, that's not exactly what was on my mind at the moment per se, only seconds away from falling flat on my face, but the truth of the matter was that this guy was the best drug I'd ever had, and I wanted him most of the time.

"Yeah," I cooed back, my eyelids half shutting like a junkie with an empty syringe in her hand. J's arms divided like an army on maneuvers, without any external signal or command, his right hand moved swiftly under my skirt to the front and his left hand shifted to the rear rubbing my ass in smooth slow circles. In his right hand, he had the clitoral controls at his finger-tips, doing the work of a master conquering what little resistance I had. In the far far reaches of my "what if your parents could see you now" mind, was the simple fact that we were standing outside our apartment building half naked and gyrating against his car, and at any time could be either heard or spied on or shot. We did not live in the safest part of town, which only added to the erotic tension that already twisted us into a kinky Kama Sutra knot.

J whispered something hot and sexy into my ear while slipping his shorts down to his knees and waiting for me to beg for it before sliding his very hard and handsome dick into my juicy slice of pie.

I was slipping deeper into my animal-sized Go For It Slut breathy voice while that part of me that had been the president of my junior class was hoping we didn't go to jail on charges of breaking some repressive southern sex law. But nothing could stop me now. I wanted it baaaaaaad. And he knew it.

J was in total control. He was grinning a cool, sexy, self-satisfying smile the whole time, holding me up against the car, watching and waiting and working me into a frenzy with shameless and shocking dirty talk, gently rocking us back and forth, pushing and pulling in a slow-motion rhythm, punctuating his lusty sentences with every thrust. I waited just about as long as I could (which was all of about four minutes on average from cock and cunt talk to orgasm with this mad sex scientist) before exploding into fiery little fits and tremors that shook me from my toes to my fingertips. J loved coming (or as he called it "going" as in "did you go yet?", which made me laugh hysterical-ly the first time he said it in the middle of one of those quiet orgasms that sneaks up on you and almost disappears without notice) only after pleasing me. And the whole time we were at it, banging against the car in the parking lot, where dead, stuffed and glassy-eyed marlin, snook, and big mouth bass were hanging on the other side of the concrete wall that separated us from the hospital where I would eventually land, aborting our twin babies, J never took his eyes off mine, his hot tongue licking my lips and making little sipping and biting sounds all in harmony with the rhythmic rocking of the rusting car we called the "Love Boat."

J and I broke up because he started shoplifting. I could live with just about anything kooky and wild. But I couldn't live with a thief.

I remember reading an article in the *New York Times* magazine a while ago about a woman who had a miscarriage while visiting Japan and was told to make offerings to a deity named Jizo or O'Jizo-San while trying to reconcile her emotional turmoil about having lost her second pregnancy in three years. Apparently in the folk-Buddhist belief, O'Jizo-San comes to the aid of all those in need, particularly travelers and grieving mothers or mothers who might have been. Divine guardian and protector of children, both the living and the dead (including miscarriages, abortions, and stillbirths) this benevolent deity vows to bring healing and happiness to all those in need. Although there is no real word for miscarriage or abortion in Japanese, the word *mizuko*, or "water child", is used. Special prayers and offerings are made to the Jizo, who helps the *mizuko* find another time and pathway for entry into this life. In Japan, abortion, considered a "regrettable necessity," is neither shameful nor politicized. Acknowledgement is made that a *mizuko*, a formless life was lost and would someday return, true to the Buddhist belief in reincarnation. Mizuko kuyo, or the ritual of "apology and remembrance" originally developed and practiced almost entirely by women, is a way of wishing the formless life well on its way to a yet-unknown future.

Making lunch for the new parents and their twins I thought about my *mizuko*, my water babies, never meant to be. I wonder if I will ever find closure to the difficult decisions that drag close behind my past. At this age I am aware that there are too many things I will never know. I can't say that I'm at peace with myself, yet. Apology, yes. Remorse, yes. I am stepping tenderly toward forgiveness. When I look back into the cloudy background of my twenties, I see a confused, scared, and lonely young woman running fast and hard and not knowing where to go. I'm making offerings in small ways to both that young woman who still lives in me, and the *mizuko* that would never be. Simple prayers like a silent nod and a smiling welcome to the butterflies and hummingbirds that flit and seem never to quite land on or take hold of the big red blooming hibiscus outside our bedroom window long enough to find roots.

One never knows what form the soul will take.

I made a few sketches of some Jizo I want to sculpt in clay and then cast in glass to commemorate my fragile *mizuko*. I want to crochet little red hats for them or maybe ask my Mom to help me. She first taught me how to knit and crochet when I was twelve. Sitting next to her on the couch, my fingers wrapped around a plastic pink needle and a strand of red wool, I felt like the most important girl in the world—my mother teaching me the fine art of making something out of nothing— true women's work.

The tomatoes washed, the papaya peeled and sliced, I glanced once more over my shoulder and out the window, stopping to wipe my hands on the towel that hangs on the refrigerator. The sky that looks over my backyard, my menopausal garden, is growing streaked with thin ribbons of fuscia pink, not unlike the color of my wrap-around skirt (which is probably in a box in the attic marked "memorabilia" along with my emerald-green string bikini and my leather mini-skirt) on the night I conceived two little souls that would never find form in my life.

My mother started pacing or rather shuffling toward the front door, letting me know it was time to get on the road. "You're daydreaming again," she said tenderly, as if she can read my thoughts. I watch her stout little body running fast and hard and I realize that we share more than DNA and the blood of our ancestors. We have secrets that, like my *mizuko,* are still wandering in the liquid spaces of time, looking for a home.

I am learning how to live in the open skies of delicate gray that gather between the black and white edges of life and death.

December 4
9:14 am

Wednesday

A delightfully scarlet-red cardinal rests for a moment, scritch-scratching on the windowsill just outside the bedroom window, trying to take hold on the narrow ledge. He lands, looking at his reflection in the window, tilting his head from side to side like a dog watching TV, then falls back, catching himself in mid-drop, lifting his wings as if he, just that moment, remembered that he had them, and flies away.

Take your time, he says.
You have all the time you need.

I am talking to birds these days, and listening to their songs in return.

I think about all the bird-headed goddesses I've visited in museums throughout Europe and Turkey. Archaeological facts, artifacts, some thirty thousand years old, made of clay, and all of them female, placed on altars, kept in shrines and carried in ritual and ceremony. Woman as bird goddess, messengers of dawn and bringers of light, harbingers of death that carry the souls of the deceased to a new place in time. When we say that spring is in the air, it is because the robins, for sure, are bringing the spring with them, foretelling of seasonal changes. I think of how many bird names are used now to diminish women, particularly older women: biddy, hen, crow, not-a-spring-chicken.

Above my desk is an altar filled with dozens of female figures, sculptures that I've created and those I've collected for many years. The Owl Goddess from the island of Cyprus calls out for my attention. She is made of rich orange clay, standing with her hands on her hips, a baby bird in her left arm. Her protruding nose is hooked like a big beak (a sign of strong character!) and her wide ears (better to hear!) are pulled flat and straight out from her head, with two large holes on each side. Earrings loop through three of the holes, adorning and making prominent her vital presence. Her eyes are wide, mouth is open, too, as if in the middle of a very important message. Her little fledgling, too, is wide-eyed, her head turned, staring directly and intensely at Mother. I remember when this image was used to grace the cover of Buffie Johnson's book, *Lady of the Beasts: Ancient Images of the Goddess and Her Sacred Animals.* I wanted to hold this art-fact in my own hands. As if driven by the voice of my bird soul, I began re-creating this image, molding that part of myself in the image of a Bird Goddess. I didn't sell many. But she is still my favorite. I imagine I am both Mother and Child.

And so I am.

Nearly ten years after first making this sculpture I feel like a different woman. I am different. I am learning how to fly again, touch down and feed what I create. I cannot give up artmaking, no matter what the challenges are in the marketplace. This is truly my gift to the world. But first, it is my gift to me, my communion with my soul.

Something new is being born of my mind, body, and spirit now. My creativity will take on a new form as I emerge. I am hatching a new egg. I am giving birth to myself, renovating me again and again.

Hormones are the mediators of inner wisdom, arriving at mid-life just in time to see things anew and awaken to a fully honest and healthy life. Our brains, during the menopause and perimenopausal years, go through dramatic changes, "catching on fire", as Christiane Northrop, MD, calls it, for deeper intuitive guidance, and insight for life-enhancing decision-making.

If we're willing to listen.

Where's the Menopausal Instruction Kit, anyway?

L knows or senses that not only I am changing. I found a few notes on his desk for a playlet based on our life with Mom. I got scared when I read "after her mother dies, they divorce." Are the birds of change calling out to both of us?

How can we change and stay the same at the same time? I do not know.

L and Mom are due home any minute. These few quiet hours are a true gift, silence singing her way into my being. I scare myself with the force of this yearning for solitude, and the roar of a fire to dance around, and enough space to lift my wings and soar.

December 5
8:14 am   Thursday

Suddenly called B in the middle of changing the sheets. I had to talk with her for no real reason. I trust this inner directive, but today I tried to ignore it and succeeded for almost an hour before the urge was so strong that I couldn't concentrate on anything else until I picked up the phone. My gut wanted to talk to B. B answered immediately, which is unusual. I often have to leave a message and wait to hear from her. Sometimes it might take days.

She's busy now with new projects and I envy those that get to spend time with her. She laughed when she heard my voice. We have this sisterly way of just laughing when we're together, about nothing and everything all at the same time. We chatted for a long time. Just girlfriend talk.

After complaining to B about, well, just about everything, she just laughed. "Wow, Nanc, your anger is really right on the surface."

"Hel-*lo*. Better than burying it under my ribs."

"It's draining, Nanc."

"Does it sound like I want to be angry? Because I don't." Now I'm angry at B for rubbing my nose in it. "I just don't know what else to do with it."

"I got real angry a couple days ago." B's voice got real low and I leaned into thin air just to feel a bit closer, even though she was on the other side of the country. "Did I tell you about my last therapy session?" We hadn't talked in almost a week. I can't believe she didn't call me immediately. My stomach started to tighten as B told me that she had another "recovered memory" about her father. I'm already mad at him; so bad I want to choke him, and I can feel my fists start to clench up real tight because she's about to tell me something that confirms, once again, that men are evil. She told me that this time, during the session, she had a distinct and disgusting memory of his penis in her mouth. She cried so hard as the memory surfaced and said she couldn't breathe. She almost threw up. I wanted to give her a hug. Mostly I wanted to walk up to her father and punch him in the face, then kick him in the dick. I hate this man only because B can't.

Now I'm doubly angry and I can't shake it; can't pull myself out of my feelings. L can feel it and I try to make small talk. I don't tell him about my call to B. Don't want to repeat what I don't want to hear said out loud again. Don't want to get reinfected with feelings. I hate this most about what men can do to children.

I need to talk to my brother. Something is urging me to find out what happened when he was fifteen and I was five and we were left alone in the house on Fletcher Street. There is a looming shadow that won't go away, a plea for healing from a very small voice in the past.

Have to pack up my sculpture for museum show. L and I and three other artists in a group show: *Liquid Sand: Contemporary Glass Art*. The museum is on its last legs, holding on by a thread. The director just resigned over conflicts with the board of directors. Board wants museum to be self-sufficient with membership. Board is run by business people who run lives by the bottom line. I think the bottom line is just a little too closely related in thematic implications to one's asshole.

But that's an artist's opinion.

Packing up my glass "Ancestors" and "Self-portrait in Blue." This last series was particularly challenging. It took almost three years to finish.

4:21 am

Decided that "Altar to the Wise Wise Woman" has to go in the exhibit, too. I am scared because it is so different for me. It's part of a series of furniture and ritual object sculptures I've just started doing. I had to use L's bureau because it's so perfect for the piece. Can't really afford to go out and buy furniture for an exhibit. Then what would I do with it? Store it in the garage? L graciously unloaded it, stacking his clothes in an open suitcase. "Only for four weeks," I tell him, sounding grateful for the loan. He just smiled. He understands so much my art mind that I truly am grateful for this abiding friendship, even if we're in a marital trough. The altar consists of three large, glass bell jars with knick-knacks of grannies holding a basket of apples under the two jars on the end. Under the center bell jar I had a large golden apple, as big as the grannies with a gold-leaf snake nestled right up alongside. But this morning, while loading it up I found the glass uterus with the gold-leafed ovaries that I cast when out in Seattle, and decided at the last minute to wrap it and take it too. I don't know why, but I want my self-portrait uterus to also be included in the show. Will be interesting to see where it ends up.

I am beginning to like my art. If nothing else, this is one of the biggest changes finding its way into my heart. In the past I'd been so judgmental, so critical of what I create, dismissing my efforts, the outcome and the energy it took to do it, before I even had a chance to listen to what I needed to learn. But I feel this overwhelming sense of acceptance washing through me. I feel gentle and kind about what I give birth to. It feels so much better in that big round space in my belly. L says, as artists, it's not our job to judge what we make. Our job is simply to create. I used to be really mad at him when he said this. Not because I disagreed with him, but because he knew this and I didn't.

In the past, I have been so misguided about valuing myself.

December 6
8:13 pm

Spent an hour with diabetic education counselor today. Mom looking like a first-grader, cheery and sitting up straight and looking into nurse G's glasses like she was looking at her own reflection, shifting her head from side to side to get a better view of her herself and all the time Nurse G is explaining blood sugar and insulin and how the pancreas works and combining "mushy" foods with hard foods and getting enough protein and carbohydrates in the same meal, but not too much, and how exercise and a good diet can go a long way to helping Mom get off her diabetes medication and always eat protein with a fruit like apples with cheese or peanut butter. Nurse G may as well have been talking Krypton into the miniature decoder ring on her right hand.

When we got back into the car I asked, "Now, what do you eat your apple with?"

So proud, so happy to have been to school and eager to get an A in listening comprehension, my mother says cheerfully, "The skins on."

Testing my mother is a very bad idea.

December 7
3:23 am

Breathwork session on Sunday. Tomorrow? Anxious and trying not to think about it. I never know what's going to come up and not knowing is hard to live with. I don't like surprises. I am praying purposefully for inner peace. Again.

Called P late last night. Left message: "Hi P. You're not home and I think I'm going crazy. I can't stand taking care of the one who's supposed to be the mother. I'm not getting anything I want. Probably won't ever get a new couch either. The refrigerator keeps me up all night, torque pulsations thrumming and vibrating in my chest, a painful and agonizing groan. I toss and turn and stick my fingers in my ears and hope that just because I can't hear it that it's not still throwing off my karma. It's barely audible, but by midnight sounds like a freight train. It's awful and it's constant and L can't hear it. Well, he says he hears it, but it doesn't bother him. Nothing bothers him. I'm definitely losing my noodle. I almost unplugged it, but L said the ice cream will melt."

December 8
9:54 pm

Sunday

Before starting the breathing session I asked K if it was necessary to the healing process to actually know *all* the details of your story before you can finally let them go. Like if there was something I didn't know but my body was holding onto, could I just say, OK, be gone with you bad memory? Or do I have to dig it up like an old familiar relic and only after piecing it all together and cataloging it can I toss it in the midden of one's life? She said I'd probably find out exactly what I need to know. *Breathing In. Breathing Out.*

Before entering the interior of my breathing meditation I smile, I remember what P said not too long ago: The more you stir the shit, the longer it stinks. Or, was it the harder the dirt, the deeper you dig? I can't remember now. Oh well, I'm looking for a mental distraction so I don't have to take the dive down the long shamanic tunnel to my shit within.

I am in my crib. I am crying. My back is pressed up against the vertical wooden slats. I am pushing myself as far away from the man who is standing next to my crib; a stranger. My hands are flapping out in front of me. There are no words. I am screaming.

I shake clear the image in my mind. K hands me a tissue and I sob for what seems like eternity. My baby within saw too much. Knows too much. K encouraged me to keep writing, "Let whatever wants to surface have a voice." Your body will thank you. She handed me a card with affirmations on it, and I cried even deeper, setting some chained part of my soul free.

I allow love to wash through me, cleansing and healing every part of my body. I am changing. I am safe.

December 11
3:39 am

Wednesday

L and I out on our Wednesday night date. All alone. We hardly talk any more when we're driving. P says she's decided that even if she has to read the warranty on the toaster oven she won't sit in silence when they're in the car. And another thing that's got me all strung out: L hasn't touched me in days. I can't believe how dependent I am on him wanting me. My self-esteem wrapped up in his desires. How crazy is that? But after twenty years of lusting after my body almost every day I feel suddenly marooned on one of those carnival rides that looks like a spinning pirate ship. I'm floating alone in someone else's space, upside down. And he won't talk to me about it no matter how I tip-toe around the obvious with tiny hints like, "Are you OK? Is there something wrong? Do you have the flu?"

L just shrugs. Says he doesn't know.

Feels weird to ride in silence when my head is having a thousand conversations with itself, all at once. G says that L is changing, too, "Male menopause, Nanc. It happens." Mental-pause is more like it. I'm not cheered by the prospects of both of us going through it at the same time. He's younger than I am. "He's right on schedule. Call it a mortality attack," G tries to buoy my mood. "Gotta give him room to explore. You two have been together, what—forever?" I'm not sure what it means to give him room, but I'm trying not to obsess about these whiny, insecure feelings that bubble up out of nowhere simply because he's spending a great deal of time shut up in his studio listening to Bruce Springsteen's "Born to Run." G says I shouldn't try to get all my exercise by jumping to conclusions. But I just can't help it. I feel like I have a huge rubbery periscope that rises up out of the top of my head and gloms onto L's every move like a spy ship in heat (no, definitely not heat), more like a paranoid submarine without a destination. I just hate feeling so…clingy.

Down periscope, please. I need to get a close-up look at my own floating life.

And I know this is all wrong, but I decided to call S and wish her a happy birthday while we're driving along, virtually turning our date night into a girlfriend chat session. But I can't stop myself. S tells me her birthday was yesterday. Oh well. Her gift will be late. Got her a copy of *The big book of FILTH; 6500 sex slang words and phrases*. Will wrap it in plain, brown wrapping paper (cut-up grocery bag), attach a bar of chocolate and include a bottle of hot sauce, and one of Mom's painted birds. Mom and I walked over at about 9 am before sun starts to bake the top of my head. Mom asks again, "Now, who is S and where does she live?" We'd been by there the night before and I pointed it out then. I am growing more and more patient. I understand something that I don't really want to understand. I know in my heart that this isn't a game. And I wish this knowing could stop the sorrow that crawls up into my throat when I least expect it.

December 12
4:14 pm

Did yoga this morning, running out at the last minute hoping I could leave Mom alone for two hours and not worry too much. Left my cell phone number just in case. In the middle of Child's Pose heard a phone ringing. Thought it was the teacher's phone in the other room. It sounded so far away.

Oh no. It's my cell phone tucked into my purse. Didn't know whether to get up and shut it off or get up and walk into other room to answer it or just forget it. Kept ringing. Who could be calling? I never get calls on the cell phone. Oh. My mother. That's who. I finally got up very slowly, not to disturb the class and tiptoed away wanting to scream. If my mother is calling, she's all right. Didn't cut off her arm or a leg. She must have something very important to tell me.

"Hello. Mom." Whatever relaxation yoga has brought to my hungry bodymind is now gone, gone, gone. I feel it exit swiftly like a sudden breeze and a door slam behind it.

"Nancy?" She sounds breathless and child-like. Amazed at technology. The fact that I am not at home but talking to her through a piece of plastic boggles her mind.

"Yes. Mom. I'm in yoga."

"I know," she starts whispering, thinking the class can hear her.

"What's up?" I am a little concerned, but not too much.

"L's Mom just called and they want to let you know that they're on their way to the airport in Philly and he'll be arriving on time, I guess."

"OK. That's good. Is that it? Because I'm in yoga now. OK?"

"I think that's it." I can hear her thinking a little harder and I'm sure her head is bowed.

"Good. Okay, " I'm now sounding like a mother with a kindergartner who has stolen candy.

"Yes," she says and I'm sure her head is bowed.

"I love you Mom. Are you OK now?"

"Oh, yeah. I'll be all right. You'll be home soon, won't you?" We agree that she can call me for emergencies. I remind her I'll be home in one short hour.

We hang up and I notice a Missed Call in glowing digital green. I wish I could ignore it and get back to Warrior Pose, but check my messages. "Hi Nancy." It's my Mom. I must have missed her first call. "J called. She's going out to, to...well, some store I can't remember the name and she wants to know if you want anything. I told her to...well, I don't know what I told her, but maybe she'll call you. OK. That's all. Yoga's good, I hope. G'bye dee-uh," she says, her Maine accent oozing affection.

Maybe it's what yoga does to my already overly aware state of being, but I had a strange sensation of my mother's voice hanging in cyberspace. Voice here. Body not here. An overwhelming ache of "gone forever" came over me. As if she had already died and all I had left was this message left inadvertently on the cell phone, her molecules dangling somewhere on the information highway. Her voice, a thin vaporous message left behind.

To hear this message again press 1. To delete this message press 3. To save it in the archives press 2.

Pressed 2. My mother's voice is now in the archives. Decided to ask her to make a recording. I remember saving and taping a voice message she left years ago. "This is your Mom, I love you." It was the first time she said, "I love you," without being prompted by me. I still have it and wonder where it is. Felt frantic for a few moments, thinking of ways to remember her.

Must do a video of her and me talking.

Do a plaster cast of hands, feet, and face.

Take more photos of her just sitting and smiling.

Love is all there is.

December 13
(Will not buy into Friday the 13th crap)
11:32 pm

Mom cannot be left alone. Even using the microwave, her favorite cooking utensil (I never use it) has become a bit confusing for her. The other day I gave her explicit instructions on how to warm up her bowl of soup (home-made with fresh veggies and chicken) while I took a shower. I even set the timer and said, "OK, Mom, whenever you're ready just place your dish in here and push START." She nodded and appeared to have taken it all in, saying "Yup, yup, I know. Yup, yup." Nod, nod. "Of course." Mind you, I know she has a little memory problem, but I kept it real simple. No one, two, three. Just one. Press here. The other thing about my mother is that she has no patience. When she's hungry she has to eat. Now. (Well, this is where we are truly joined: the appetite.) So I was in a hurry to get us both fed, get my paperwork together, finish up the bills, go over the grocery list, make four phone calls (two to her doctor to both cancel and confirm future appointments, one to Medicare, and one to her insurance company) and she was in a hurry to go nowhere but to her lunch plate, fast. I figured I'd eat on the run and still had to put together a little sack of road food for me. (Yes, taking care of my mother is like running a small business.) She wanted to "make" her own lunch. Says I'm taking away her independence. Says she needs to do more to take care of herself. Why she thinks this is important I don't know. She will stay with us until she doesn't recognize me any more and then will be taken care of by someone else (I don't want to go there right now).

OK, I say. Here's the deal on lunch. I'll get ready to go out. You get your lunch ready. We finish the instruction session. She's "got it." I feel relatively convinced that we're making some progress and move out of the kitchen, looking back to see my mother leaning on her elbows, staring into the microwave as if she's just come upon a meteor in the middle of a desert and is trying to convince (her, him, it) to fork over some food. I scramble into the shower.

Slow down, Nancy, I remind myself. No need to rush. Take a deep breath.
Life is not an emergency.

Ahhh. The shower feels like a vacation. A quick get-away. Just me and a waterfall of cool water. A calming flow of liquid luxury from my head to my toes.

Shhhhhhh. Shhhhhhh. Shhhhhhhh.

I am a water baby. Lap, lap, lap, licking and smoothing and scrubbing.

I think about the dolphins I saw the day before, riding the surf during my afternoon walk. I saw the smaller dolphin first; the mother close behind, rising up like a sleek, living rock, surfacing only for a second and then back under. There's something about seeing dolphins, appearing out of, where? nowhere, that makes me smile and feel all free and childlike and happy inside. I look for them whenever I walk, sing a little dolphin chant, wait, walk, and wait some more. I also like that the word "dolphin", in Greek, means "womb." As in, giving birth live from the womb, like human mothers. Yesterday I was lucky. Apparently the blues (bluefish) are running and this means the dolphins are close behind, along with the other cooperative fishing crew, the brown pelicans. I like how they all work together. This time perhaps a mother showing a baby how to circle fish and ride waves at the same time to make a daily "have to" into a fun event. Usually when I see a few pelicans working the surface, I know there are dolphins not too far from the ocean lunch line. These clues are everywhere, I guess, when we pay attention. Clues. I like this word, too, which originally meant "ball of thread" referring to how Theseus found his way out of the Minotaur's (king bull) labyrinth because the Goddess Ariadne gave him a ball of thread to trace his steps.

Clue sounds like glue, the invisible goo that binds us all together, as we bump our way around the a-mazing map of life.

I emerge from the shower wondering how to make time with Mom more playful. She is happier than she's ever been. Last night, after tucking her in, she held my hand in both of hers and said, "You know something?"

"Nope. What?" I think she is stalling for time, the way kids ask for everything they ever wanted just before you turn off the light and say goodnight.

She lifted her head off the pillow and said, "I'm happy I'm here."

She caught me by surprise and I leaned over and said, "I'm happy you're here too, MaZen. If it weren't for you, I wouldn't be here either."

"No," she said correcting quietly. "I mean I'm happy I'm *here*. Right here, with you and L."

My mother knows how to live in a place called Here and Now. She is my instruction kit; my live-in wisdom keeper.

Coming around the bend with my towel wrapped around me, Mom is exactly where I left her, leaning over the big black stranger of a microwave, her new alien friend. She succeeded in getting her soup into the oven, but got stuck there. "You look tired, Mom," I said, trying to divert her attention and not making it too obvious that she was stymied. "I'll take over."

"Well, I'm trying to read the directions here. And it doesn't say anything about chicken soup."

"Let's see if I can convince it." I shuffle her over to the table and return to the micro monster to find that she had put a tissue over her soup (she thought it was a paper towel) and didn't get much further. The tissue was now sinking into the middle of the bowl and soaking up the juice like a dry sponge on water. Only here the sponge was turning to mush. I chuckled a bit. "So Mom. What's with the Kleenex? Chicken soup got a runny nose?"

"Guess so," she laughs then gets real serious and sad. "What's happening to me, Nancy? What is it that has a hold of my mind?" I walk back across the kitchen and wrap my arms around her, bending to kiss the top of her head.

"Everything is going to be all right, Mom." I whisper into her shiny gray hair. "Everything is going to be fine."

I am lying.

December 15
3:13 am

Sunday

Breathwork session with K yesterday. I (desperately) wanted to call and cancel, and if I knew what I was going to uncover I would have stayed home and crawled under my bed. Think I must be nuts to want to spend a Sunday afternoon flat out and sobbing when everyone else I know is whimpering privately or sunning themselves on the beach. Except I just don't know where to file the mixed-up emotions that float and fire up all around me, unexpected, unannounced, unbidden. I'm told this is good. Not that I'm fired up all the time, but that I'm willing to shed some light on the unknown so I can make some room for joy. And I'm hoping I'm not wasting my time throwing money at someone else's vacation. There's nothing wrong with letting sleeping dogs lie, especially if it's looking like a hungry pit bull on steroids.

Gandhi said that anger transformed can heal the world.

Since B told me about her father molesting her I have wanted to single-handedly sneak into his room at night and slowly torture him, which, of course, is just what he did to her. Another case of becoming what I despise. I'll just seethe in my skin and wish she never told me. No. That doesn't make any sense either. B said that when she told her lover that she was sexually abused he said that he hasn't met a woman who wasn't. He held her and held her and she cried for what she said felt like forever and this new boyfriend never stopped soothing her and stroking her hair and patting her back. I almost cried when she told me. She is happy with S and I hope they can share special fun times, too.

Still don't want to go to my therapy session. Something tugging at the underside of my rib cage; a wild and resonant howling welling up from the full Moon of my heart. When the Goddess Inanna, she of gentle rains and terrible floods, descends into the underworld to "find herself" she tells her attendant, "If I'm not back in three days, send for help." I call B and tell her I'm on my way to my session. "Nanc, the Big Mama didn't bring you here for nothing," she says reassuringly. "You'll get exactly what you need. You're becoming Inanna." No consolation there. Inanna was hung on a meat hook to rot for three days as the illusions of her changing life dissolved before her. I can feel another FGE (Fucking Growth Experience) rising up from hell.

Take your finger out of the fan. Breathe. You are innocent.

I packed a snack for the ride home, sliced apples with almond butter (I am now using my diabetic education wisely), and a big bottle of cold water, which will be lukewarm by the time I get there. It's almost 90 unseasonal degrees and a storm is rolling in from the west. Iridescent white thunderheads are stacked up on top of each other like colossal cosmic cauliflower. A bold gray veil pushes itself in front of the Sun and rushes out to sea, casting a quick shadow across the car. I have an hour of drive time ahead of me. One hour. Completely alone. I turn off the radio and head north on A1A. Kids with their parents, little girls in pink, two-piece bathing suits and strawberry-colored jelly sandals, holding their mom's hand, and little boys with sand on their bellies, wait to cross the street. Young men with surfboards tucked under their arms stand alongside young women in bikinis (tiny bikinis) looking like an ad for suntan lotion. I want to open my window and yell out to the innocent girlfriend staring goofy-eyed into her surfer boy's biscuit-brown and self-confident smile, "Get your own life." But I say nothing for fear of sounding like Dr. Laura on an unsolicited drive-by.

The sky thickens ahead and a few big raindrops splash the windshield.

I will be a different woman when I return. I will know something that I don't know now. My eyes fixed on the gray ribbon pavement in front of me, driving down the road to my future, looking through the rearview mirror; I have no idea that the storm I'm driving into moved onto my path many years ago.

I drive very carefully.

The session begins the same as usual. Talking about nothing really.

I'm aware that talking delays the breathing part of the therapy and the descent into my fruitful shadowy caverns. "Are you ready?" K asks suddenly, cutting off a rambling jag that could have gone on for hours. She stands up and unfolds her left arm, holding it out like an usher, guiding me to the massage table.

"Of course not. I'm never ready," I laugh. But I am very serious.

"Remember, enthusiastic inhale, easy exhale." She is tender and caring. A wise woman at the crossroads, guiding me—re-minding me, home. "Relax your jaw."

"Now that's a new concept."

I am returning, going back to the crib, to the baby who is screaming and scared and pressed hard against the corner of her small world. The room is dark. Her eyes are wide open. I lift her quietly into my arms. She is trembling. I sway gently back and forth.

The man appears. He is wearing overalls with blue stripes. He is carrying bottles of milk, clanging against a metal case. He is smiling, whistling. He is a nice man? My little girl shakes her head. No, he is bad. I don't like him. He moves on past us. He is unzipping his pants. No. He is not a nice man. He is chasing the boys in the other room. He is after them. He is laughing. They are running away. He grabs the little boy next door. My baby girl hides her head, turning her face into my shoulder. She doesn't want to see any more. She has seen enough. She knows what this man does to little boys.

K holds me in her arms. I am sobbing. I know what I came to find out in the house of shadows. It all came flooding back to me. Our hasty move from the house on Fletcher Street to the trailer park. My parents must have found out about the milkman who liked little boys. My parents, living by leaving.

Of course they knew what happened when I was five years old.

Breathing In. Breathing Out.

December 16
11:01 pm   Monday

Mom woke up late this morning. We both had to rush around to get her ready for Bingo and lunch. Halfway out the door she runs back toward the bathroom yelling, "Wait, I've got to check my Polaroids." She shuffles around the corner and disappears into the bathroom.

"Mom, the photos aren't in there. They're next to your desk."

"Not photos, dear, my Polaroids are hurting again."

"Polaroids?" Now I'm the one completely confused. "You mean hemorrhoids?"

"Yes. Of course, dear," she says confused. "What do you think I said?"

"Never mind."

I made her a breakfast of waffles (crunchy) and chopped apples (hard) and almond butter (mushy). She's on an antibiotic for a bladder infection so I make sure she has acidophilus as a chaser, so she doesn't end up with diarrhea, more hemorrhoids (please Great Mother of Mercy no more hemorrhoids) and the itch "down there." It was a long night. I feel so desperate when she's hurting. Woke up at 4 am thinking about life after Mom. As if I have any idea what that looks like. Decide I'm wasting my time on the future, so I get up and check in on her. I sneak up just to make sure she's still breathing. She lifts her head and starts talking to me as if we're at the kitchen table having tea and biscuits, "My great grandfather used silver. My grandfather used gold. Not leaf, no, not leaf. He used it right out of the jar. Yes he did." She's been on a roll for three days in and out of time and space, like a bad acid trip, which makes me grateful for those long, late nights I spent calming friends who overdosed on Window Pane (or was it Sunshine or Purple Barrels?). At least something from the era of sex, drugs and rock 'n' roll has now come in handy. I crawl on top of the blanket and lay down beside her, stroking her hair and massaging her head. I want to get my fingers in there, under her scalp and pluck out the bad spark plugs and get my mother's engine running clean and smooth and real again.

It is not your job to fix your mother.

I know, I know. Her journey is not up to me, does not belong to me. It's so much easier to give myself advice than it is to follow it. I don't want to think about dying. Not now. Not when she's breathing and I'm breathing and it looks like life is still prancing around the meadow and lifting her tail, snorting wildly.

I massage and breathe and send love, pure liquid daughter love into her beautiful old body, my mother, my creator.

I am forgiving and letting go. The past holds no power over us. Not now. Not ever. This moment is all there is.

Listening to her breath I stay present to the woman who gave me her blood and bones. I let go of hoping for an outcome I can't control. I am simply, quietly, *with* her. The Full Moon is waning. An eggy shape hangs just outside the long, horizontal window above our heads. We are bathed in the changing lunar light.

She changes everything she touches. Everything she touches changes.

Mom is asleep, finally. I return to bed after hearing a soft snuffle and snore. I crawl in next to L. Eyes wide open I count on my fingers one, two, three, four, five, six, seven. I made seven calls (including emails) to ask for help today: P volunteered to take Mom to church this Sunday, I've hired B to drive Mom to Bingo three days a week, rescheduled a doctor's appointment for Mom so it better fits into my yoga schedule, called for another therapy session (sooner rather than later), called Mom's church for caregiver relief for Thursday nights, made a massage appointment *for me*, and called about Adult Day Care, which we will check into.

This is my prayer: Thank you. Thank you. Thank you.

I see now that everything arises as an opportunity to better take care of myself.

Everything is a gift. Or it is nothing.

I doze off thinking about an old story from South India about soap. It's said that soap is the dirt we buy, and when we introduce it to the dirt we have the two are so happy to see each other that they fall in love and run away together.

I want more spiritual soap in my life.

More joy. Not less.

December 17
4:34 pm

Tuesday

Did yoga this morning. Yes. Yes. Yes. How I love this simple practice, letting my breath breathe me, as my yoga teacher says. Did not answer the phone or the doorbell while in meditation. Good for me. I'm getting better at staving off interruptions. Menopause is a post-graduate program in self-care. I am learning to protect and keep sacred my time alone, my time of diving deep and listening closely. Who would have thought that at age 50, almost 51, I'd be learning how to say those simple, one-syllable baby words again, Yes and No.

Taking Mom to Adult Day Care for the first time today. It's run by the Alzheimer's foundation. I'm nervous about it. Actually stalling all morning. I'm afraid she'll see the word Alzheimer's on the sign outside the door and get really upset. Mom is anxious, too. She sees me doing strange activities, frecking and fussing around the house and going nowhere but in larger circles. She can't handle new ideas, changes, long conversations, or too much information. L got a call for an interview yesterday at a college in NY. *Please, Mother of All Mothers, make this job happen for him, for us.* I think I'm supposed to be more specific here, but I'm not sure. Specific can be too narrowing, limiting the possibilities. Do I simply surrender my supplications and let some unimagined better, best option unfold? I opt for Best. I back up my plea and restate:

Please, Mother of All Mothers, I accept the best in all ways every day. And while I'm at it, make this Adult Day Care the best for Mom. And me. OK? We'd really like that it's clean and no one is pooping in their pants or screeching cuss words at us when we walk in. Let the nurses be kind and gentle and patient. Let them be caring daughters. That's all I ask. Oh, and one more thing. It's a big one, but can you make the food just a little al dente? Not too mushy. She needs to chew. Raw veggies are not a bad thing.

"Remember when you took me to nursery school?" I try to comfort her.

"Yeah, but I had to go to work." Her defense is a hair trigger. As if I'm blaming her for something I don't even know about. "I cleaned houses." She pauses and stares at me squinting. "Didn't I? Isn't that what I did?"

"Yes. You worked very hard, Mom," I sound too patronizing already. "And I do, too. Only I work at home." She can't make the connection here. Home=Work? Does not compute. "You'll really like this new Senior Center (like, how the hell do I know what she'll like. I wince when I hear myself, but don't want to say Adult Day Care. It sounds so…terminal.) "New friends. Bingo." With Bingo I'm hoping to snag her attention.

"Bingo?" Her spirits are lifted. Alas. Bingo is the best I can hope for.

And please, Great Mother of Aging Mothers, don't let it smell like a port-o-let.

December 18
8:14 am

Wednesday

Woke up feeling like I could really enjoy the second half of life for absolutely no rational reason at all, and in spite of the fact that I have an itchy pimple on my vulva that stings when my thighs slap shut. The fact that the Adult Day Care experience was totally depressing for Mom and me doesn't weigh as heavily on my shoulders as it did yesterday. I dropped her off in the morning for a "visitors' day" freebie. When I picked her up four hours later she was all happy and bubbly when the nurses aides (bless their hearts) kissed her goodbye and said enough I love you's to last a lifetime, hugging my little Mom, following her to the door and waving bye-bye through the window until we were out of sight. All the time my mother smiling from ear to ear and waving back, and me thinking Yes. Yes. Yes. It worked.

"You must've had a good time," I bubbled with great hope, opening the door and helping her climb into the car. "They want you to come back."

"Of course they want me to come back," my mother snapped, not the slightest trace of a smile left on her face. "They're all vegetables in there. I'm the only one with a brain."

Back to square one. Like so many parents of young children, I've learned that if it doesn't work for my mother, it doesn't work for me.

I'm in my office trying to read, which with my wandering menopausal mind is at best a challenge. I didn't sleep much last night. I am worried about what was and what will be. This morning when I woke up I couldn't even remember what I was worrying about. And feel somehow relieved of whatever it was that weighed me down. I do remember sighing about four hundred thousands times and rolling around for about an hour. Tossing and turning is so boring. Then, and only then, did I decide to practice three-part yogic breathing. Why does it take so much energy to help me remember what I already know? Inhale to count of four. Fill up bottom of lungs first, then middle lungs, then upper lungs. Gently hold to count of seven. Release to count of eight from top of lungs, then middle lungs, then lower lungs. Gently hold to count of four. Repeat. Sinking my brain into my belly, I hop aboard a new rhythm, smoothing out the carnival yin-yang ride in my mind. It must have worked. I woke up at 7:17. Total of five hours sleep, maybe six: from 12-3 and 4-7. I can always nap in the afternoon.

My cat within says naps are good for the nerves.

December 19
9:13 am

Thursday

It's been raining for days. Huge and tumultuous afternoon thunderheads gather in the west and storm their way across the river. And this isn't even rainy season. After the long and hard drought, the downpour is longingly soaked into the smiling Earth. It occurred to me on my walk this morning that perhaps I am molding (molting?) in my damp and secret special-purpose parts. Either that or my delicate yoni flower has a case of diaper rash. I have taken to wearing housedresses. Mu mu's. Big tents. Loose and flowing and letting my twazoo breathe free and easy. *Au naturel*. I started doing this really wildass morning trance dance to some very luscious music with bells, drums, and sensual rhythms strong enough to coax the last drop of pheromones out of a mole. I close my bedroom door (I'm feeling like a teenager when I shut out the rest of the world. But I like it. It works for me) and do an improv dance around the bed, all the time staring at the flame bush in the backyard, buzzing with scarlet trumpet flowers and yellow and black zebra-striped butterflies. The lizards, too, are dancing up and down the branches as I wiggle, jiggle, and wind my arms around myself like a snake up a pole. It's my Menopause Power Dance, a blessing to my body, to the first day of the rest of my life, to my

Goddess self, to the wild natural world that is my teacher. This dance of ecstasy is my morning meditation. I just can't sit still.

In the beginning was not "the word." In the beginning was a song and a dance and a soft lullaby.

And I hope my neighbor isn't parked outside his porch with a pair of binoculars.

December 20
3:01 am

Friday

"Are these pants too revealing?" I asked L while walking out of the bathroom after having spent a good sweaty few minutes in front of the mirror twisting myself backwards to see what my ass looks like in a pair of new, tighter capris. We're going out on a date. Two workaholics practicing how to have fun.

"I refuse to answer that question." Obviously, this is why I married him.

"Is this the artist formerly known as Should Have Been a Lawyer speaking?" I smile, smoothing out my thighs. I'm becoming a round and voluptuous Goddess woman. Either that or I'm returning to my dimpled baby butt self.

"That question has no answer." I think he's trying to protect my self-esteem, giving wise counsel. But I suspect he is protecting his own interests. One false move and he knows he won't get laid tonight. Chances are slim to none anyway. He's holding out hope and refusing to engage in my body image sickness. Thank goodness someone is on my side.

It's incredibly hard to believe I used to be a topless dancer, baring all and caring not.

The capris can stay, but the pull-on bra has to go. The skinny hard straps dig a deep ravine into my shoulders, and the elastic around the bottom edge cuts into my rib cage, and my breasts are smooshed together looking like a landscape berm rising off my chest. My breasts, my precious, sensitive, sensual breasts are howling for freedom. Does this mean I'll never be able to get a job where I have to be in the public eye? I can hear my on-lookers, "Will someone throw this old hag a bra?"

Can't some middle-aged woman design a decent outfit that is comfortable (number-one priority), doesn't cost a week's wages, and comes in colors other than gray and black or acid orange with lime-colored flowers emblazoned all over it? And can this menopause trousseau be tossed in the washer with the towels and come out looking like I just bought it? Oh, and it has to be 100 percent cotton, too. Those synthetics are way too flammable next to my barbeque grill within. And for the sake of my global kin please will someone pay the people who make my clothes a decent wage?

And while I'm at it, can someone please consider the environment?

That's all I ask. Today.

11:15 pm

I'm hot flashing (if this is a power surge, hook me up, I can generate power all the way to California, where they need it the most) all over the place today after not having a single case of the sweats for almost two weeks straight. As usual, my menopausal friends, Acute and Irrational, introduce every fevered flush, searing the inside of my chest like a propane torch on sugar. There is no Al Qaeda more effective than the one that sits inside my mind, terrorizing me with spontaneous attacks on my sense of well-being. The duration of the assault, thank Goddess, is manageable. I can handle anything for a minute or two. Only four or five more years and it will be over.

Interesting that listed under the word anxiety in the thesaurus are: intentness, desire, yearning, longing, aching.

I am begging the Crone at the Crossroads: *Can I have retroactive credit for the nearly nine years of perimenopause? Can you go easy on me with the anxiety and just hand over a hot flash a la carte?*

I may have to give up chocolate. It's a last-ditch effort. I've been paying close attention to the timing of hot flashes. Caffeine and sugar seem to incite a riot around the frayed edges of my nerves just seconds before spontaneous beads of sweat land on my upper lip. Ignorance surely is bliss. I've outsmarted chocolate right off my plate. What next?

Last night L and I were doing the hokey pokey in the living room and Mom came out shaking her little ole hiney like she was doing the rumba. She was so cute, smiling and holding her hands in little fists and jiving her way across the floor. It was a moment of the sublimest happiness. I was laughing so hard the tears were streaming down my cheeks, singing at the top of my lungs.

That's what it's all about. Hey!

December 21
Solstice! Let the Sun shine.
Let the Sun shine in.
But don't make it too hot please.
3:29 am

I walked around naked all afternoon, wearing only my red reading glasses (so I can see the magic living in the details of life!) and my gold wedding band. Every day I fall deeper in love with the color red, even though it looks bad against my skin. I like the vibrancy of it. Life. Passion. Fire. Feels wonderful to be alone in the house. Besides that, lunch for Mom was a great success: canned, cream of mushroom soup over a thick slice of deli turkey, a few very red and ripe cherry tomatoes, red jello and two of her favorite sugar-free chocolate wafers (yes, with all the chemicals!). She was so happy to get exactly what she loves, even if it was the fourth time this week. It's all new to her. And I was happy to give it to her. And why not? She's not going to die young. She and L then went off to the grocery store for more sugar-free ice cream while I popped on the Pointer Sisters CD and jiggled my booty all over the kitchen singing, *I'm so excited and I just can't hide it. I'm about to lose control and I think I like it.* My thighs flapping like loose sheets in the wind. Felt really good too to jiggle free and easy, round and soft and strong in all the big places that are wonderfully womanly. Breasts, hips, thighs. I like that I am solid, round, like the Earth, and low to the ground. Grounded. And one more thing, I like my ample butt. Soft is not bad. Soft is comforting and serene. I love my badass butt. This butt was born of a long line of courageous women who worked hard in the fields, in smoke-filled factories, in the scrub sinks and kitchens of their own homes to feed their babes. Besides, fat contains estrogen and it isn't a bad thing to have a few extra pounds to help when the ovaries retire. I love Susun Weed, author of *Menopause Years: The Wise Woman Way,* for suggesting that we put on an extra ten pounds. Not all at once, mind you, but a pound a year (ha!) through the forties so we can have a little back-up estrogen to wind our way through menopause. Lo and behold, I'm right on target! I wonder if this is one of those cases where more is better?

I can love all of me, even if it's only for a few minutes at a time.

Pamela Wyn Shannon sent me her new CD, "Nature's Bride" and I just love it, especially the first cut, *world in my arms.* I've played it a hundred times this morning, her words running around in my head like a freedom song, *Damn to the years of melancholy! To dwelling in your misty gray hours with a longing in my belly. Damn to the catalog of weepy songs, that I held as my companion for far too long! Cause I've got better things to do than to pine away my days!*

December 22
8:32 am

Today I will eat whatever I damned well please. I am so tired of listening to what I *should* eat, diet prescriptions flung at me by the latest food marketeers that by the time I've run down the list of breakfast foods that are *supposed* to get me up and running in the morning, I've fallen back into a swirling stupor, having resentfully lost my appetite in the meantime.

The only food I need to eat is food I really love and that truly loves and nourishes me in return. Food is pure vibration. If I eat what I *should* eat and don't really like what I'm eating, then the energy of *not liking* it will have an injurious impact on what I'm eating. Doesn't that make sense? In my menopausal mind most diet prescriptions look like a kind of torturous slow suicide in the name of following the rules, and doing what's *right* according to someone else's research. Food as punishment is what it all adds up to. Besides, all that scientific research changes constantly, depending on who funds the research. What builds strong bones one day clogs your corpuscles the next.

NO MORE DIETS.

I read somewhere that resentment is like taking rat poison and waiting for the rat to die. I say no more resentful breakfasts.

So this is what I came up with today and it feels really good to me: I hereby take full responsibility for my food choices. Besides, I trust my body knows what it, no *she* (no more referring to my body as *it*) wants. She *wants* and I shall *obey*. Last week I was craving steamed collards with a drizzle of garlic oil and balsamic vinegar and for lunch I ate just that. Nothing else. And it tasted really good. During yoga meditation this morning I was listening intently for some food clues and I heard, to my own breathless marvel and wonder, the words Chocolate Chip Cookies. I stretched into Cobra Pose like a spandex snake with a divine issuance I can live with and love. Yes. My body knows exactly what she wants! There is nothing more wonderful than looking forward to happiness you can be sure of. I got so freakin' excited giving myself permission to have what I want that I nearly rose up off the floor a couple inches while dancing into the kitchen, when normally I slog my way to the refrigerator and hope some kind, Grandmother Elf spent the wee hours of the morning preparing my meals and left me a delicious and healthy breakfast, ready to eat. Today, with guidance from the Chocolate Chip Grandmother I couldn't have been more euphoric if I'd just sold a piece of art to the Guggenheim. Listening a little closer I got all kinds of guidance for a happy, easy, *Yes, This Is Exactly What I Want Today* breakfast.

> *2 chocolate chip cookies* (my favorite: organic, no milk, no wheat, no hydrogenated oils, no heartburn)
> *1 big scoop (about 1 tbsp) each raw almond butter and raw sesame butter (tahini)*
> *1 heaping tbsp of freshly ground, golden flax seed* (I love this nutty stuff)
> *1 tbsp chocolate chips* (I always buy organic chocolate)

Arrange each of the above items on a favorite, pleasing plate with colors that soothe. This is a breakfast ceremony dedicated to Happily Trusting Self, so keep conscious about it, smiling and paying attention to thoughts and feelings.

Food ritual is a sacred necessity. Body responds to joyful attitude with untold gratitude. Bring plate to table. Best sit with a beautiful view of garden while eating. Watching butterflies mate is good for digestion. Break off a piece of cookie and spread with a little of each nut butter. Pay attention closely here. With deep understanding I bless the rain on the fields that soaked the roots of the almond trees, and the forever-giving fruited branches. The sun's warm and greening breath. The choreography of clouds that at one time passed through my piece of the sky eventually opened up and rained on the ground of my breakfast far, far away. That same dance of rain exists in every wondrous bite. Ponder the power encased in a single sesame; ancient food of my kin. Yes. Yes. Yes. Open Sesame. Open fully, says me. This day is mine, all mine to live it the way I want it, fully connected to what is wholly true for me in this very moment and every moment born of it. Yes. Speak to me, sesame. With pure joy singing from the heart, yes, my heart, I hear you too, press cookie into little golden hill of ground flax to give a crusty, crunchy surface. Immediately press cookie into pile of chocolate chips, magic manna from the Cocoa Mama, for a chunky rich topping, a miniature dark mountainscape of pure ecstasy and pleasure. Enjoy with a cup of warm, soothing tea. Flavor to be determined at the time. Every day is different, so I may want a different flavor every day. Give in to what I want, and whisper a prayer with the first bite:

May this food nourish me in bodymind and spirit, in all ways. Always, I give thanks, in return with joy in my heart. I find great satisfaction and meaning in food that is meaningful for me. I trust my body knows.

December 23
11:32 pm

Monday

I'm peeling a hard-boiled egg for lunch, standing at the kitchen sink this morning listening to my belly rumble, Hungry, Hungry. Feed me. Now. The tree frogs in the backyard drone a low throbbing chant, like monks doing voice practice in Nature sounds. Trying my darnedest to get a hold of that thin white skin just below the shell and above the soft white embryonic eggy flesh. I know that once I catch hold it will make peeling this egg really easy, but each tugging lift of the thin brown shell pulls off a small chunk of egg white with it, leaving a little hole where a nice bite might be, and less of my afternoon meal for me. Today I want eggs. Never again will I eat only the whites of eggs, separated out from the gooey golden centers. My eggs will be eaten whole, intact, yolk clinging to wrap-around white. Cooked fresh and peeled, my lunch eggs are looking all rough and dug out, like a spongy soft, opalescent

Moon rock. I pop it, ragged and excavated, in my mouth and absorb this gift of hen-wholeness. It is no less satisfying for being unreasonably difficult.

The tree frogs are yelping *smazzzz smazzzz akkkkkk raaaaaaam* from some hidden branches in the scrub oaks. Anxious squirrels mimic the neighbor's cat, *mow mow mow*, giving a word of territorial warning. To whom? The male cardinal, who's been hanging out near the silver gazing ball in the middle of my menopause garden, is determined to hop on and hold fast to the slippery-silvered surface. But no matter how hard he tries, he keeps sliding off before he's able to realize that the bird that is threatening him is his own reflection. Finally he flits off to a branch in the vitex bush and calls out *vreet vreet keedo keedo keedo,* as if finishing up a morning workout and now on to other more important bird business. A lawn mower starts up somewhere in the neighborhood. A yellow and black zebra-striped butterfly is doing a breezy, looping dance across the flame bush covered in rich, golden-orange trumpet flowers and then onto the hibiscus. Another butterfly, just like it, catches up and together they spiral out of sight in a tornadic pas de deux.

The zizzz zizzz zizzz chorus of cicada join the early winter symphony of semi-tropical backyard sounds. Turtle season is over. The Moon and the Sun and a mysterious, migratory map of invisible Earth energy lines guides the Turtle Mother toward another shore, where she will roll and dive and soak up the ocean pulse that will eventually send her back to our beach. Endless cycles turning in time.

Breathing In. Breathing Out.

Hurricane season is long past. Big sigh. I can feel the cool, damp winds of a nor'easter press against my aching hipbones; my weather station within. I take another bite of my lazy lunch. The yolk is just the way I like it, soft, yummy, rich, warm, golden orange, dripping down my chin. As we spiral into winter it will get cooler, clearer. The cloudless sky will go on forever. Wherever I may be next month, next year, or even tomorrow, this is my home today. Right here, right now. In the middle of a sand bar, only a hurricane's breath away from nothingness, where my lunch tastes like love, and the birds know my name, and every moment that ever was is folded into the happy frog voices lapping up last night's storm. I am home. And I don't care what time it is and may never care again. It is my time; my menopausal changing time, wild with possibilities.

Yes. Change is good.

In a few minutes I'll have to get dressed for a gallery talk at the museum, where my new series of glass sculptures, "Ancestral Voices," and the "Shaman Jars" are on exhibit. L is talking, too, about his new conceptual works on paper. We are mystic misfits, married to the same visual path and passion: creating the world the way we see it. The way we want it. A hazy creative mission that changes meaning on a moment's whim and whiplash.

Maybe I won't wait for a future special dinner to wear the flowing white "milk" linen jacket that is so soft and comfortable. Special is happening right now. I'm not waiting for anything called future. NOW is where I live.

I hear the words of Uvavnuk's poem in my heart, an Eskimo shaman woman chanting:

> The great sea
> Has set me adrift
> It moves me
> As the weed in a great river
> Earth and the great weather
> Move me
> Have carried me away
> And move my inward parts with joy